Challenges to the Global Trading System

International trade continues to expand robustly in East Asia and elsewhere, but global trade negotiations have collapsed and globalization is widely criticized. One line of argument is that 'real world' trade policy favours rich countries and the strongest producers within them. Another sees globalization as the cause of varied social ills, including income inequality, environmental degradation, violations of labour and human rights, and the destruction of culture.

In this book, the participants of the 30th Pacific Trade and Development Conference—including the then-Director General of the World Trade Organization, leading government officials, academics and executives from a dozen major Pacific Rim economies—debate whether global negotiations have ended once and for all, or are suffering temporarily from 'globalization fatigue', whether East Asia's new regional partnerships will advance or undermine the global trading system; and whether the region's trade tensions with the United States will intensify or subside. They provide new empirical evidence on how trade affects the distribution of income, the location of pollution-intensive industries, the causes of 'outsourcing', the structure of the intellectual property regime and international security. They also probe the implications of adjustment to globalization: how can countries reap the benefits of trade while controlling the risks faced by the poor and, perhaps more importantly, the politically strong?

Offering an unusually wide-ranging perspective on the adjustment problems caused by trade, as well as strategies for managing these problems, *Challenges to the Global Trading System* is an invaluable resource for students and scholars of Asia-Pacific studies, international relations and development studies, as well as those with a more general interest in Asian studies.

Peter A. Petri is the Carl J. Shapiro Professor of International Finance at Brandeis University.

Sumner J. La Croix is a Senior Fellow at the East-West Center and professor and chair of the Department of Economics, University of Hawaii.

Pacific Trade and Development Conference Series

Edited by Peter A. Petri and Sumner J. La Croix

Titles published by Routledge in association with the PAFTAD International Secretariat and the Australia–Japan Research Centre, The Australian National University include:

Business, Markets and Government in the Asia Pacific

Edited by Rong-I Wu and Yun-Peng Chu

Asia Pacific Financial Deregulation

Edited by Gordon de Brouwer and Wisarn Pupphavesa

Asia Pacific Economic Cooperation/APEC: Challenges and Tasks for the 21st Century

Edited by Ippei Yamazawa

Globalization and the Asia Pacific Economy

Edited by Kyung Tae Lee

The New Economy in East Asia and the Pacific

Edited by Peter Drysdale

Competition Policy in East Asia

Edited by Erlinda M. Medalla

Reshaping the Asia Pacific Economic Order

Edited by Hadi Soesastro and Christopher Findlay

Challenges to the Global Trading System

Adjustment to globalization in the Asia-Pacific region
Edited by Peter A. Petri and Sumner J. La Croix

Challenges to the Global Trading System

Adjustment to globalization in the Asia-Pacific region

Edited by
Peter A. Petri and
Sumner J. La Croix

LONDON AND NEW YORK

First published 2007 by Routledge
2 Park Square, Milton Park, Abingdon, Oxon, OX14 4RN

Simultaneously published in the USA and Canada by Routledge
711 Third Avenue, New York, NY 10017

Routledge is an imprint of the Taylor & Francis Group, an informa business

First issued in paperback 2011

Publisher's note: This book has been prepared from camera-ready copy
provided by PAFTAD International Secretariat.

© 2007 PAFTAD International Secretariat for selection and editorial
matter; individual chapters, the contributors

British Library Cataloguing in Publication Data
A catalogue record for this book is available from the British Library

Library of Congress Cataloging-in-Publication Data
Pacific Trade and Development Conference (30th : 2005 : Honolulu, Hawaii)
Challenges to the global trading system : adjustment to globalization in the Asia-Pacific region /
edited by Peter A. Petri and Sumner La Croix.
p. cm. — (Pacific Trade and Development Conference series ; 8)
Includes bibliographical references.
ISBN 978-0-415-42986-3 (hardback : alk. paper) 1. Asia—Commerce—Congresses. 2. Pacific
Area—Commerce—Congresses. 3. International trade—Congresses. I. Petri, Peter A., 1946- II. La
Croix, Sumner J., 1954- III. Title.
HF3751.7.P32 2005
382.095—dc22
2006039009

ISBN 10: 0-415-42986-2 (hbk)
ISBN 10: 0-415-66641-4 (pbk)
ISBN 10: 0-203-44186-9 (ebk)

ISBN 13: 978-0-415-42986-3 (hbk)
ISBN 13: 978-0-415-66641-1 (pbk)
ISBN 13: 978-0-203-44186-2 (ebk)

Contents

Figures

Tables and boxes

Contributors

Narongchai Akrasanee is Chairman of Seranee Holdings Co., Ltd, and Chairman of MFC Asset Management plc. He is former Minister of Commerce and Senator of Thailand, former member of APEC Eminent Persons Group and APEC Business Advisory Council, and is currently an adviser to the Thai Finance Minister.

Doug Bereuter is President of The Asia Foundation. He served as a member of the US House of Representatives for 26 years, and as member, vice chairman and chairman of several House committees.

Chad P. Bown is Okun-Model Fellow in Economic Studies at the Brookings Institution in Washington, DC, and Associate Professor in the Department of Economics and the International Business School at Brandeis University.

Inkyo Cheong is Professor of Economics and a Director of the Center for FTA Policies, Inha University, Incheon, Korea, and Research Fellow at the Korean Institute for International Economic Policy (KIEP). He is actively involved in FTA studies on behalf of the government of Korea.

Chi-Chen Chiang is Assistant Professor in the Department of Political Science, Soochow University in Taipei, Taiwan, an Adjunct Research Fellow in the Taiwan Institute of Economic Research (TIER), and a Consultant to the Foundation on International and Cross-Strait Studies and the Foundation of Medical Professionals Alliance in Taiwan.

Lisa Coen is Director for the G8 at the National Security Council (NSC). Previously she worked at the Office of the US Trade Representative (USTR) as Deputy Assistant USTR for Southeast Asia and the Pacific and Global Pharmaceutical Policy, and as Deputy Assistant USTR for Congressional Affairs.

Peter Drysdale is Emeritus Professor of Economics and Visiting Fellow in The Crawford School of Economics and Government at The Australian National University, and Director of the PAFTAD Secretariat.

Arthur L. Goldstein recently retired as the Chairman and Chief Executive Officer of Ionics, Inc. He is a director of several corporations.

Geir H. Haarde is Prime Minister, and was previously Finance Minister and Foreign Minister, of Iceland.

Douglas A. Irwin is the Robert E. Maxwell '23 Professor of Arts and Sciences in the Department of Economics at Dartmouth College, and a Research Associate of the National Bureau of Economic Research.

Denise Eby Konan is Interim Chancellor of the University of Hawaii at Manoa, and Professor, Department of Economics, University of Hawaii at Manoa. She specializes in international trade theory and policy.

Sumner J. La Croix is Professor in the Department of Economics and the Population Studies Program, University of Hawaii at Manoa, and Adjunct Senior Fellow, Research Program, East-West Center.

Dorothea C. Lazaro is a Research Analyst at the Philippine Institute for Development Studies, and a consultant to the Asian Development Bank.

Justin Yifu Lin is Professor and Founding Director of the China Centre for Economic Research (CCER) at Peking University. He also serves on several international committees, leading groups and councils on development policy, technology and environment.

David McClain is President of the University of Hawaii, where he previously served as Vice President for Academic Affairs, Dean of the College of Business Administration, the First Hawaiian Bank Distinguished Professor of Leadership and Management, the Henry A. Walker, Jr. Distinguished Professor of Business Enterprise, and Professor of Financial Economics and Institutions.

Rachel McCulloch is the Rosen Family Professor of International Finance at Brandeis University. She currently serves on the Academic Advisory Council of the Federal Reserve Bank of Boston, and the Advisory Committee of the Institute for International Economics, Washington, DC.

Erlinda M. Medalla is a Senior Research Fellow at the Philippines Institute for Development Studies, and the Project Director of the Philippine APEC Study Center Network (PASCN).

Yumiko Okamoto is Professor of Economics in the Department of Policy Studies, Doshisha University, Japan, and a specialist in international economics and development economics.

Pang Eng Fong is Practice Professor and Director of the Wee Kim Wee Center at Singapore Management University (SMU). He is also the Director of SMU's Lee Kong Chian Scholars Program. He has served as the Head of Singapore's diplomatic missions in Seoul, Brussels and London.

Mari Pangestu is Minister of Trade of Indonesia, and a member of the Board of Trustees of the Centre for Strategic and International Studies (CSIS), Jakarta.

Supachai Panitchpakdi was WTO Director-General from 2001 to 2005, and is currently Secretary-General of UNCTAD.

Yung Chul Park is a Professor of Economics at Korea University, and Co-Chairman of the Public Fund Oversight Committee of the Korean Ministry of Finance and Economy.

Hugh Patrick is Director of the Center on Japanese Economy and Business at Columbia Business School, Co-Director of Columbia's APEC Study Center, and Robert D. Calkins Emeritus Professor of International Business at Columbia University.

Peter A. Petri is the founding Dean of the International Business School and the Carl J. Shapiro Professor of International Finance at Brandeis University. He is a consultant to the World Bank, the OECD and the United Nations, and an Economic Adviser to the Government of Bulgaria.

Richard M. Rosenberg is the retired Chairman and Chief Executive Officer of BankAmerica Corporation, and has also served as President and Chief Operating Officer of Seattle-First National Bank and Seafirst Corporation, and as Vice Chairman and Director of Wells Fargo Bank.

Chyuan-Jenq Shiau is Professor of Political Science at the National Taiwan University, specializing in political economy, political and economic changes in Taiwan, and economic cooperation in the Asia Pacific.

Hadi Soesastro is the Executive Director of the Centre for Strategic and International Studies (CSIS) in Jakarta. He also lectures at the University of Indonesia, and is Adjunct Professor at The Australian National University.

Kim Song Tan is Associate Professor, School of Economics and Social Sciences at the Singapore Management University (SMU). He is the Vice President of the Singapore Economics Society.

Ying-Yi Tsai is Assistant Professor, Department of Applied Economics, National University of Kaohsiung, Taiwan, and was previously a Research Economist at the Development Fund, Executive Yuan in Taiwan.

Shujiro Urata is Professor of Economics in the School of Social Sciences, Waseda University, Research Fellow at the Japan Center for Economic Research, and Faculty Fellow at the Research Institute of Economy, Trade and Industry in Tokyo.

Rong-I Wu is chairman of the Taiwan Futures Exchange. He previously served as Senior Adviser to the President and the Vice Premier of Chinese Taipei, President of the Taiwan Institute of Economic Research, and Professor and Director of the Institute of Economics at National Chung-Hsing University. He has served on many advisory boards, including as Director General of the Chinese Taipei Pacific Economic Cooperation Committee and Executive Director of the Chinese Taipei APEC Study Center.

Preface

The Pacific Trade and Development (PAFTAD) Conference series has been at the frontier of analysing challenges facing the economies of East Asia and the Pacific since it was first established in January 1968 in Tokyo. The thirtieth conference, which examined new criticisms of trade, was co-sponsored by Brandeis International Business School's Rosenberg Institute of Global Finance, and the East-West Center. It was held on 19–21 February 2005 at the East-West Center in Honolulu.

This volume collects the contributions of a distinguished group of economists, policy makers and business leaders from around the region. In the PAFTAD tradition, their papers underwent rigorous review and revision following the conference. We are very grateful to all the contributors—paper writers, discussants and referees—whose work is reflected here, and to the PAFTAD International Steering Committee, and especially Hadi Soesastro, its Chair, and Peter Drysdale, the head of its Secretariat, whose efforts made this volume possible.

In organizing the conference and the publication, excellent services were provided by Alberto Posso, Minni Reis and Adrian Rollins, and, more generally, by the PAFTAD Secretariat at the Crawford School of Economics and Government of the Australian National University. We greatly appreciate also the unwavering support of Charles Morrison, the President of the East-West Center, the outstanding work of Jane Smith-Martin, and the valuable assistance from Jane Ho, Scot Griep, Anna Tanaka, Marshal Kingsbury, Jonathan Chow, and other members of the East-West Center staff. Many graduate students from the University of Hawaii and East-West Center volunteered to help during the conference and provided us with large doses of enthusiasm, energy and humour. We thank Somchai Amornthu, Mayumi Bendiner, Amonthep Chawla, Hu Che, Michael Kimmitt, Ming Liu, Sang-young Park, Sittidaj Ponkijvorasin, Fu Shifu, Akihiro Tamura, Kiyoyasu Tanaka, Lubomir Toth and Kristen Uyemura for volunteering their time. And we are most grateful for excellent editorial services from Simon Sherrington at Brandeis and Gaye Wilson at Gryphonworks.

In addition to the Rosenberg Institute at Brandeis University and the East-West Center, the PAFTAD conference and overall programme benefited from the generous support of a consortium of international donors. We greatly appreciate the contributions of the Ford Foundation, the Canadian International Development Research Centre (IDRC), the Japan Research Institute of Economy, Trade and Industry

(RIETI), the Korea Institute of International Economic Policy (KIEP), the Australian Government's Aid Agency AusAID, the Asia Foundation, Toronto University, Victoria University (Canada), the National University of Singapore, the Taiwan Institute of Economic Research, Columbia University (New York), the Centre for Strategic and International Studies (Jakarta), Seranee Holdings (Bangkok), the Philippine Institute for Development Studies, the Institute of Southeast Asian Studies (Singapore) and the Australian National University.

Peter A. Petri and Sumner J. La Croix
September 2006

Abbreviations

AFL-CIO	American Federation of Labor and Congress of Industrial Organizations
AFTA	ASEAN Free Trade Area
ANZCERTA	Australia New Zealand Closer Economic Relations Trade Agreement
APEC	Asia-Pacific Economic Cooperation
ARF	ASEAN Regional Forum
ASEAN	Association of Southeast Asian Nations
ASEAN+3	ASEAN, China, Japan and South Korea
ATC	Agreement on Textiles and Clothing
ATM	Automatic Teller Machine
ATPA	Andean Trade Preference Act
ATPDEA	Andean Trade Promotion and Drug Eradication Act
CA	capital accumulation
CAFTA	Central American Free Trade Agreement
Caltech	California Institute of Technology
CBD	Convention on Biological Diversity
CCAMLR	Commission for the Conservation of Antarctic Marine Living Resources
CEO	Chief Executive Officer
CEPA	Closer Economic Partnership Arrangement
CER	Closer Economic Relations Agreement
CFCs	chlorofluorocarbons
CGE	computable general equilibrium
CITA	Committee for the Implementation of Textile Agreements
CITES	Convention on International Trade in Endangered Species
CJK	China, Japan, Korea
CMI	copyright management information
CTC	changes in tariff classification
CTEA	Copyright Term Extension Act
CUSFTA	Canada–United States Free Trade Agreement
DDA	Doha Development Agenda

DMCA	Digital Millennium Copyright Act
DR–CAFTA	Dominican Republic–Central American Free Trade Agreement
DTA	discriminatory trade agreement
EAEG	East Asian Expert Group
EAI	Enterprise for the Americas Initiative
EASG	East Asian Study Group
EC	European Community
EFTA	European Free Trade Association
EIA	Environmental Impact Assessment
EPA	Economic Partnership Agreement
EU	European Union
EUCD	European Union Copyright Directive
EUROSTAT	Statistical Office of the European Communities
FDI	foreign direct investment
FSA	Fabless Semiconductor Association
FTA	free trade area
FTAA	Free Trade Area of the Americas
GATS	General Agreement on Trade in Services
GATT	General Agreement on Tariffs and Trade
GCC	Gulf Cooperation Council
GDP	gross domestic product
GM	General Motors
GSP	Generalized System of Preferences
GTAP	Global Trade Analysis Project
GVC	global value chain
ICCAT	International Commission for the Conservation of Atlantic Tunas
IDM	integrated device manufacturer
IMF	International Monetary Fund
IP	intellectual property
IPR	intellectual property rights
ISO	International Organization for Standardization
ISP	internet service provider
IT	information technology
ITC	International Trade Centre / US International Trade Commission
JCCT	Joint Commission on Commerce and Trade
JETRO	Japan External Trade Organization
JSEPA	Japan–Singapore Economic Partnership Agreement
JSFTA	Japan–Singapore Free Trade Agreement
KCFTA	Korea–Chile Free Trade Agreement
LDCs	less-developed countries
MBA	Master of Business Administration degree
MBIs	market-based instruments

MEA	multilateral environmental agreements
MEFTA	Middle East Free Trade Area
MERCOSUR	Mercado Comun del Sur (Southern Cone Common Market)
MFA	Multi-Fiber Arrangement
MFN	most-favoured-nation
NAFTA	North American Free Trade Agreement
NAICS	North American Industry Classification System
NASA	National Aeronautics and Space Administration
NEAT	Network of East Asian Think-Tanks
NGO	non-governmental organization
NIE	newly industrialized economy
NIH	National Institutes of Health
NOAA	National Oceanic and Atmospheric Administration
NSF	National Science Foundation
NTB	non-tariff barriers
NYSE	New York Stock Exchange
ODA	Official Development Assistance
OECD	Organization for Economic Cooperation and Development
OEM	original equipment manufacturing
OMA	orderly marketing agreement
OTEXA	Office of Textiles and Apparel
PAFTAD	Pacific Area Forum on Trade and Development
PCT	Patent Cooperation Treaty
PLT	Patent Law Treaty
PNTR	permanent normal trade relations
PPMs	Processes and Production Methods
PTA	preferential trade arrangement
R&D	Research and Development
RCA	revealed comparative advantage
ROO	rules of origin
ROW	Rest of World
RTA	regional trade agreement
RVC	regional value content
SACU	South African Customs Union
SARS	Severe Acute Respiratory Syndrome
SC	semiconductor
SIPRI	Stockholm International Peace Research Institute
SITC	Standard Industrial Trade Classification
SITCR2	Standard Industrial Trade Classification Revision 2
SME	small and medium-sized enterprise
SPLT	Substantive Patent Law Treaty
TIFA	Trade and Investment Framework Agreement
TK	Traditional Knowledge
TL	trade liberalization

TMB	Textile Monitoring Body
TMD	theatre missile defence
TNC	transnational corporation
TPA	Trade Promotion Authority (US)
TRIPs	Trade Related Intellectual Property Rights
UAE	United Arab Emirates
UC Berkeley	University of California, Berkeley campus
UC Los Angeles	University of California, Los Angeles campus
UC San Francisco	University of California, San Francisco campus
UN COMTRADE	United Nations Commodity Trade Statistics Database
UNCTAD	United Nations Conference on Trade and Development
UNDP	United Nations Development Programme
UNIDO	United Nations Industrial Development Organization
US	United States (of America)
USTR	United States Trade Representative
VER	voluntary export restraint
VIE	negotiated voluntary import expansions
WCT	World Copyright Treaty
WHO	World Health Organization
WIPO	World Intellectual Property Organization
WMD	weapons of mass destruction
WPPT	WIPO Performances and Phonograms Treaty
WTO	World Trade Organization

1 New challenges to the global trading system

Sumner J. La Croix and Peter A. Petri

The opening line of Charles Dickens' great novel, *A Tale of Two Cities*, that 'it was the best of times, it was the worst of times, it was the age of wisdom, it was the age of foolishness, it was the epoch of belief, it was the epoch of incredulity …' might well have been written about the global trading system in 2006. It is the best of times, as international trade is robust, many countries are opening their economies to trade and foreign investment, and it is now a commonplace that countries, companies and individuals are destined to compete in markets that span the globe. And yet it is also the worst of times, as multilateral trade negotiations have seemingly collapsed, a growing welter of regional and bilateral trade agreements are bypassing the central GATT rules banning non-discrimination in trade, and interest groups, academics and the press are broadly engaged in vitriolic attacks on trade.

This book presents revised versions of several papers presented at the 30th Pacific Trade and Development conference held in Honolulu, Hawaii in February 2005. The conference participants examined the broad array of problems that confronts trade policy today, especially the criticism levelled against free trade. Is the criticism justified? Even if it is not, has it nonetheless influenced trade policy across a spectrum of countries?

There are two principal threads to the criticism. One thread is that trade *policy* is flawed because negotiations in the 'real world' are unduly influenced by the larger economies and the stronger interest groups within their borders. As a consequence, trade agreements are not structured to create a level playing field, but rather simply create rules that favour these powerful countries and their well-organized producer interests. A second thread is that *globalization* itself is the villain, rather than trade in particular. Globalization is considered to be problematic because its well-known achievements are thought to give rise to adverse social side-effects such as greater income inequality, environmental degradation, violations of labour and human rights standards, and the destruction of older long-established cultures by an all-encompassing global popular culture.

These arguments are being made in increasingly sophisticated ways and have captured significant popular attention. As segments of the public have come to accept some of these arguments, the public has also begun to view 'regulated trade'—as portrayed in the popular press, in many academic discussions, and by government policy reports—as the reasonable, middle ground between protectionism and the 'religion' of free trade.

What can we say about this shift in public opinion against free trade? Does it reflect new insights from trade economists into the relationship between trade and economic welfare? Is the mounting criticism of free trade providing new insight into the contentious and drawn-out world trade negotiations and the changing distribution of trade's benefits and costs, or is it a cover for protectionism, or merely a collection of errors and misconceptions?

The authors in this volume, representing a dozen major trading economies, were asked to address the various dimensions of the academic and popular criticisms of trade. They have responded to this challenge by providing both theoretical and econometric analyses of the changing patterns and structure of trade and foreign investment flows in the Asia-Pacific region over the last decade; by pondering the effectiveness of international economic institutions; by considering the present and future impact of Asia's new rising giant on regional trade and investment; and by searching for the formula that might lead trade negotiators to announce a successful conclusion to the Doha Round. The authors typically used their analysis to develop critical evaluations of trade and investment policies and, in some cases, to suggest policies for reducing adverse domestic spill-overs from changes in trade flows, for balancing innovation and access to pharmaceuticals, and for reducing protectionist backlashes to surging trade flows.

GLOBALIZATION AND TRADE POLICY

The book opens with a set of essays designed to probe the depth and character of opposition to the further opening of multilateral trade. Dr Supachai Panitchpakdi, who was the Director-General of the World Trade Organization when he addressed the 30th PAFTAD Conference in February 2005, provides an overview of the international political issues that were slowing the Doha Round of trade negotiations. His concerns for the future of the Doha Round centre on his perception that the governments of leading developing and developed countries lacked the will to make the politically risky commitments needed to bring it to a successful conclusion. His essay is understandably couched in careful language, but Dr Supachai leaves the reader with little doubt that the preoccupation of the large trading powers—Europe, Japan, and the United States—with their narrow domestic interests made it impossible for them to focus on the critical global public good: markets that are open to trade, entry and investment. The potential losses of powerful domestic interests increasingly deflected these governments from searching for comprehensive agreements—which most initially believed to exist—that would be welfare-enhancing for all WTO members.

Douglas A. Irwin addresses the same issues from a historical perspective. His review of the protectionist backlashes in the United States and Europe induced by the globalization of capital and product markets in the late nineteenth century led him to conclude that recent concerns regarding the potential for a broad-based political backlash are largely unjustified. This conclusion stems partially from his sense that the opponents of globalization represent a wide range of political positions and have been unable to organize effectively within the political systems of their home countries. Moreover, Irwin sees many of the recently developed arguments against trade and investment liberalization as poorly articulated and unlikely to convince voters and officials to attempt to slow globalization. He finds that the extensive trade liberalization achieved in the second half of the twentieth century has been coupled with considerable technological change. He argues that this combination increased the importance of trade to most countries and their businesses. At the same time, Irwin finds that many countries have been slow to undertake the large adjustments—say, in educational investments—required to respond to such rapid changes. Rather than backlash, he believes that the trade policy environment is characterized by 'globalization fatigue', or a lack of desire to undertake additional changes in institutions and individual choices until adjustments to current developments are more fully completed.

Yung Chul Park, Shujiro Urata and Inkyo Cheong take a deeper look at the trade policy objectives of East Asian countries and find a more specific problem: the lack of multilateral trade initiatives is tied to the widespread interest among East Asian governments in regional trading arrangements. The motives of individual countries differ, but East Asian countries are concerned about competition from products produced in North American and European regional trade and investment zones. Park *et al.* find that the trade policies of East Asian countries are related not only to their long-term economic interests but also to their efforts to achieve greater influence in the global economy. This is spawning smaller free (preferred) trade areas and might eventually lead to larger regional groupings. There is, however, some evidence that East Asian governments are not firmly committed to this path. The authors find that the regional free trade agreements in place have done little to improve economic performance, primarily because they have generally been unambitious, in the sense that they regularly provided full or partial exemptions for politically sensitive products. The authors conclude that current regional agreements serve more as placeholders for potentially more effective future agreements than as effective mechanisms for stimulating current trade.

An even more detailed view of the political mechanisms at work is provided by Chad P. Bown and Rachel McCulloch, who address America's specific concerns and actions against important East Asian trade partners. They show that the United States has discriminated against Chinese exports by its widespread use of antidumping actions and safeguard measures, and by establishing stringent quotas on Chinese exports in many product markets. As a result, China has established export taxes to ward off US pressure to restrict Chinese exports of low-quality clothing and textiles, which are labour-intensive products. These events are similar to those involving Japan two decades ago, even though Chinese products have not yet achieved the penetration of American markets that Japanese products had reached in the late 1970s and the 1980s. Bown and McCulloch suggest that policy makers operate with a 'conservative welfare function' that serves to prevent or slow change. Their chapter highlights the many unintended consequences of such interventions, including the deflection of Chinese exports to third-country markets where they create unintended competition for American products exports to these markets.

Together, these authors offer insight into how domestic interest groups in large countries influence trade policy both by countering liberalization efforts and by deflecting policy initiatives away from global negotiations. They further argue that, given the decline in the hegemonic power of the United States, no country or institution is currently providing the 'public good' of access to a large market open to trade. The authors are unsure whether the decline in the provision of this public good is temporary or permanent, but they do see the reduced provision of this public good as negatively affecting the Doha Round.

EXTERNALITIES

The book's second major group of essays addresses criticisms of trade from the perspective of maximizing the welfare of society. Yumiko Okamoto deals with perhaps the most common criticism, that trade skews the income distribution in favour of individuals with skills that are in demand in international labour markets, at the expense of many others who are less well equipped to compete internationally. However, her evidence does not fully support this view. She finds that the growth in trade today is driven by a new kind of trade that is *not* associated with the expansion of income differentials. She calls this trade 'intra-mediate trade', to reflect the fact that the fragmentation of production increases both exports and imports of intermediate goods. She notes that intra-mediate trade is generally associated with increases in growth and productivity, and finds that countries that globalize through intra-mediate trade experience more modest income differentials than countries that do not. Indeed, Okamoto's concern is that the least developed countries may be too slow to adopt this new kind of trade, because it requires relatively high investments in human capital.

Erlinda Medalla and Dorothea C. Lazaro provide a clear look at environmental issues in the Philippines and other developing countries. Does trade shift the production of pollution-intensive products to poor countries? Does the competition for products among such countries lead to a 'race to the bottom' in environmental regulations? Medalla and Lazaro find no evidence for this hypothesis. If anything, developing countries tend to produce somewhat *fewer* pollution-intensive products than developed countries. Measures of environment quality appear to improve *earlier* today than they did in developed countries at similar income levels in the 1980s and 1990s. They argue that the production processes of products that have had the largest increases in trade volumes are not particularly pollution-intensive, and stress that environmental concerns are often motivated by protectionist interests, and may ultimately result in more harm than good, even from an environmental perspective. In general, they favour addressing environmental concerns with appropriate environmental regulation rather than with more general trade policies.

The effects of 'outsourcing' and related wage impacts are addressed in a novel joint product of Mainland Chinese and Taiwanese researchers, Justin Lin and Ying-Yi Tsai. The authors note that in some cases outsourcing may be due to the presence of economies of scale in intermediate goods production. In other instances outsourcing may simply be due to the operation of the principle of comparative advantage in highly competitive industries. Outsourcing occurs when production technologies permit production chains to be divided into finer segments and to be located—barring massive transportation costs—in relatively distant geographic areas. Economists have generally found the effects of outsourcing to be relatively modest and, as for any trade based on comparative advantage, generally positive. Whether or not outsourcing reduces the wages of unskilled labour in developed countries or the overall welfare of unskilled workers has still not been settled. However, the authors do find an interesting difference between the division of labour that now characterizes the manufacturing process in East Asia and earlier forms of comparative advantage. They argue that the new trade patterns involve a high degree of risk-sharing along the supply chain, presumably to offset the greater volatility of markets, and to provide high-powered incentives to critical producers in the product's supply chain.

The essay by Sumner J. La Croix and Denise Eby Konan examines the global intellectual property (IP) rights regime and its implementation in the Asia-Pacific region. The authors note that the global IP regime is regularly criticized from two different perspectives: developed country producers, who complain about the poor protection of IP in developing countries, and developing country consumers, who argue that they are denied access to essential medicines—in some cases life-saving medicines— in order to enrich large pharmaceutical firms in developed countries. Both sides have argued passionately for their viewpoints, each of which has some merit from the viewpoint of important stakeholders. La Croix and Konan argue that a strong and efficient global IP regime would only be adopted by WTO members if it were part of an overall deal that provides adequate compensation to poor- and middle-income countries for paying the higher prices on patented products. The authors argue that compensation agreed to during the Uruguay Round was the phase-out of the Multi-Fiber Arrangement (MFA), which created—in principle at least—a major export opportunity for developing countries. In the event, the gains from dismantling the MFA have been concentrated among just a few developing countries, and Europe and the United States have pursued antidumping actions and imposed safeguard measures on particular categories of textiles and clothing. Thus, many developing countries have been dissatisfied with the outcome of the IP–MFA deal and the global IP regime remains in dispute.

In the final essay of this group, Rong-I Wu, Chyuan-Jenq Shiau and Chi-Chen Chiang explore the connections between trade and security issues. Here there is a potentially positive externality: greater interdependence should raise the value of cooperation and therefore should diminish the prospect of conflict. The authors find, however, that the relationship is more complex—several causal mechanisms are at work, and they operate in both directions. For example, economic interdependence has also generated new possibilities for conflict through the transmission of economic volatility, and by creating new channels for the spread of disease and terrorist activities. The authors argue against complacency; nations must consciously intensify international political cooperation to manage the implications of increased contacts, which include both positive and negative externalities.

POLITICS OF TRADE AND ADJUSTMENT

In a series of shorter essays, policy makers, business leaders and academics proceed to translate these academic insights into the context of 'real world' trade policies. Richard M. Rosenberg, the former CEO of Bank of America, summarizes how major trade policy issues play out in California—a state with an economy similar to that of a large country in both scale and complexity. California has strong interests in open trade because of its exports of agricultural products, high-technology goods, and entertainment products. Still, even this internationally oriented economy cannot escape conflicts among competing interests. In fact, California's 'trade policies' are not as open as one might predict. Environment, immigration and national security concerns all overshadow trade relationships. Another leading executive, Arthur L. Goldstein, notes that business management finds it particularly troublesome that there are large differences across borders in the enforcement of intellectual property rights, in environmental regulations and in the prevalence of corruption. Countries and companies that maintain high and effectively enforced ethical, environmental and IP standards frequently find themselves at a disadvantage when they compete for sales in many parts of the world. Similarly, they face unfair competitive pressures from countries that manipulate their exchange rate to improve the positions of their export businesses. Such frustrations help to explain, according to Goldstein, why support is weakening for free trade, even among market-oriented executives, and in trade-oriented economies such as the United States.

The adjustment requirements of global economic integration are significant, including in the private sector. Pang Eng Fong observes that nations need to make difficult choices to take advantage of global markets—he expects success in countries, like Dubai, that have invested heavily in defining their international competitive position, and worries about others, like Georgia, that are still mired in political conflict. Kim Song Tan explains that even successful globalizers like Singapore need to adjust—in this case with additional investments in technology and greater receptivity to foreign workers. David McClain examines interesting examples of adjustment to globalization within the institution he leads, the University of Hawaii. The university is taking new steps to focus on its comparative strengths, such as oceanographic research, and professional and academic disciplines that take advantage of Hawaii's unique 'island culture' in their research and teaching.

The essays of government leaders and policy analysts provide insight into how these economic and political pressures translate into trade policy initiatives. In frank and detailed comments, Mari Pangestu, the Minister of Trade of Indonesia, explains that while her government recognizes the benefits of fostering increased globalization in Indonesia, it must also control the risks stemming from globalization. More liberal trade policies open opportunities for increased overall welfare, but Pangestu believes that a responsible government must also develop complementary policies to raise the productivity of groups harmed by increased imports (such as farmers and SMEs). Dr Hadi Soesastro calls such complementary policy measures 'second order' liberalization and argues that they must accompany 'first order' trade liberalization to ensure that the first-order reforms are politically acceptable to a country's legislature.

Geir H. Haarde, then Finance Minister and now Prime Minister of Iceland, notes that important domestic industries (for example, the fishing industry in Iceland) often have a profound influence on the course of a country's trade policies, even in advanced countries. Lisa Coen, a senior official in the US Trade Representative's (USTR) office, notes that the executive's US trade policy also depends on close cooperation with the US Congress, and with industry and non-governmental organizations. In this complex setting, the USTR pursues a multi-track policy by conducting both regional and global negotiations. Doug Bereuter, the President of The Asia Foundation and a former US Congressman who participated in the 1999 WTO meetings in Seattle, theorizes that these policy trends, reflecting similar developments in many countries, represent the 'bifurcation of the world order'—a gradual shift of power away from national governments toward more fragmented citizen groups and non-governmental organizations (NGOs) on the one hand, and supra-national bodies on the other.

What, then, accounts for the disintegration of government and political party control over trade policy? Some observers have pointed to the effects of the rapid technological change that has revolutionized how products and services are produced. Narongchai Akrasanee writes of a shift to a new 'cyberstate' that has made it virtually impossible for companies or countries to control markets, even in services, which are now frequently provided via the Internet. He also notes that the 'corporate state' means that managing cannot be done at the border, since corporations now frequently span borders and make internal decisions about where to locate production, raise capital or pay dividends. Peter A. Petri emphasizes that these technological changes create more volatile markets, and thereby induce rapid changes in the number of firms producing for the market, employment levels in an industry and firm investment decisions. Since the cost of adjusting the firm's capital and labour stocks depends on how quickly adjustment is effected, the cost of adjustment to producers has typically increased with the rate of technological change. This increased cost of adjustment to technological changes, market changes, and changes in the rules of the game may be one reason for the current 'rest' in multilateral trade liberalization efforts. It may also explain the popularity of bilateral and regional agreements: countries find these easier to control and manage than the trade policies mandated by the WTO.

With these concerns in relief, the book refocuses on the implications of current trends for trade policy and the conduct of international negotiations. Peter Drysdale describes today's approach to trade negotiations as highly vulnerable to misdirection. Trade negotiations are biased towards bilateralism, since there are few international controls on what countries may or may not negotiate away from the multilateral negotiating table. Bilateral negotiations, in turn, are biased toward the issues of the larger, dominant economy. In fact, bilateral and regional agreements are biased towards pairings that consist of members of unequal size, so that the stronger can impose its preferences on the weaker. This generates 'hub and spoke' trade arrangements. All this points to a serious fragmentation of the trade negotiation process that, in Drysdale's view, leads to large economic losses and potentially serious political tensions. Hugh Patrick echoes these concerns and argues that governments need to pay more attention to these trends. At a minimum, he wants them to ensure—regardless of current policy directions—that bilateral and regional trade agreements are structured to permit a smooth return to a multilateral, non-discriminatory framework in the future. For example, preferential trading arrangements should contain built-in sunset provisions, or open access provisions, which allow discriminatory effects to fade away when the benefits of multilateral approaches are again widely recognized.

CONCLUSION

At the 30th PAFTAD conference in Hawaii, the conference participants reached broad agreement in their discussions that the case for free trade remains very strong, especially in the Asia-Pacific region. The region's economies are robust and increasingly open to trade and investment, notwithstanding some flirtation with regional arrangements. However, the state of the multilateral trading system is much more precarious. The participants could not agree on whether the difficulties of the WTO system are grounded in the shortcomings of the global negotiations process, or in the (perhaps temporarily) limited willingness of governments and other stakeholders to absorb change. They did, however, broadly agree that the WTO and its accompanying institutions regulating world trade are critical to global prosperity and deserve to be strengthened. The decade-long rush to bilateral and regional initiatives is only a second-best alternative to much more productive multilateral agreements. Bilateral and regional agreements have diverted the attention of governments from global negotiations. At worst, they are establishing a discriminatory 'spaghetti bowl' that will long frustrate the creation of truly global markets. Thus, the policy community should redouble its efforts to advance the global WTO negotiations and to ensure, at a minimum, that bilateral and regional agreements leave the door open for future multilateral liberalization efforts.

2 The challenge of policy in the era of globalization

Keynote address by the WTO Director-General Supachai Panitchpakdi

LADIES AND GENTLEMEN

I am delighted to join this auspicious gathering. Sometimes it may appear that we economists devote too little of our attention to really analyse and discuss criticisms levelled at the benefits of freer trade and its role in globalization. But I believe that a debate of this nature is both timely and essential. Trade policy and the multilateral trading system have taken centre stage in both the media and the public eye. No doubt this scrutiny will intensify over the course of this year. Not only are we at a critical phase in the Doha Development Agenda round of trade negotiations, but this year we are also celebrating the 10th Anniversary of the World Trade Organization. This anniversary has already stimulated a good deal of reflection about the multilateral trading system's benefits and challenges.

I should like to focus my brief comments here today in an area in which I perhaps have a comparative advantage: that is in providing an overview of the challenges facing WTO Members in concluding the Doha Development Agenda. Given the overarching theme of this conference, let me, first of all, reflect on the role and objectives of the multilateral trading system. I believe these are too frequently misunderstood and too often the target of misguided criticism. In this respect I will focus on three issues, which I am sure you will be taking up in greater detail over the course of this conference. Firstly, the importance of the multilateral trading system as a body of agreed, predictable and enforceable rules; secondly, the role of the WTO in fostering trade liberalization, and finally, the WTO's aspirations to become a truly universal organization.

I would argue that the core role of the WTO as a body of multilateral trade rules, underpinned by a binding dispute settlement mechanism, is often forgotten or taken for granted. Perhaps this is because few of us can remember a time when there was a serious and sustained breakdown in international trade relations resulting from random and protectionist interventions by governments. Of course, trade spats often capture the headlines. These, however, are isolated incidents which are, for the most part, eventually resolved. This is to the great credit of the multilateral trading system, and is proof that it is functioning effectively.

Certainly, one of the most impressive achievements of the multilateral trading system has been the members' record of compliance with dispute settlement rulings, particularly since the system was strengthened and reformed as a result of the Uruguay Round. Over the last ten years (1 January 1995–31 December 2004), 323 complaints have been filed with the Dispute Settlement Body, leading to the creation of 162 panels and the circulation of panel reports in 115 cases. Around 75 per cent of these panel reports have been appealed. More disputes have been brought to the WTO in a decade than were brought to the GATT in nearly five decades of its existence. Members have, in general, implemented the recommendations and rulings made by panels and by the Appellate Body within a 'reasonable period of time'. It is clear that WTO Members have confidence in the WTO dispute settlement system and respect it. What also stands out is the fact that over half of the disputes brought to the WTO do not reach the panel stage, with many of these cases being resolved through bilateral consultations. Diplomatic solutions are often found before litigation is necessary.

As concerns the role of the WTO in fostering trade liberalization, I would like to take off my hat as Director-General just for a moment and speak to some of my experiences and observations in Asia.

It is now well accepted that all Asian countries open to trade have benefited from globalization. Japan has risen from the devastation of World War II to be one of the richest countries in the world. Korea has grown from poverty to being an OECD member in some thirty years. More recently China has grown at almost 10 per cent a year, lifting millions out of poverty. India is following a similar path.

A common characteristic in each of these economies has been the ongoing programmes of structural reform, in which trade liberalization has played an integral part. These structural reforms, embedded in generally stable macroeconomic environments, have allowed resources to move into their areas of comparative advantage. It has been widely shown that the sectors in the Asian economies that have been liberalized—manufacturing, and particularly electronics—have done better than those sectors that have remained protected. Moreover, Asian economies have been largely successful in devising policies to compensate the losers that inevitably result from structural reform.

The Asian experience has demonstrated that, more than any other policy approach yet tried, openness to trade is an important component as an engine for rapid economic growth. Granted, however, there is space for debate about the scope, sequencing and pace of reform, and most importantly, trade openness alone will not generate economic success. Other accompanying policies are required to create the right conducive environment.

I would argue that multilateral trade negotiations are by far the best route to achieve trade liberalization and to maximize the potential benefits of freer trade. The multilateral route also provides the broad trade-offs which make liberalization politically digestible. It gives all players a voice, and allows smaller and poorer countries to exercise greater clout by banding together. We have seen this recently with the emergence of the G20 and growth of a stronger alliance between the G90 countries. Our experience has also shown that only multilateral trade negotiations have succeeded in tackling the more sensitive and politically charged issues—where regional and bilateral agreements have singularly failed to make headway. Two particular examples are textiles and clothing, and agriculture.

An important achievement of the Uruguay Round was the agreement to integrate textiles and clothing fully into normal multilateral disciplines by the progressive phasing out of quotas that were held by some members. 2004 saw the end of that phase-out period, ending the special and discriminatory regime that had lasted for more than 40 years. The elimination of these quotas will benefit the global economy through welfare and efficiency gains, and through increased market access opportunities. While there are some concerns and anxieties about the adjustment costs likely to result from the abolition of quotas for some members, the removal of these distortions should be seen as a major achievement. Efforts are being made with the World Bank and the IMF to explore and identify ways to address liberalization-related adjustment challenges, among other things.

Although agriculture was covered under the GATT, related disciplines were rather weak. As a result, trade in many agricultural products was impeded by high tariffs, a host of non-tariff measures and increasing recourse to trade-distorting subsidies. The Uruguay Round signalled a collective U-turn in the direction of agricultural protection and support that had been developing, and greater transparency in agricultural trade regimes through tariffication of non-tariff barriers. The Uruguay Round also included a commitment to continue the process of agricultural reform that began in the year 2000, and is continuing through the Doha Development Agenda. And I must say that the current DDA negotiations provide a historic opportunity to inject real substantive changes to agricultural policy around the world. Agriculture is *the* crucial issue for so many countries in the DDA that it will be central to a successful outcome to the negotiations.

As I mentioned before, regional and bilateral deals have failed to make headway in advancing agricultural reform. They are not a viable policy alternative for multilateral trade liberalization. While regional and bilateral agreements, if they are open, may help to advance the cause of trade liberalization, we should also be cognizant of their inherent risks. One major risk is that they may, in fact, serve to divert more trade than they create. Another is that they may create vested interests and divert focus and resources away from multilateral negotiations. Thirdly, there is the issue of the systemic impact of these deals on one of the most valuable principles of the WTO—that of non-discrimination. Certainly as bilateral and regional deals proliferate, the world becomes a more complex place to do business globally. Differing rules of origin are of particular concern in this regard.

Turning to my third subject, we are also making headway in achieving the multilateral trading system's goal to be a truly universal organization. At the GATT's inception there were 23 contracting parties, most of whom were either developed or large developing countries. Today, the WTO has 148 members, which accounts for more than 90 per cent of world trade. Three-quarters of WTO members are developing countries—ranging from the smallest and poorest countries to the big players like China. Over 25 additional countries are queuing to join, also involving large players such as Russia and Saudi Arabia, and a number of least-developed countries, as well as countries such as Iraq and Afghanistan.

But true universality must involve more than simply the fact of membership. It must involve real integration into the system and a sense of drawing real benefits from the rights and obligations taken on board. In many respects we have seen some positive developments, particularly over the last ten years: one example is developing countries' use of the dispute settlement mechanism to protect their rights under the system. Around one-third of the disputes brought to the dispute settlement body are from developing countries. Among the ten biggest users of the dispute settlement system, at least half are developing countries.

We have also seen developing countries as a whole becoming much more assertive in the WTO, and pushing hard for their interests, both in terms of rule-making and market access within the context of the Doha Development Agenda.

Another positive development is the greater emphasis that has been placed by members on helping developing countries to participate more fully in the negotiations and regular work of the WTO through technical assistance and capacity building. There has been a huge increase in the scope and quantity of trade-related technical assistance activities. In 1995, 84 activities were provided on a budget of two million Swiss francs (around US$1.7 million). In 2004, 501 activities were organized on a budget of 30 million Swiss francs (around US$25 million). Efforts are also being made to coordinate with other institutions where joint action can be positive and more efficient. An arrangement to cooperate with UNIDO, for example, is geared towards addressing supply-side constraints. Another example is the Integrated Framework programme for least-developed countries, which is aimed at helping poor countries mainstream trade into their development and poverty reduction strategies. We are working with five other agencies in this effort: UNCTAD, the ITC, the World Bank, UNDP and the IMF.

Without question, however, the most important action that can be taken to more fully integrate developing countries into the trading system is to conclude as rapidly as possible the Doha Development Agenda. The DDA holds the opportunity for all members to strengthen their economies and help improve the international trading environment. An ambitious outcome in these negotiations would also be a considerable contribution to the global fight against poverty. Better market access for poor country exports, steep reductions in trade-distorting farm subsidies, and more equitable trade rules would present developing countries with a major opportunity to help use the trading system as a vehicle for their development. So let me briefly report to you on the state of play of the DDA negotiations and what I see as being the key challenges ahead.

As you will know, the Doha Development Agenda has been under way for over three years. It has been a rocky road, with both disappointments and successes. Two steps forward in the DDA have often been followed by one step back. On the one hand we have seen deadlines missed, including the original target deadline for the end of the round, which was set for 1 January 2005. On the other hand, we have seen members show real leadership and political courage in narrowing their differences on sensitive issues, one example being a waiver decision taken before the Cancún Ministerial meeting on TRIPs and public health. This provides additional flexibility to poor countries with an insufficient manufacturing capacity to make effective use of compulsory licensing, so as to provide essential medicines at cheaper prices.

Another, more recent, example is the so-called July package. Following the setback at Cancún, the aim in 2004 was to make up lost ground and make substantial progress, particularly in the market access negotiations, by agreeing on frameworks for modalities in agriculture and non-agricultural goods, as well as to make progress on other areas of the negotiations. We scored a major success, particularly in agriculture where members agreed to eliminate export subsidies by a date to be decided. They also agreed to make substantial reductions to domestic support, and determined the kind of approach they would apply for cutting tariffs. We now have the foundations in place to negotiate the finer details. Members also agreed to launch negotiations on trade facilitation (as one of the so-called Singapore issues) as well as the treatment of cotton within the negotiations. Inability to bridge differences on these issues in the past had caused major roadblocks to progress.

As a result of the July package, the negotiations have now entered a new phase, whereby we need to move from clarification of issues to real negotiations. We now have in our sights the WTO's Sixth Ministerial Conference which will be held in Hong Kong in December 2005. We must have an ambitious outcome from that conference if we are to conclude the Doha Development Agenda in 2006, which appears to be a realistic and generally agreed new timeline for the negotiations.

In order to make the Hong Kong conference a success, we need to achieve a balanced outcome across the negotiations. In particular, we must have a substantial breakthrough in Hong Kong on five key issues: modalities in agriculture; modalities in non-agricultural goods; a critical mass of market opening offers in services; significant progress in areas such as rules and trade facilitation; and finally a proper reflection of the development dimension. In this respect, I believe that we must see July 2005 as an important marker in our progress. By that time we must have made significant progress in each of the areas I just mentioned. In July we should have a reality check to determine how far we have moved and whether we are on course for a significant outcome in Hong Kong.

As I have emphasized to ambassadors in Geneva, we need to keep ministers continuously and closely involved in the process over the course of this year. It is ministers who will ultimately make the major political decisions that will determine the fate of the Doha Development Agenda. Indeed, I would argue that agriculture would not have moved as far as it did last year without some procedural innovation, which also involved intensive involvement by ministers. Already this year I have met with ministers on the fringes of the World Economic Forum Annual meeting, as well as African and Nordic ministers in Tanzania. I am very encouraged by the level of commitment and determination they have expressed towards moving these negotiations forward. A number of gatherings of ministers are being planned in the coming months, and we must ensure that their attention is firmly on the key issues.

Ministers have some very tough decisions in front of them. Tough, in part, because they are all politicians who are accountable to their constituents. Some of these constituents may be negatively affected by trade liberalization, and may oppose conclusion of the negotiations. It is for governments to find ways outside of the negotiations to alleviate any such negative impacts, as a successful and ambitious outcome should be in wider interest to their economies as a whole. For other constituents and sectors of society, concerns about the WTO and trade liberalization may be based upon a lack of understanding of the role and objectives of the WTO and the DDA negotiations. That is why your discussions over the next two days are so important. I would urge you to disseminate the outcome of this conference in a way that is digestible to the general public. We need their support. In order to secure their support and confidence, we need to have an informed debate about the critiques of trade and its role in globalization. The WTO can make a big contribution to improving the prospects of the global economy.

Thank you.

3 Globalization fatigue, not globalization backlash

Douglas A. Irwin

The aim of this paper is to examine an issue that lurks behind many discussions of globalization. That issue is whether there is now or will be a serious backlash against increased worldwide economic integration that will lead to a retreat from trade liberalization and a possible return of protectionism.

The fashionable answer among many academic observers and prognosticators is to express concern (and perhaps even fret) about the current state of trade relations, to issue a warning about impending protectionism, and to suggest that the world trading system could collapse without renewed efforts on its behalf.

In this paper, I offer a mild dissent. I do not think that there has been or will be a serious backlash against globalization. Indeed, I am surprised by the lack of 'push back' or resistance to greater economic integration in the United States and other industrial countries over the past 20 years, even as such integration has accelerated.

Before explaining this benign view, I would like to answer the question of why so many observers are concerned about such a backlash. The reason is the fear that history could repeat itself. What many people have in mind is the experience of the first half of the twentieth century when the first wave of globalization (from 1870 to 1913) was followed by the inter-war period (from 1919 to 1939). The first wave of globalization was characterized by increasing world trade, the free flow of capital around the world, and the migration of substantial numbers of people from Europe to the New World. By contrast, the inter-war period saw the rise of barriers to trade, the interruption of capital flows, and new obstacles to labour migration, all of which helped to stifle the world economy. The reduction of these barriers was part of the work of the post-war generation of policymakers, who created the Bretton Woods system and the General Agreement on Tariffs and Trade (GATT). The effort to reduce trade barriers continues to the present in the World Trade Organization (WTO) and elsewhere.

The lesson that some observers have drawn from this turn of events is that even high degrees of economic integration can be reversed by policy and that globalization can sow the seeds of its own destruction.

For example, the economic historian Jeffrey Williamson (1998) has written provocatively on 'globalization backlash'—that the high degree of economic integration achieved by 1913 around the world was reversed in the 1920s and 1930s. In his view, increased economic integration generated income distributional conflicts because trade and migration benefited some groups but harmed others. Therefore, open markets created aggrieved domestic interests that fought back politically and succeeded in partially closing markets. As he writes, 'these distributional events helped to create a globalization backlash which caused a drift to more restrictive immigration and trade policy prior to World War I'.

This interpretation of events can be questioned. By 1913, there was not really any significant globalization backlash. Tariff levels were stable, capital flows were free, and although there was some tightening of immigration restrictions in the United States, the world economy was functioning smoothly. Transportation costs were declining, the telephone was beginning to proliferate, automobiles were about to break into the consumer market, and aeroplanes were poised for commercial service. In short, there was no end in sight to this first era of globalization.

What happened was World War I, a failure of political leadership after the war in the 1920s, and the Great Depression of the 1930s. The war forced governments to take a greater economic planning role, including trade controls, a role that they were reluctant to give up after the war. The 1920s were littered with international conferences designed to reduce trade barriers, but there was little political enthusiasm for them. The Great Depression then sparked an outbreak of protectionist pressures, quite understandably, and reinforced the view that trade controls were an essential part of economic management since capitalism (the market economy) was so inherently flawed—though now of course we understand that it was precisely the failure of governments' monetary and financial policies (not the market) that so severely exacerbated the economic downturn.

So we have to put the first era of globalization into perspective. It did not sow the seeds of its own demise; there was no globalization backlash, but rather war and depression disrupted its continuation.

Still, the historian Niall Ferguson (2005) has recently warned of the historical parallels between globalization then and now. He suggests that just as pre-1914 globalization was reversible (at least in part), so is today's globalization. Ferguson argues that a major worldwide conflict could occur, meaning that 'the possibility is as real today as it was in 1915 that globalization, like the *Lusitania*, could be sunk'. As he puts it, 'the end of globalization after 1914 was not unforeseeable … As the economic parallels with 1914 suggest, today's globalization shows at least some signs of reversibility'.

Although there are many threats to world peace in the Middle East and in East Asia (China and Taiwan in particular), such conflict—and with it the demise of globalization—is not inevitable. It is impossible to predict or foresee a World War III akin to World War I.

Still, an appropriate lesson to be drawn from history is that if we do not wish the current era of globalization to be faced with an ending similar to that of the first era of globalization, then a major global conflict and another economic depression should be avoided. This sounds glib, but it is not meant to be. In particular, economic growth and sound macroeconomic management are fundamental reasons why there has not been a globalization backlash despite the increased integration of the world. Economic growth eases the pain of dislocation, creates new opportunities for those who face the downside risks of globalization, and thereby reduces the pressures on policymakers to close markets or render costly assistance. In addition, social safety nets are a feature of economic policy today that helps mitigate any backlash, and these policies were almost wholly absent in 1913.

Indeed, barring a global war or a major depression, globalization today is probably irreversible as the steady march of technology brings economies together. The technology behind increased international communications, from the telephone and Internet to the Boeing 747 and Airbus A-380, cannot be undone. Even if trade policies were to be used in an attempt to offset this shrinkage of the world, they cannot put the globalization genie back into the bottle because the toothpaste is out of the tube (to mix metaphors). To use a historical analogy, when railroads ran deep into the Midwestern United States and Russia in the late nineteenth century, grain prices fell across Europe. Agricultural tariffs rose somewhat in response, but this policy response failed to offset the rapid decline in transport costs. In the end, grain markets were integrated to a much greater degree than before.

Furthermore, the momentum of global economic policy is towards the continued opening of markets, more through bilateral and regional arrangements than through the multilateral process, an issue to which I will return shortly. This makes it difficult to see a revival of protection on the horizon, but economists have not refrained from crying wolf on this score for many years.

Consider the case of the United States. In 1961, the great economist Jacob Viner said that 'in Congress … the tide is running in a protectionist direction'. In the early 1970s, Fred Bergsten warned that 'US trade policy has been moving steadily away from the liberal trade approach which had characterized it since 1934'. Around the same time, Harald Malmgren stated that 'we are seeing a resurgence of mercantilism'. In the late 1970s, Robert Baldwin argued that 'the Carter Administration is facing protectionist pressures from particular industries and labor groups that are stronger than at any time since the early 1930s'. In the early 1980s, the same was said about the Reagan administration. Indeed, the Reagan administration was routinely denounced as the most protectionist administration since Herbert Hoover. In 1982, Mike Aho and Thomas Bayard published an article 'The 1980s: Twilight of the Open Trading System?' in *The World Economy*.

All of these quotes come from Robert Pastor's classic 1983 article entitled 'Cry and Sigh Syndrome', the repeated statement that trade liberalization efforts are in peril, only to have these fears remain unrealized. All the concerns mentioned above may have resulted in short-term protectionist actions, but were designed to be temporary and indeed faded away. What these economists said may have had value at the time as warnings, but surely not as predictors of the actual turn of events. How many economists would exchange the trade policies of 2005 for those of 1985 or 1975 or 1955?

But are the threats to the open world trading system more powerful today? Are industry groups waiting to battle any move to open markets further? Industry pressure groups are, in fact, relatively quiet in terms of pressing for closed markets. The farm lobby in most countries is trying to cling to the status quo, while other manufacturing industries demand protection only to the extent that they have not become multinationals or are sourcing from foreign suppliers, an ever diminishing set of firms. With the possible exception of the apparel industry, China in the 2000s is not stimulating the same protectionist reaction as Japan did in the 1980s, in large part because multinationals operate much more freely there.

But are the anti-trade non-governmental organizations (NGOs)—or the New Millennium collectivists, as David Henderson (2001) calls them—a threat to open trade? This was a concern after the WTO ministerial meeting in Seattle in 1999, but since then such groups have not posed the obstacles that were once feared. These groups are relatively weak, are certainly divided, and many have no positive agenda for the future.

If the anti-globalization forces appear to be underwhelming, why is progress on trade liberalization proceeding so slowly? There is no doubt that the Doha Round has stalled or is proceeding sluggishly (as of 2005), and that there are deep concerns about the future of the multilateral trading system. Yet let us remember that the world trading system has been through serious difficulties in the past. Does anyone remember the deep and pervasive pessimism of the late 1970s and early 1980s, particularly after the failure of the GATT ministerial conference in 1982? I vividly recall reading an essay by John Jackson called 'The Crumbling Institutions of the Liberal Trade System' in the *Journal of World Trade Law* in 1978. At that time, Jackson was not alone in arguing that the GATT was in tatters, its rules routinely ignored, unable to stem the spread of voluntary export restraints (VERs), and its membership incapable of making progress on trade liberalization.

However, the Uruguay Round followed. Now the WTO has a more solid institutional base than the GATT and a much stronger set of rules—rules that are taken seriously— than the GATT had in 1978. Some now think that the institution is too strong in the realm of dispute settlement. In any event, the institution did not crumble in quite the way Jackson wrote nearly 30 years ago.

The lack of progress in the Doha Round is lamentable, but not surprising. Multilateral trade liberalization has never, ever, been easy. We seem to think of the 1950s and 1960s as the halcyon days of trade liberalization, when there was consensus and political will, and everything was easy. This is a false reading of history. Each of the GATT negotiating rounds was an extremely difficult task. From about 1947 until the end of the Kennedy Round in 1967, the GATT accomplished virtually nothing. History indicates that progress at the multilateral level should be measured in terms of decades, not years. Doha may be behind schedule; so what else is new? Most trade rounds take about a decade to conclude, and as this text is being written (2005) it has only been less than four years since the commencement of the Doha Round.

It is instructive to go back and read the pronouncements before the conclusion of the Uruguay Round. The same frustration and pessimism that we see today was pervasive. In 1991, Jagdish Bhagwati wrote a book entitled *The World Trading System at Risk*. About the same time, the American economist Lester Thurow (1990) said that

GATT was dead because it had failed to move for so long. Yet MIT's Rudiger Dornbusch got it right: the GATT, he once remarked, is resting (personal communication).

Indeed, while I do not think there is any globalization backlash, there is definitely globalization fatigue, in part because the world trading system is still digesting the Uruguay Round, with the major changes in dispute settlement and intellectual property rights protection that it brought, along with the abolition of the MFA. In addition, China has been folded into the world trading system, a major accomplishment. This, along with the lingering effects of the NAFTA debate, has created indigestion in terms of US trade politics. There is little political enthusiasm for major efforts at trade liberalization in the United States and elsewhere.

Even if the WTO achieves nothing in terms of trade liberalization over the next few years, it is still an invaluable institution for the rules, structure and policy bindings that it provides. Even if it ceases to be a forum for trade liberalization, which I doubt, the integration of markets will proceed with the steady march of technological change and smaller regional trade agreements.

Will the WTO be supplanted by regional arrangements? The movement towards bilateral agreements can be seen in the light of globalization fatigue. They are relatively easy to do. They involve like-minded countries; they do not eat up much political capital, because the stakes tend to be smaller; they can exclude politically sensitive sectors here and there (the EU is particularly good at this, but also the United States); and they seemingly accomplish something for trade ministries around the world at a time when there is little action at the WTO. They are clearly an inferior way of achieving trade liberalization in comparison to the multilateral route, but should not be considered a victory for the protectionist forces that want markets closed.

The biggest threat to the WTO as a trade liberalization body comes from its membership. Alan Oxley, Australia's former ambassador to the GATT, says the reason is that a core value is under threat—that everyone must liberalize for the common good. In his view, the developing countries that form half of the WTO do not view the institution as a place to liberalize, but as a place to get trade charity in the form of unreciprocated preferences (Oxley 2005). This approach is not good for developing countries, or for developed countries.

Without a common political commitment to reduce trade barriers, there is little that can be accomplished in the WTO. The WTO risks becoming like the United Nations: a forum for debate but not much action. The WTO is nothing more or less than what the membership wants it to be, and can collectively achieve. The WTO rules are important and are taken seriously, but as a forum for liberalization, the action—for the time being—is taking place elsewhere. The WTO's inaction is not the result of inactivity. The WTO holds more than 3,000 meetings a year, but with little to show for it. Perhaps the representatives are trying to accomplish too much across too many issues.

Let me conclude by saying that, despite the challenges ahead, we should view the pervasive pessimism about world trade negotiations with some degree of scepticism. At the risk of being accused of complaisance, I take comfort from the fact that policy efforts—however erratic—are being made largely in one direction: the opening of world markets. There is globalization fatigue, but not globalization backlash. And it simply takes time to recover from fatigue.

John Maynard Keynes (1923) might object to this sanguine approach: 'economists set themselves too easy, too useless a task if in tempestuous seasons they can only tell us that when the storm is long past the ocean is flat again'.

What I am trying to suggest is that, despite the problems that now confront the world trading system, the ocean has never really been flat at any time in the past, and yet the ship of world trade has not sunk, and has even managed to sail forward.

REFERENCES

Bhagwati, J. (1991) *The World Trading System at Risk*, Princeton, NJ: Princeton University Press.

Ferguson, N. (2005) 'Sinking Globalization', *Foreign Affairs*, 84: 64–77.

Henderson, D. (2001) *Anti-liberalism 2000. The Rise of New Millennium Collectivism*, London: Institute of Economic Affairs.

Jackson, J.H. (1978) 'The Crumbling Institutions of the Liberal Trade System', *Journal of World Trade Law*, 12: 93–106.

Keynes, J.M. (1923) *Treatise on Monetary Reform*, London: Macmillan.

Oxley, A. (2005) 'The WTO is in Trouble', available at <http://www.techcentralstation.com>, entry for 10 February; accessed 15 August 2006.

Pastor, R. (1983) 'The Cry and Sigh Syndrome: Congress and US Trade Policy', in A. Schick (ed.), *Making Economic Policy in Congress*, Washington, DC: American Enterprise Institute.

Thurow, L. (1990) 'GATT is Dead', *Journal of Accountancy*, 170: 36–9.

Williamson, J. (1998) 'Globalization, Labor Markets and Policy Backlash in the Past', *Journal of Economic Perspectives*, 12: 51–72.

Wolf, M. (2003) 'Is Globalization in Danger?', *The World Economy*, 26: 393–411.

4   The emergence of 'intra-mediate trade': implications for the Asia-Pacific region

Yumiko Okamoto

INTRODUCTION

We have seen a dramatic integration of the global economy through trade in the last few decades. What is distinctive is not the sheer volume of trade but novel features of modern international trade: the vertical disintegration of the industry and the concomitant increase in intra-industry trade largely consisting of trade in intermediate inputs (Feenstra 1998: 31, Krugman 1995: 333).

Companies are now finding it profitable to produce a good in a number of stages in a number of locations, adding a little bit of value at each stage.[1] They are also outsourcing increasing amounts of the production process, a process which may occur either domestically or abroad. The combination of both vertically disintegrated modes of production and the increasingly global outsourcing activities of firms is considered to be one of the important factors for the recent expansion of world trade.

This paper examines empirically both the extent and consequences of the emergence of this new type of international trade in the Asia-Pacific region. The novel features of modern international trade are considered to become even more important in the future. Unlike in the past when inventions and innovations were considered breakthroughs, today they are a regular occurrence (Asian Development Bank 2003: 208). This means that the transformation process of each economy is continuous and the production process of goods and services, especially manufactured goods, will become increasingly more complex, which will make a substantial impact on the modes of production and international trade.

Recent empirical studies have tended to focus too much on the relationship between trade and growth at the macro level, as discussed in the literature survey below. We may need to investigate the empirical relationship between trade and growth at the more disaggregated level, although it is very hard to work out at what level of disaggregation such an exercise can best proceed (Commander 2004: 525).

The relationship between globalization, inequality and poverty has received considerable attention in recent years, especially its impact on wage inequality. It is interesting to observe empirically the relationship between outsourcing and wage inequality in the Asia-Pacific region.

This paper reviews both theoretical and empirical studies investigating the relationship between trade, growth and inequality. The first section observes the extent to which novel features of international trade have emerged in the Asia-Pacific region particularly since the beginning of the 1990s. The following section empirically analyses the relationship between trade, growth and inequality using simple regression techniques. Finally, the paper considers the implications of globalization for the least-developed countries of the Asia-Pacific region such as Cambodia, Laos and Vietnam. With the arrival of the new wave of globalization, the distinction between the winners and the losers has become clear even among developing countries. Some have begun to break into the world markets. To many in the developing world, however, globalization has not brought the promised economic benefits. It is important to observe which force is stronger in the Asia-Pacific region.

LITERATURE SURVEY

Trade and growth

Theories

Economists seem to agree that the removal of barriers to free trade and the closer integration of national economies *can be* a force for good, and that it has the potential to enrich everyone in the world.[2] Economists believe that countries can specialize and do better. The significant gains from specialization through trade have been considered to be a potential source of growth for a long time.

Ever since Adam Smith, economists have suggested that the size of the market matters for growth: scale economies in production can be exploited when trade expands markets. This seems to be particularly relevant for small-sized and poor economies (Bhagwati 2004: 61).

A larger market matters for growth for other reasons as well. A larger market may intensify competition, which can spur innovation and growth. It may also give access to more ideas, allows for investment in large fixed-cost investments and enables further division of labour (World Bank 2002: 36). The importance of the ability to import ideas from richer countries is usefully emphasized by Romer (1993) (see also Rodrik 1999: 25). One advantage of backwardness is that ideas can be imported from abroad.

A larger market may enhance growth through widening choice. This will matter more for firms than for consumers in developing countries, since the larger size of the market gives wider access to better-quality machines and a much greater variety of specialized intermediate inputs (World Bank 2002: 36). Since the work of Krugman (1979), product variety has played a central role in models of trade and growth.

More recent theories of endogenous growth, going beyond models of static comparative advantage, have substantially deepened our knowledge of the channels through which trade can affect growth. The new models demonstrate how benefits of scale economies and imports of high-quality inputs and technology can generate cumulative growth impact over the long term (Rodrik 1999: 25). Rodrik emphasizes, however, that according to the new growth theories, openness may also increase the risk of specialization in technologically less dynamic sectors in which developing countries may have an initial comparative advantage.[3] Both cases can occur in existence of multiple equilibria.

The immiserizing growth is a classic example of the case against free trade for small open economies. The development of new growth theories has made it even harder to derive an unambiguous relationship between trade and growth. Although the review of both traditional and modern trade theories implies the existence of a huge potential of benefits through trade, the relationship between the two is far from clear. We need to investigate further the mechanism by which trade enhances growth, and to understand under what conditions the risk of specialization in undesirable activities becomes large.

Empirical evidence

The last two decades produced a large body of cross-country regression evidence for openness and growth: see, for instance, Dollar (1992); Sachs and Warner (1995); Edwards (1998); Rodriguez and Rodrik (2000); Frankel and Romer (1999); and Dollar and Kraay (2001). World Bank (2002), Baldwin (2004) and Hallak and Levinsohn (2004) have reviewed some or all of the previous empirical studies. These three reviewers agree that it is difficult to find a rigorous relationship between trade and growth, at least at the macro level, and that the growth process is far more complex than we generally think. Trade is, therefore, not sufficient for growth.

This suggests the importance of future research in two directions. One is to investigate the relationship between trade and growth at a more disaggregated level, although it is hard to determine the best level of disaggregation. The other is to pay more attention to the mechanism by which trade impacts growth and to test it empirically.

Trade and wage inequality

The relationship between trade and the distribution of income also remains a hotly debated issue. This is partly because the link is very complex and influenced by many other factors (Milanovic and Squire 2005: 3). The link may be even more complex than that between trade and growth.

The standard theoretical framework such as the two-factor, two-country Heckscher–Ohlin (H–O) model leads to an unambiguous prediction between free trade and wage inequality.[4] In this model, freer trade will increase the relative price of the abundant factor, which is usually considered to be unskilled labour in the case of developing countries. This in turn is expected to lead to the reduction of inter-occupational wage inequality in developing countries.

This type of model does not, however, reflect the complexity of today's globalization. The H–O model presumes the expansion of inter-industry trade as countries resort to freer trade. Feenstra and Hanson (1996) focus on a different form of globalization: trade through outsourcing. In their model, the wage gap between skilled and unskilled workers enlarges in both developed and developing countries. The reason is that outsourcing is expected to reduce the relative demand for unskilled labour in developed and developing economies: the outsourced activities are unskilled–labour–intensive relative to those in the developed countries, but skilled–labour–intensive relative to those in the less developed economy. Other models also predict the rising wage inequality between skilled and unskilled labour in developed and developing countries.[5]

Whenever theory leads to different predictions, empirical evidence is required to help choose among alternatives. Winters, McCulloch and McKay review some of the most recent empirical studies with respect to skill gaps in developing countries (Winters, McCulloch and McKay 2004: 101–2). Most of the recent empirical evidence concerns Latin America. A large number of studies[6] found an increased skills gap following liberalization in Latin America. Wood (1997) argued that Latin America's increasing wage gap between the different skill levels contrasts with the early experience of East Asia, where liberalization was accompanied by a narrowing of the gap. The recent empirical evidence is scant, however, except for Latin America. Besides, the exact cause of the widening wage gap is still unknown. Although the growth of outsourcing over the 1990s is often pointed out as an important factor for the growing gap, its exact impact is as yet unclear. The combination of a complex phenomenon and data inadequacies seems to make it difficult for empirical studies to show the robust relationship between trade and wage inequality (Milanovic and Squire 2005: 3).

NEW ASPECTS OF INTERNATIONAL TRADE IN THE ASIA-PACIFIC REGION

Conventional measures of the degree of trade openness

The merchandise trade as a share of merchandise value-added (trade in goods to goods GDP ratios) in addition to trade–GDP ratios are often used as a measure of openness.[7] This is because GDP figures include not only goods but also the services sector, which hides the increasing integration of trade through outsourcing in the manufacturing sector. The degree of openness of the services sector is still less by far than that of the manufacturing sector.[8]

Both ratios for the Asia-Pacific countries (Table 4.1) indicate that the degree of economic integration increased substantially in the 1990s in the Asia-Pacific region, except in Chile and Pakistan. Chile had become very open by 1990, but there was no change in the 1990s.

In addition, the degree of economic integration is much greater in goods than in services. The best examples are Japan and the US: trade–GDP ratios of both countries were not only small in 1990 in the absolute term, but also did not show much increase over the 1990–2000 period. This is especially the case with Japan. Trade–GDP ratio was very small (19.8 per cent) in 1990. The ratio increased only up to 20.1 per cent in 2000 (Table 4.1). Merchandise trade as percentage of goods GDP tells a different story. The merchandise trade ratio went up from 44.1 to 60.3 per cent in Japan, and from 44.8 to 70.4 per cent in the US during the same period.

The degree of economic integration substantially differs among sub regions in the Asia-Pacific. For instance, countries in Southeast Asia are not only highly integrated but also the degree of integration increased substantially in the goods sector in the 1990s. This is even applied to such a big country as Indonesia in which the merchandise trade to goods GDP ratio exceeded 100 per cent in 2000. The speed and the degree of economic integration are still very low, on the other hand, in Latin America and in South Asia, except Sri Lanka.

Table 4.1   Ratios of trade to GDP (%)

	Trade–GDP ratios		Trade in goods – goods GDP[a] ratios	
	1990	*2000*	*1990*	*2000*
Australia	33.5	45.7	68.7	98.0
New Zealand	53.8	70.8	121.0	132.6
Japan	19.8	20.1	44.1	60.3
Korea	57.4	78.5	102.7	152.9
China	31.9	49.1	47.4	65.9
Hong Kong, China	255.9	287.4	772.3	1,380.8
Taiwan	88.5	106.6	164.4	263.9
Singapore	NA	NA	750.1[b]	889.6
Indonesia	49.1	76.4	68.1	100.5
Malaysia	147.0	229.3	232.3	365.0
Philippines	60.8	108.9	84.7	201.8
Thailand	75.8	124.9	132.2	210.1
Cambodia	18.9	113.9	64.9	155.7
Vietnam	81.3	112.5	88.1	149.3
United States	20.6	26.3	44.8	70.4
Canada	52.0	86.8	115.1	187.3
Mexico	38.3	63.9	78.9	159.7
Bangladesh	19.7	33.2	33.3	59.5
India	15.7	28.5	24.3	48.0
Pakistan	38.9	34.3	68.9	55.4
Sri Lanka	67.2	88.6	117.3	186.3
Chile	66.0	58.5	100.5	98.1
Peru	29.6	34.1	NA	NA

Notes
a   Goods GDP combines agriculture, mining, manufacturing, construction and public utilities.
b   1995 figure.

Source: World Bank, *WDI Indicators Online* (except Taiwan). Data of Taiwan were obtained from Asian Development Bank, *Key Indicators*, downloaded from www.adb.org.

The emergence of 'intra-mediate trade'

Many countries in the Asia-Pacific region are distinctive, not only because the degree of economic integration in the goods sector has substantially increased but also a new mode of international trade has emerged over the last decade. Although there is no single perfect measure to indicate the degree of vertical disintegration of production process and integration through trade, the shares of both exports and imports by end-use categories could be one measure (Feenstra 1998; Irwin 1996). There the values of both exports and imports are divided into five categories:[9] (1) food, feeds and beverages; (2) industrial supplies and materials; (3) capital goods (machinery, parts and components); (4) consumer goods (except auto); and (5) automotive vehicles and parts.[10] The capital goods are used by firms not only for investment (such as machinery) but also as intermediate inputs.[11] Outsourcing takes on greatest value when the products being imported or exported are neither basic raw materials nor finished consumer goods, but are at an intermediate stage of processing. In this case, 'it is very plausible that stages of the production process (or value chain) shift across borders as new trade opportunities emerge' (Feenstra 1998: 38).

Table 4.2 shows the shares of products at an intermediate stage of processing (category 3) both in exports and imports by country. Most countries in Northeast and Southeast Asia demonstrated a new pattern of trade in the 1990s: a sharp increase in the share of capital goods (category 3) in trade. What is striking, though, is that the dramatic expansion of trade in capital goods concentrates on intermediate inputs such as parts and components[12] rather than on machinery (see Table 4.2). This concurrent increase in the share of intermediate inputs both on the export and import sides is here termed 'intra-mediate trade'.[13]

Certainly, the intra-firm trade of the multinationals is an important factor for the emergence of 'intra-mediate trade'. Urata (2001), for instance, analysed the changing structure of foreign trade and direct investment in East Asia and its impact on growth. He calls it the formation of an FDI–trade nexus in East Asia. As emphasized by Feenstra (1998: 36), however, the imports of multinational firms are too small to account for observed wages and employment changes. Thus, analysing the multinationals alone (or business transactions internal to a firm) does not provide a full perspective on what is happening in trade.

However, the higher degree of openness observed in Table 4.1 does not take the form of 'intra-mediate trade' in Australia and New Zealand. Table 4.3 shows shares of exports and imports by end-use categories for these two economies. It reveals that the inter-industry specialization continues to be an important part of trade for Australia and New Zealand. The bulk of exports consists of primary commodities or industrial supplies, and for imports the greatest expansion is observed in the category of final consumer goods and the automotive sector. This indicates that distance may still be a very important determinant of the pattern of international trade.

DO NEW ASPECTS OF INTERNATIONAL TRADE DELIVER A PROMISING RESULT?

Trade and productivity growth

The review of literature summarized above implies that the vertical disintegration of production and integration of trade will lead to higher productivity growth in the manufacturing sector, for several reasons. First, it is expected to enhance the vertical specialization and generate gains through specialization. Second, the new pattern of trade will widen the variety of intermediate inputs in which the most modern technology is embodied. Firms can enhance productivity growth through wider access to good-quality capital and intermediate inputs. Third, the new pattern of trade will enable firms to enter global production networks at their own level of capability and climb

Table 4.2   Shares of capital goods, parts and components and machinery (%)

	Capital goods				Parts and components				Machinery			
	Exports		Imports		Exports		Imports		Exports		Imports	
	1990	2000	1990	2000	1990	2000	1990	2000	1990	2000	1990	2000
Oceania												
Australia	7.0	8.4	32.4	28.6	4.3	5.3	15.6	16.9	2.7	3.0	16.8	11.7
New Zealand	5.8	8.5	26.3	23.7	2.6	4.5	12.3	12.4	3.2	4.0	14.0	11.3
Northeast Asia												
Japan	40.1	48.3	11.8	23.3	25.2	33.8	7.5	19.2	15.0	14.5	4.3	4.1
Korea	24.6	42.1	32.7	34.3	16.9	32.2	17.8	26.6	7.8	9.9	14.8	7.8
China	7.3	23.3	29.9	38.0	4.9	18.8	12.0	27.5	2.5	4.5	17.9	10.5
Hong Kong	17.9	31.7	19.5	34.4	14.1	28.2	14.7	30.3	3.7	3.5	4.8	4.1
Taiwan	29.0	51.7	29.3	45.4	21.0	38.3	18.8	33.9	8.0	13.3	10.5	11.5
Southeast Asia												
Singapore	40.1	63.6	37.5	56.7	32.6	58.9	27.3	49.5	7.4	4.7	10.2	7.2
Indonesia	1.1	13.1	35.8	21.1	0.7	11.6	12.8	9.8	0.4	1.5	23.0	11.4
Malaysia	27.5	51.3	49.5	61.5	23.7	47.7	32.3	53.6	3.8	3.6	17.2	7.9
Philippines	13.4	72.6	25.5	47.6	13.1	71.4	15.6	42.4	0.3	1.2	9.8	5.2
Thailand	16.8	35.5	33.6	40.1	15.2	30.9	19.6	32.4	1.6	4.7	14.0	7.7
South Asia												
Bangladesh	0.9	0.7	14.5	17.0	0.6	0.4	7.7	5.3	0.3	0.2	6.7	11.7
India	5.7	6.0	20.9	15.7	3.3	4.1	12.5	10.2	2.4	1.9	8.4	5.5
Pakistan	1.0	0.9	19.2	14.8	0.5	0.5	10.6	7.1	0.6	0.4	8.6	7.7
Sri Lanka	2.6	5.9	12.1	13.1	0.7	3.3	6.5	6.7	1.9	2.6	5.6	6.3
NAFTA												
Canada	16.2	17.7	29.8	32.2	10.7	11.6	19.8	22.6	5.5	6.1	10.0	9.6
USA	39.4	44.5	23.5	27.8	23.3	31.1	16.7	21.1	16.1	13.4	6.9	6.8
Mexico	13.5	31.9	30.5	38.7	10.3	26.4	14.5	30.6	3.3	5.6	16.0	8.1
LA												
Chile	0.9	1.4	31.4	20.3	0.2	0.7	12.1	11.6	0.6	0.8	19.4	8.7
Peru	0.9	0.9	25.8	20.9	0.6	0.7	11.0	12.3	0.3	0.2	14.8	8.6

Note: Capital goods include both machinery and parts and components.

Source: The author's calculation based on UN COMTRADE.

the technology ladder along global value chains. If globalization results in the outsourcing of activities, skill upgrading would be a direct consequence of trade. In other words, trade and technological change could be observationally equivalent (Feenstra 1998: 6).

Figure 4.1 shows a simple relationship between changes in the magnitude of new forms of economic integration and industrial productivity growth in the Asia-Pacific region. The change in the degree of new forms of economic integration is defined in this paper as follows:

Table 4.3   Shares of exports and imports by end-use categories in Australia and New Zealand (%)

	Exports		Imports	
	1990	*2000*	*1990*	*2000*
Australia				
Food, feeds and beverages	21.8	20.9	4.7	4.4
Industrial supplies and materials	66.3	62.3	34.6	32.9
Capital goods	7.0	8.4	32.4	28.6
(parts and components)	4.3	5.3	15.6	16.9
Consumer goods (except autos)	3.3	5.2	18.4	21.5
Automotive vehicles and parts	1.6	3.3	9.9	12.7
New Zealand				
Food, feeds and beverages	45.6	45.7	6.3	7.3
Industrial supplies and materials	43.6	38.9	39.1	39.1
Capital goods	5.8	8.5	26.3	23.7
(parts and components)	2.6	4.5	12.3	12.4
Consumer goods (except autos)	4.4	6.0	17.4	18.9
Automotive vehicles and parts	0.6	1.0	10.9	11.0

Source: See Table 4.2.

$$\text{INTEG}_{(1990-2000)} = (d\,(\text{export share of intermediate inputs}) + d\,(\text{import share of intermediate inputs}))\,/2.$$

In other words, the variable of INTEG is defined here as the simple average of changes in the shares of intermediate inputs in the total values of exports and imports respectively.

Figure 4.1 indicates that there is a positive and statistically significant relationship between the degree of integration in intermediate inputs and manufacturing productivity growth in the Asia-Pacific region.[14] There is a simple relationship between changes in the degree of openness measured in a conventional manner such as increases in trade in goods to goods GDP ratios[15] and industrial productivity growth rates between 1990 and 2000. Figure 4.2 shows the result. It demonstrates that there is no statistically significant relationship between the openness of the goods trade and industrial productivity growth.

These two simple exercises imply that although the rigorous relationship between the growing importance of 'intra-mediate trade' and productivity growth remains to be derived, the pattern of trade may have a higher predictability of productivity growth than a simple measure of trade openness in the goods sector.

Figure 4.1   The new pattern of trade and productivity growth

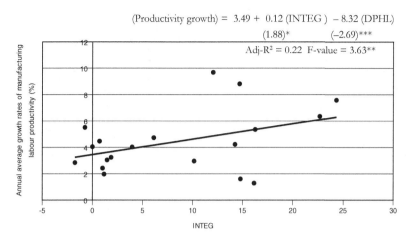

(Productivity growth) = 3.49 + 0.12 (INTEG) − 8.32 (DPHL)

(1.88)*   (−2.69)***

Adj-R² = 0.22 F-value = 3.63**

Notes: DPHL represents a dummy variable for the Philippines. Figures in parentheses show t ratios.
* indicates statistical significance at the 10 per cent.
* indicates statistical significance at the 5 per cent level.
***   indicates statistical significance at the 1 per cent level.

Source: Author's construction.

Figure 4.2   Conventional measure of trade openness and productivity growth

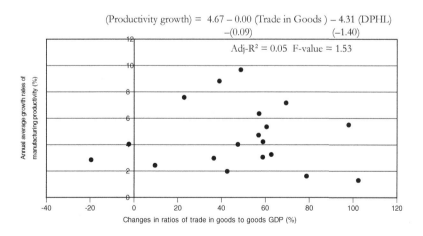

(Productivity growth) = 4.67 − 0.00 (Trade in Goods) − 4.31 (DPHL)

−(0.09)   (−1.40)

Adj-R² = 0.05 F-value = 1.53

Note: See Figure 4.1.
Source: Author's construction.

Mechanism by which trade impacts growth

The recent models of the endogenous growth theory demonstrate how the benefits of scale that economies reap through participation in world markets and imports of technology can cumulate into faster growth over the long-term (Rodrik 1999: 24). The direct empirical testing of the mechanism described in the new models will not be possible, however, unless the testing is conducted at the individual firm level. What this paper examines instead is whether intra-mediate trade will contribute to reinforcing economic fundamentals of Asia-Pacific countries.

Rodrik (1999) argues that, in the long run, investment is key to economic performance, and the openness of trade has a significant positive impact on long-term growth performance only when economic integration enhances investment activities, especially in developing countries. Participation in the global value chain may lead to a higher level of investment activities for several reasons. First, to climb the technology ladder countries need to continue to import new technology or invest in innovation. The former will lead to the higher importation of new capital goods and intermediate inputs, while the latter is expected to lead to increases in R&D activities. New capital goods and intermediate goods are often a good source of new technology. Second, to continue to climb the quality ladder also requires the upgrading of skill levels of labour. That will enhance investment in human capital.

Figures 4.3, 4.4 and 4.5 show the impact of increased trade integration on investment activities. A higher degree of integration in the form of intra-mediate trade has no impact on investment in physical assets (Figure 4.3). There is no statistically significant

Figure 4.3   The link between the degree of integration and changes in investment ratios

(Changes in investment ratios) = 1.11 −0.26 (INTEG) +   8.96 (DPHL)

(−1.53)   (−1.04)

Adj-R^2 = 0.02 F-value = 1.17

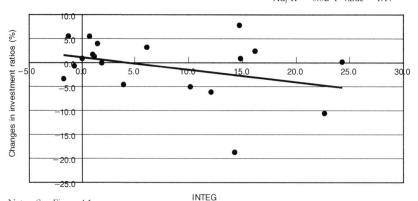

Note: See Figure 4.1.

Source: Author's construction.

relationship between the two at all. On the contrary, there seems to be even a negative relationship.

The growing importance of intra-mediate trade, however, is more compatible with the increases in investment in human capital and innovation. Figure 4.4 shows the relationship between the changes in the degree of integration and enrolment ratios in tertiary education—there is an upward sloping relationship between two variables, although the correlation between two variables is not statistically significant.

A robust relationship is found between the changes in the degree of trade integration and R&D activities measured in R&D–GDP ratios (Figure 4.5). The higher degree of integration in intermediate inputs corresponds to more innovation activities.

Although it is very difficult to discover the exact mechanism by which trade impacts growth, the above simple exercises indicate that if globalization results in outsourcing activities, trade, skill upgrading and technological changes could be observationally equivalent. In other words, a higher level of integration into the global economy through intra-mediate trade may stimulate countries' demand for a higher level of skills and innovation activities.

Trade and wage inequality

Trade theories do not lead to an unambiguous relationship between trade and wage inequality. The more recent model incorporating the breakdown of the production process and outsourcing activities, however, predicts the rising inter-occupational wage equality both in developed and developing countries. What happened, then, with the

Figure 4.4   The link between the degree of integration and skill upgrading

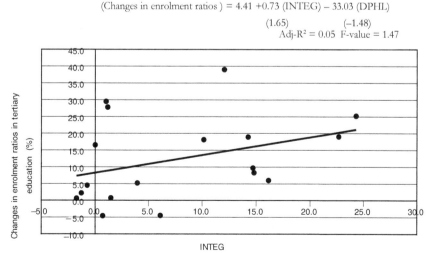

(Changes in enrolment ratios) = 4.41 +0.73 (INTEG) – 33.03 (DPHL)

(1.65)   (–1.48)

Adj-R^2 = 0.05 F-value = 1.47

Note: See Figure 4.1.

Source: Author's construction.

Figure 4.5   The link between the degree of integration and innovation activities

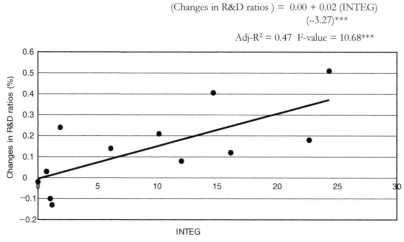

$$(\text{Changes in R\&D ratios}) = 0.00 + 0.02 \ (\text{INTEG})$$
$$(-3.27)^{***}$$

Adj-R^2 = 0.47   F-value = 10.68***

Note: See Figure 4.1.

Source: Author's construction.

inter-occupational wage gap in the Asia-Pacific region as the new pattern of international trade emerged in the 1990s?

Data inadequacies, especially those of wage data, make empirical work both hazardous and partial in many cases. I used inter-occupational wage data of workers in the manufacturing sector in Asia employed either by Japanese companies or Japanese affiliates overseas. The Japan External Trade Organization (JETRO) has published the range of wages for three types of workers in Asia by country since 1995: production workers, engineers and managerial class workers.[16] JETRO collects wage data by interviewing Japanese companies directly. Since Japanese companies have been some of the main drivers of intra-mediate trade in East Asia, the analysis of those wage data could be useful in illustrating impacts of trade on wage gaps.

Table 4.4 shows the results. Countries in Northeast, Southeast and South Asia are divided into three groups: Group 1 includes countries in which the wage gaps between unskilled workers (such as production workers) and skilled workers (such as engineers and managerial-class workers) have increased unambiguously since the mid-1990s; Group 2 includes those in which the inter-occupational gaps have narrowed unambiguously since the mid-1990s; and Group 3 includes countries in which the trend of the wage inequality is ambiguous. Each group divides countries further into globalizers and non-globalizers. The definition of globalization in this table is whether a country demonstrated the new pattern of international trade in the 1990s or not, as observed in Table 4.2.

Table 4.4   Wage inequality: decreased or increased?

	Group 1 *Unambiguously increased*			
	Wage gap (Production workers = 100)			
	Engineers		*Managers*	
	1996–98	*2000–02*	*1996–98*	*2000–02*
Globalizers				
Japan	137	146	184	201
China	191	193	318	325
Taiwan	140	181	224	269
Singapore	211	288	336	474
Non-globalizers				
India	166	192	564	581
Pakistan	198	288	455	584

	Group 2 *Unambiguously decreased*			
	Wage gap (Production workers = 100)			
	Engineers		*Managers*	
	1996–98	*2000–02*	*1996–98*	*2000–02*
Globalizers				
Korea	126	118	189	177
Malaysia	387	297	723	640
Thailand	252	206	604	431
Hong Kong	195	123	235	189
Non-globalizers				
Indonesia	298	225	910	619
Sri Lanka	260	187	371	366

	Group 3 *Indeterminate*			
	Wage gap (Production workers = 100)			
	Engineers		*Managers*	
	1996–98	*2000–02*	*1996–98*	*2000–02*
Globalizers				
Philippines	209	217	461	359

Notes: Globalizers and non-globalizers are defined depending on international trade. See Table 4.2 for details.

Source: Author's own construction based on data from *JETRO Sensor*, various years.

Table 4.4 shows that there is no rigorous relationship between trade and wage inequality. Globalizer or not, some countries showed an increase in wage gaps while others showed the opposite. This implies that the link between trade and wage inequality is far more complex than theoretical models predict. What is interesting, however, is that the *level* of inter-occupational wage gaps between 2000 and 2002 is far greater in non-globalizers such as India, Pakistan and Indonesia than in globalizers (except Sri Lanka). Besides, although someone may be nowadays concerned very much with the increasing income inequality as a result of globalization in such countries as China, Table 4.4 shows that the magnitude of inter-occupational wage inequality in China is far smaller than in many other developing countries such as those in Southeast Asia.

Although it is too dangerous to make conclusions just from the above simple exercise, it seems that there is no reason that we should worry too much about the impact of trade on wage inequality.

IMPLICATIONS OF GLOBALIZATION FOR LEAST-DEVELOPED PARTS OF ASIA

The last part of this paper considers implications of globalization for new ASEAN members such as Vietnam, Cambodia, and Laos. These are the least-developed areas in the Asia Pacific and their development is one of the most pressing issues in the region. Since the 1990s, they have begun to opt for integration into the world economy through joining ASEAN, and unilateral trade and investment liberalization. All three countries applied for membership to the World Trade Organization (WTO), into which Cambodia was accepted as a member in 2004.

New economic geography also suggests that many of the least-developed countries may become increasingly marginalized from the dynamics of international production in the era of globalization (Henderson, Shalizi and Venables 2001). The removal of restrictions to trade and investment alone may not bring long-term growth, nor alleviate poverty. It is, therefore, interesting to analyse whether openness has created a growth momentum and a convergence force between these three countries and the rest of the Asia-Pacific region, and if so, how fast they are converging.

Analysis of the trade patterns of Cambodia, Laos and Vietnam

Both Cambodia and Vietnam have increasingly integrated into the world economy since the beginning of the 1990s (see Table 4.1). Between 1990 and 2000, trade in goods–goods GDP ratios increased from 65 to 156 per cent for Cambodia, and from 88 to 149 per cent for Vietnam. The degree of openness is significantly higher than that of countries in South Asia. Has trade openness created a growth momentum for new ASEAN members?

The discussion above concludes that there is no empirical evidence to show that trade openness measured by merchandise trade–GDP ratios alone leads to high rates of productivity growth. Changes in the pattern of trade seem to have a much more significant impact on growth. Since none of the new ASEAN members report trade data to the UN at the disaggregated level, I have estimated the shares of both exports and imports by end-user categories using those of their trading partners. Table 4.5 shows the comparison.

Cambodia, Laos, and Vietnam have one commonality in their trade structure: in the 1990s, all of them became successful in shifting away from being exporters of primary commodities only to exporters of manufactured goods, especially consumer goods (see Table 4.5). The export expansion of consumer goods is concentrated in the textile and apparel industries, though it is not shown in Table 4.5.[17] This shift makes economic sense since these three countries are considered to possess a comparative advantage in the labour-intensive sectors.

The change in trade structure, especially export structure, seems to be too drastic, though, in Cambodia and Laos. While Vietnam was successful in diversifying the type of export commodities, the other two countries seem to have changed their main export items from one commodity to the other. They may end up creating another enclave.

Table 4.5 also indicates that there is one more big difference between Vietnam, and Cambodia and Laos. While Vietnam started to reveal the new mode of international trade as observed in East and Southeast Asia in the 1990s, the others did not. Shares

Table 4.5   Shares of exports and imports by end-user categories for new ASEAN members (%)

	Exports				*Imports*			
	1990	*1995*	*2000*	*2002*	*1990*	*1995*	*2000*	*2002*
Vietnam								
Food, feeds and beverages	41.6	34.7	20.3	19.0	11.2	11.1	8.0	8.2
Industrial supplies and materials	53.4	31.5	36.3	30.0	41.1	46.9	54.3	48.5
Capital goods	0.1	1.3	5.8	6.3	22.7	22.1	22.7	28.7
(parts and components)	0.1	0.9	4.9	5.3	9.9	10.5	14.6	15.9
Consumer goods (except autos)	4.7	32.3	37.2	43.8	14.3	10.3	6.4	8.4
Automotive vehicles and parts	0.2	0.2	0.4	0.8	10.7	9.6	8.5	6.2
Cambodia								
Food, feeds and beverages	1.0	1.0	0.7	0.3	39.2	17.0	7.4	8.7
Industrial supplies and materials	94.0	77.7	7.7	3.9	27.7	35.4	66.9	60.8
Capital goods and intermediate inputs	1.1	0.3	0.2	0.2	14.0	17.4	8.8	12.4
(parts and components)	0.2	0.1	0.1	0.1	3.8	6.0	3.3	5.5
Consumer goods (except autos)	3.8	20.9	91.3	95.6	8.3	11.9	11.3	13.4
Automotive vehicles and parts	0.1	0.1	0.1	0.0	10.9	18.4	5.6	4.7
Laos								
Food, feeds and beverages	3.5	11.9	11.4	9.3	11.3	18.5	12.4	23.0
Industrial supplies and materials	85.1	50.6	36.5	10.7	34.4	38.2	48.2	23.9
Capital goods and intermediate inputs	0.7	0.3	0.5	0.2	30.9	17.9	11.0	18.3
(parts and components)	0.3	0.2	0.3	0.1	16.5	5.4	4.9	12.1
Consumer goods (except autos)	10.3	37.3	51.5	79.8	11.3	10.9	11.8	14.0
Automotive vehicles and parts	0.5	0.1	0.1	0.0	12.2	14.6	16.6	20.8

Source: Author's calculation.

of intermediate inputs in the total values of exports and imports started to increase, especially after the mid-1990s in Vietnam: from 0.1 to 5.3 per cent in exports and from 9.9 to 15.9 per cent in imports between 1995 and 2002. This implies that only Vietnam started to participate in global value chains (GVCs), although the magnitude of its participation is still low compared with other original ASEAN countries (see also Table 4.1). Vietnam could gain substantially through its entry into the GVCs for the reasons mentioned above, and catch up with the more advanced nations in the Asia-Pacific region.

However, neither Cambodia nor Laos have yet shown new aspects of international trade. In Cambodia, as the share of imported industrial supplies and materials increased, so did the share of exported consumer goods. This indicates that Cambodia still imports a bulk of raw or low-processed industrial materials and export consumer goods after a certain stage of the simple production process. Trade openness alone does not yet seem to be generating a dynamic long-term growth process.

Trade openness does not seem to promise much, especially in the case of Laos. Table 4.5 shows that, while the share of exported consumer goods increased dramatically, the expansion of imports concentrated on food, consumer goods and automobiles, but not on industrial supplies or capital goods (including both machinery and intermediate inputs). This implies that export revenues are not spent on the purchase of goods and services for production purposes. Laos has not only failed to reveal a new pattern of trade, but has also failed to generate the import structure compatible with long-term growth and development.

Trade openness alone is not enough

Table 4.6 confirms the above analysis: it shows the growth performance and some important economic fundamentals such as physical investment ratios and human capital development of Cambodia, Laos and Vietnam in comparison with the original ASEAN members. According to the table, Vietnam has grown faster than any other ASEAN country since the early 1990s, and its fundamentals are strong. This indicates that the potential benefits of globalization are being realized in Vietnam. The entry into intra-mediate trade may enhance its growth performance through increasing demand for a high level of skills and technological progress.

Trade openness per se may not, however, generate promising results for Cambodia and Laos. Despite the increasing degree of openness and the change in export structure, they are not growing faster than other ASEAN members. They are catching up with Indonesia and the Philippines, not because Cambodia and Laos are growing fast, but because Indonesia and the Philippines have been growing slowly, especially since the 1997–98 Asian crisis. Cambodia and Laos are not catching up with relatively better performing ASEAN economies such as Malaysia, Thailand, and Singapore. One serious problem of Cambodia and Laos is that investment in human capital is extremely poor (Table 4.6). The secondary-school enrolment ratio of Cambodia even dropped between 1995 and 2000. This means that the swift shift to a new form of globalization may be difficult. The reason is simple: even labour-intensive activities have often needed to be combined with new technologies and advanced skills (United Nations 2001: xvii)

Table 4.6   Growth performance of ASEAN countries

Country	Per capita GNP in US dollars	Annual average of per capita GDP growth rates (%)		Gross fixed capital formation as percentage of GDP (%)			School enrolment ratios (%)			
							Secondary		Tertiary	
	2003	1991–2000	2001–2003	1995	2000	2002	1995	2000	1995	2000
Cambodia	310	3.5	4.4	14.2	18.7	22.7	26.5	18.1	1.9	2.2
Laos	320	3.5	2.8	NA	NA	NA	26.8	37.6	2.7	3.2
Vietnam	480	5.8	5.8	25.4	27.6	30.0	47.0	67.1	4.1	9.7
Indonesia	810	2.7	2.4	28.4	21.8	20.3	51.5	56.8	11.3	14.4
Philippines	1080	0.7	1.8	22.2	21.2	19.2	77.5	77.1	29.0	30.5
Malaysia	3780	4.5	1.1	43.6	25.6	23.2	58.7	69.3	11.7	26.3
Thailand	2190	3.5	4.0	41.1	21.9	22.9	54.1	82.8	20.1	35.6
Singapore	21230	4.7	-1.2	33.4	30.1	25.8	73.4	NA	33.7	NA

Source: *World Bank Development Indicators* (online).

in recent years, especially in the machinery sector. Unless they put a large effort into developing human resources, both Cambodia and Laos may end up staying at technologically non-dynamic activities.

CONCLUSION

The review of literature suggests that the link between trade, growth and income inequality is complex and far from conclusive, both theoretically and empirically. This paper has examined the impact of trade on growth and wage inequality by focusing on a new form of globalization such as 'intra-mediate trade'. This new mode of economic integration has become important and will be increasingly so in the future in the Asia-Pacific region. It is useful to consider the economic consequence of its emergence. Past empirical studies, especially cross-country regression analyses, have focused too much on the link between trade and growth at the macro level, and may hide the dynamic growth force that is being created in the Asia-Pacific region. This paper found that the increase in the degree of vertical specialization at an intermediate processing stage has a tendency to bring higher productivity growth. It is not just trade openness, but a type of economic integration that seems to account more for high growth rates of industrial productivity. Although the mechanism by which the new mode of economic integration cumulates into long-term growth is still unknown, this paper suggests that it may do so through inducing skill upgrading and technological progress. Trade and technological change could be observationally equivalent. Future research is recommended to determine the exact mechanism, using much more disaggregated level data such as industry-level or firm-level data.

The link between a new form of international trade and the wage gap is far more complex than that of trade and growth. It is quite difficult to draw a robust relationship between the two. What it seems to suggest, though, is that we do not have to worry too much about the impact of trade on the wage gap. Many other factors could be much more important for the widening wage gap among different occupations.

The case of new ASEAN members such as Cambodia, Laos and Vietnam illustrates well that trade openness alone does not initiate a cumulative long-term growth process. Despite opening up to the world economy, Cambodia and Laos, especially the latter, have failed to catch up with original ASEAN members. They could be stuck at technologically non-dynamic sectors. It is only Vietnam that shows promising results. First, Vietnam began to enter the global value chain. Second, the new form of economic integration is accompanied by strong fundamentals such as the high level of investment activities in Vietnam.

This paper suggests that whether trade impacts growth or not depends largely on how each country integrates into the global economy. Trade openness alone does not promise a cumulative long-term growth process. The new mode of international trade that has emerged in many parts of the Asia-Pacific region in the last two decades seems to bring about somewhat more promising results by enhancing technological change and productivity growth without endangering wage inequality too much.

APPENDIX 4.1

SITC R2 Numbers classified as 'intra-mediate trade'

69733	Parts of 69731 and 69732	74149	Parts of 74141
7119	Parts of 7111 and 7112	7429	Parts of 742
712	Steam engines, parts	7432	Parts of 7431
713	Internal combustion piston engines	7439	Parts of 7435, 7436
714	Engines, motors, non-electric	74419	Parts of 74411
7169	Parts of rotating electric plant	7449	Parts of 7442
7188	Engines, motors	74519	Parts of 74511
72119	Parts of 7211	74523	Parts of 74522, 7753
72129	Parts of 7212	74526	Parts of 74525
72139	Parts of 7213	749	Non-electric parts of machinery
72198	Parts of 72191	7523	Digital central processors
72199	Parts of 72197	7524	Digital main storage units
7239	Parts of 72341 to 72346	7525	Peripheral units
72439	Sewing machine needle, parts	7528	Offline data processing equipment
72449	Parts of 7244	759	Parts of 751, 752
72454	Machinery for felt, parts	7649	Parts of 76
72469	Parts for 72451, 72452, 72453	771	Electric power machinery, parts
72479	Parts of 7247, 7751	772	Switches, fuses, etc., parts
7259	Parts of 725	773	Distributing electricity equipment
72689	Parts of 72681	77579	Parts of 7757
7269	Parts of 72631, 7264, and 7267	77589	Parts of 7758 other than 77585
72719	Parts of 72711	776	Transformers, valves
72729	Parts of 72722	778	Other electrical machinery, components and parts
72819	Parts of 7281	87429	Parts of 87421
72839	Parts of 7283	8749	Parts of 873, 8743, 87454, 8748
72849	Parts of 72348, 72721, 72842–72848	88119	Parts of 8811
7369	Parts of 736	88129	Parts of 8812
73719	Parts of 73711	8989	Parts of 898
73729	Parts of rolling mills		

NOTES

I would like to thank the participants at the PAFTAD 30 Conference for valuable comments on the earlier draft of this paper. Special acknowledgements go to Sumner La Croix, Peter Drysdale, Theresa Greaney, Akira Kohsaka, Rachel McCulloch, Seiji Naya, Eng Fong Pang, Hugh Patrick, Peter Petri and James Roumasset.

1   Krugman (1995) calls it 'to slice up the value chain'.
2   Recently, Samuelson has challenged economists' oversimplified complacence about globalization: the gains of winners from free trade worked out to exceed the losses of the losers. He argued that the different rates of technological progress among trading partners can induce for the home country a permanent loss in terms of per capita real income (Samuelson 2004: 137). Moreover, some economists have expressed a concern that outsourcing may be less likely than other forms of international trade to result in overall prosperity, as pointed out by Bhagwati, Panagariya and Srinivasan (2004: 100). The debate for and against globalization continues.
3   See, also, Grossman and Helpman (1992: Chapter 9) and Feenstra (1990).
4   Wage inequality is only one aspect of income inequality. It is frequently linked to income equality, however, because wages are the most important component of national income.
5   See Feenstra (1998) for a good review of theoretical models predicting the skilled- and unskilled-wage gap in developed and developing countries.
6   See footnote 31 of Winters, McCulloch and McKay (2004).
7   See Feenstra (1998). The difference between Feenstra and this paper is, though, that this paper includes both goods and services trade in trade–GDP ratios while Feenstra includes only merchandise trade in trade–GDP ratios.
8   Bhagwati, Panagariya and Srinivasan also state that trade in services through outsourcing is a relatively small phenomenon even in the US labour market (2004: 112).
9   The classification of trade by end-user categories is used widely, for instance, by the US Bureau of Economic Analysis, *Survey of Current Business*, various issues.
10   In this paper, category 1 corresponds to SITCR2 0–1; category 2 to SITCR2 2–6 (except 696–7); category 3 to SITCR2 7 (except 76 and 775), 69733, 77579, 77589, 87429, 8749, 88119, 88129, 8989; category 4 to SITCR2 8 (except 87429, 8749, 88119, 88129, 8989), 696–7 (except 69733), 76, 775 (except 77579, 77589); and category 5 to SITCR2 78.
11   For example, all electrical parts and components are included within the capital goods of category 3.
12   Refer to Appendix 4.1 for which products are included as intermediate inputs (parts and components) in the calculation.
13   Antweiler and Trefler (2000) term offshore sourcing of parts as 'intra-mediate trade'.
14   The Philippines is an outlier. Despite its high degree of integration into the global economy as defined in this paper, the annual average growth rate of manufacturing productivity is only 0.11, the lowest growth rate among the Asia-Pacific countries.
15   Refer to Rose (2002), for details of trade policy measurement and trade liberalization. This paper uses changes in trade in goods to goods GDP ratios as a conventional measure of openness, because it is the most comprehensive measure to represent the degree to which a goods sector became integrated into the world economy, not only due to changes in its trade policy, but also due to other factors such as the development of information technology.
16   *JETRO Sensor*, various years.
17   This is according to the UN COMTRADE data of the trading partners of new ASEAN members.

REFERENCES

Antweiler, W. and D. Trefler (2000) 'Increasing Returns and All that: a View from Trade', *NBER Working Paper 7941*, Cambridge, MA: National Bureau of Economic Research.

Asian Development Bank (2003) *Asian Development Outlook 2003*, Manila: Asian Development Bank.

Baldwin, R.E. (2004) 'Openness and Growth: What's the Empirical Relationship?', in R.E. Baldwin and L.A. Winters (eds), *Challenges to Globalization: Analyzing the Economics*, Chicago: University of Chicago Press: 499–521.

Bhagwati, J. (2004) *In Defense of Globalization*, New York: Oxford University Press.

Bhagwati, J., A. Panagariya and T.N. Srinivasan (2004) 'The Muddles over Outsourcing', *Journal of Economic Perspectives*, 18(4): 93–114.

Commander, S. (2004) 'Comment on a paper by R.E. Baldwin (2004)', in R.E. Baldwin and L.A. Winters (eds), *Challenges to Globalization: Analyzing the Economics*, Chicago: University of Chicago Press: 521–5.

Dollar, D. (1992) 'Outward-Oriented Developing Countries Really Do Grow More Rapidly: Evidence from 95 LDCs, 1976–85', *Economic Change and Cultural Change*, 40(3): 523–44.

Dollar, D. and A. Kraay (2001) 'Trade, Growth and Poverty', *Policy Research Working Paper No. 2199*, Washington, DC: World Bank.

Edwards, S. (1998) 'Openness, Productivity and Growth: What Do We Really Know?' *Economic Journal*, 108(447): 383–98.

Feenstra, R.C. (1990) 'Trade and Uneven Growth', *NBER Working Paper 3276*, Cambridge, MA: National Bureau of Economic Research (NBER).

—— (1998) 'Integration of Trade and Disintegration of Production in the Global Economy', *Journal of Economic Perspectives*, 12(4): 31–50.

Feenstra, R.C. and G. Hanson (1996) 'Foreign Investment, Outsourcing and Relative Wages', in R.C. Feenstra, G.M. Grossman and D.A. Irwin (eds), *The Political Economy of Trade Policy: Papers in Honor of Jagdish Bhagwati*, Cambridge, MA: MIT Press: 89–127.

Frankel, J.A. and D. Romer (1999) 'Does Trade Cause Growth?', *American Economic Review*, 89(3): 379–99.

Grossman, G.M. and E. Helpman (1992) *Innovation and Growth in the Global Economy*, Cambridge, MA: MIT Press.

Hallak, J.C. and J. Levinsohn (2004) 'Fooling Ourselves: Evaluating the Globalization and Growth Debate', *NBER Working Paper 10244*, Cambridge, MA: National Bureau of Economic Research (NBER).

Henderson, J.V., Z. Shalizi and A.J. Venables (2001) 'Geography and Development', *Journal of Economic Geography*, 1: 81–105.

Irwin, A.D. (1996) 'The United States in a New Global Economy? A Century's Perspective', *American Economic Review and Proceedings*, 86(2): 41–6.

Krugman, P.R. (1979) 'Increasing Returns, Monopolistic Competition, and International Trade', *Journal of International Economics*, 9(4): 469–79.

Krugman, P. (1995) 'Growing World Trade: Causes and Consequences', *Brookings Papers on Economic Activity*, 1: 327–77.

Milanovic, B. and L. Squire (2005) 'Does Tariff Liberalization Increase Wage Inequality? Some Empirical Evidence', *NBER Working Paper 11046*, Cambridge, MA: National Bureau of Economic Research (NBER).

Rodriguez, F. and D. Rodrik (2000) 'Trade Policy and Economic Growth: A Skeptic's Guide to the Cross-National Evidence'. Available at <http://ksghome.harvard.edu/~drodrik/skepti1299.pdf> accessed 20 June 2006.

Rodrik, D. (1999) 'The New Global Economy and Developing Countries: Making Openness Work', *Policy Essay No. 24*, Washington, DC: Overseas Development Council.

Romer, P. (1993) 'Idea Gaps and Object Gaps in Economic Development', *Journal of Monetary Economics*, 32(3): 543–73.

Rose, A.K. (2002) 'Do WTO Members Have a More Liberal Trade Policy?', *NBER Working Paper 9347*, Cambridge, MA: National Bureau of Economic Research.

Sachs, J.D. and A.M. Warner (1995) 'Economic Reform and the Process of Global Integration', *Brookings Papers on Economic Activity*, 1: 1–118.

Samuelson, P.A. (2004) 'Where Ricardo and Mill Rebut and Confirm Arguments of Mainstream Economics Supporting Globalization', *Journal of Economic Perspectives*, 18(3): 135–46.

United Nations (2001) *World Investment Report 2001: Promoting Linkages*, New York: United Nations.

Urata, S. (2001) 'Emergence of an FDI–Trade Nexus and Economic Growth in East Asia', in J.E. Stiglitz and S. Yusuf (eds), *Rethinking the East Asian Miracle*, New York: Oxford University Press: 409–59.

Winters, L.A., N. McCulloch and A. McKay (2004) 'Trade Liberalization and Poverty: The Evidence So Far', *Journal of Economic Literature*, 42(1): 72–115.

Wood, A. (1997) 'Openness and Wage Inequality in Developing Countries: the Latin American Challenge to East Asian Conventional Wisdom', *World Bank Economic Review*, 11(1): 33–57.

World Bank (2002) *Globalization, Growth, and Poverty: Building an Inclusive World Economy*, Washington, DC: The World Bank.

5 The political economy of the proliferation of FTAs

Yung Chul Park, Shujiro Urata and Inkyo Cheong

INTRODUCTION

Since the early 1990s there has been a concerted movement towards freer, if not free, trade in East Asia. Berg and Krueger (2003) show that individual countries in the region have achieved a great deal in reducing tariffs and lowering non-tariff barriers. In parallel with unilateral trade liberalization, East Asian countries have mounted collective efforts for region-wide free trade. In 1993, ASEAN states agreed to establish an ASEAN free trade area (AFTA). By 2003 they had managed to reduce tariffs to a maximum of five per cent among the original six members, despite a number of exceptions, and brought four new members into AFTA. In 1995, APEC leaders proposed a plan for bringing about free trade in the Asia-Pacific region by 2010/2020 in what is known as the Bogor Goal.

The most notable development in the process of trade integration has been the economic ascent of China: it has replaced the US as the most important destination of exports of all East Asian countries. Unlike other large countries, China exports a large share of its output. In recent years, its exports as a share of GDP have risen to almost 25 per cent of GDP, twice the average share of other large countries. Assuming China is able to sustain its current rate of growth, it will be the engine for increasing intra-regional trade in East Asia and promoting economic integration in the region.

In recent years, the APEC movement for region-wide free trade has lost its momentum and given way to a remarkable proliferation of bilateral free trade agreements (FTAs). ASEAN has been negotiating or discussing a number of bilateral FTAs with other Asian countries, notably China, Japan and Korea, and, from outside the region, also with the US and India. Of the ASEAN states, Singapore has been the most aggressive, as it is prepared to talk to anyone willing to negotiate an FTA. The members of ASEAN+3 have concluded or have been negotiating or discussing altogether about 40 FTAs with one another and with parties from outside the region. When all the negotiations for these FTAs are completed, East Asia will have constructed a thick web or network of FTAs. What does this FTA development imply for trade liberalization in East Asia?

If China and Japan succeed in concluding their negotiations with neighbouring East Asian countries for bilateral FTAs, they may emerge as hubs of FTAs (Baldwin

2004). Although China and Japan may be natural hubs, ASEAN has been at the centre of the bilateral FTA movement in East Asia. Indeed, ASEAN has been the most sought after partner for bilateral FTAs to China, Japan, Korea, the US and India. ASEAN knows very well that it could easily be marginalized as a spoke in either China or Japan's network of bilateral FTAs. In order to avoid this marginalization and to gain access to other export markets, ASEAN has been seeking FTA partners from outside the region, including the US, India, Australia and New Zealand.

The purpose of this paper is to analyse the causes and possible consequences of the proliferation of bilateral FTAs in East Asia. Throughout the paper, our discussion will be directed to finding clues on whether the bilateral FTAs in East Asia that are completed or under discussion could be building or stumbling blocks for regional as well as global trade integration. We first discuss some of the factors behind the increase in bilateral FTAs. The next section is devoted to an analysis of economic effects of the proliferation of FTAs. The following section discusses consequences of the proliferation of FTAs in East Asia, and examines the quality of East Asia's FTAs in terms of the coverage of tariff elimination and rules of origin. This analysis is expected to help predict whether East Asian countries will end up creating a convoluted 'spaghetti bowl', hub and spoke system of bilateral FTAs or a single regional FTA as they are entering into negotiations for a multiple of overlapping bilateral FTAs. Also, the section concludes that for a number of institutional constraints, the proliferation is not likely to lead to the creation of a single East Asian FTA. Concluding remarks are in the last section.

PROLIFERATION OF FTAs IN EAST ASIA

Recent developments

As shown in Table 5.1, the 13 members of ASEAN+3 have concluded 22 FTAs and have been negotiating or discussing another 19 FTAs. Until recently, East Asia was not active in the formation of regional trade agreements (RTAs), which include FTAs and customs unions. Indeed, the AFTA was the only major FTA in East Asia until Japan and Singapore enacted the JSEPA in 2002.

Among the East Asian economies, both ASEAN and its individual members have taken a great deal of interest in negotiating FTAs with countries within and outside the region since 2002. One FTA involving ASEAN that has received great attention is the one with China. ASEAN began FTA negotiations with both Japan and Korea respectively in 2005. Several ASEAN members have sought to establish bilateral FTAs independently of ASEAN's umbrella FTA negotiations. Singapore enacted or signed several FTAs with New Zealand, Japan, Australia, the US, the EFTA and Korea. It has also been negotiating a similar one with India. Malaysia concluded bilateral FTAs with Japan in 2005. Thailand, the Philippines and Indonesia are expected to do the same with Japan in the near future.

Japan has so far concluded negotiations for three FTAs with some of the ASEAN members and Mexico. Not to be outdone by Japan, China has been equally active in courting other Asian countries for bilateral FTAs. On 4 November 2002, China and ASEAN agreed on a framework to set up a large free trade area that would have a

Table 5.1   Progress of major FTAs in East Asia (2005)

FTA	Discussion	Joint study	Negotiation	Signed (year)	Implementation (year)
			Stages of evolution		
ASEAN					
ASEAN FTA					• (1993)
ASEAN–China (CEC)					• (2005)
ASEAN–Japan (CEP)			•		
ASEAN–India				• (2005)	
ASEAN+3		•			
ASEAN–Korea				• (2005)	
ASEAN–CER		•			
Japan					
Japan–Singapore					• (2002)
Japan–Mexico					• (2005)
Japan–Malaysia				• (2005)	
Japan–Korea			•		
Japan–Philippines			•		
Japan–Thailand			•		
Japan–Chile		•			
Japan–India		•			
Korea					
Korea–Chile					• (2004)
Korea–Mexico			•		
Korea–China	•				
Korea–Singapore				• (2005)	
Korea–Canada			•		
Korea–US	•				
Korea–EFTA				• (2005)	
Korea–MERCOSUR		•			
Korea–India		•			
China					
China–Hong Kong					• (2004)
China–Macao					• (2004)
China–Australia			•		
China–Brazil		•			
China–Chile				• (2005)	
China–GCC		•			
China–Thailand			•		
Singapore					
Singapore–Australia					• (2003)
Singapore–New Zealand					• (2002)
Singapore–US		Signed TIFA with the US			• (2004)
Singapore–EFTA					• (2003)
Singapore–Canada					• (2004)
Thailand					
Thailand–China				•	
Thailand–Australia					• (2005)
Thailand–US		Signed TIFA with the US	•		
Thailand–India					• (2004)

Note: CER–FTA between Australia and New Zealand, GCC–Gulf Cooperation Council, MERCOSUR–South American Customs Union.

Source: Compiled from various sources.

total GDP of nearly $2 trillion. They enacted an FTA on trade in goods in July 2005, and are currently negotiating an FTA on trade in service and investment. At a China–Japan–Korea summit meeting in November 2003, China proposed a study on a tri-lateral trade agreement. It has also indicated its interest in an FTA with Korea. China's eagerness for forging free trade ties with ASEAN, where Japan has invested heavily for the past four decades, may turn the region into an economic battleground between the two countries.

At the Leaders' Summit Meeting of ASEAN+3 in 1998, East Asian leaders agreed to create the East Asian Vision Group (EAVG), and the East Asian Study Group (EASG) two years later. The mandate of the EAVG, which comprised private sector experts, was to develop a long-term vision for economic cooperation in East Asia. The EAVG presented the leaders with its recommendations in 2001, which included the establishment of an East Asian FTA (EAVG 2001). The EASG, consisting of government officials, concurred with the EAVG recommendation by acknowledging the potential role an East Asian FTA could play in liberalizing trade and FDI in East Asia.

The recommendation for an East Asian FTA has not seen the light, however. The East Asian leaders have been reluctant to initiate negotiations for an East Asian FTA, as they are faced with strong opposition from non-competitive sectors of their economies. More importantly, no country has been willing or able to provide the leadership needed for creating the FTA. However, the activities of the EAVG and EASG were followed up by establishing a Network of East Asian Think-Tanks (NEAT) in 2003, which is supported by ASEAN+3. NEAT's meetings were held in 2003, 2004, and 2005 to discuss issues related to forming an East Asian Community, of which an East Asian FTA is an important component. In 2005 the East Asian FTA Expert Group (EAEG) was set up at the request of ASEAN+3 economic ministers, to study the possibility of an ASEAN+3 FTA. The EAEG is expected to submit a report with recommendations at the ASEAN+3 Economic Ministers' meeting in the fall of 2006.

Factors behind the proliferation of FTAs in East Asia

A number of developments have led to an upsurge in the number of FTAs in East Asia. Some of them are common to all East Asian economies, whereas others are country specific. One of the common developments has been the proliferation of FTAs in other parts of the world. By the mid-1990s the world's leading economies, except those in East Asia, had become members of FTAs. Indeed, both of the world's two largest economic regions—North America and Western Europe—formed FTAs. As a result of this FTA development, East Asian countries began to realize that they were being discriminated against in many foreign markets. To overcome such a disadvantage and to secure markets for their exports, East Asian economies have turned to forming their own FTAs, beginning in 2002.

Another development has been the slow progress in multilateral trade liberalization under the WTO. Despite years of multilateral efforts, trade liberalization under the WTO has become increasingly difficult and slow. With the increase in the number of

WTO members, there has been a growing divergence of views on the pace and extent of trade liberalization. The increasing difficulty in reaching consensus on trade issues delayed the start of a new round after the Uruguay Round. Although an agreement was reached in Doha to launch a new round in December 2001, it failed to initiate substantive negotiations. It was only in July 2004 that the modality of negotiations was more or less agreed. Faced with the difficulty in managing trade liberalization on a global scale, many countries opted to form FTAs with like-minded countries to open their trade regimes.

It should also be noted that the GATT/WTO rules could not adequately deal with newly emerging international economic activities such as FDI, trade in services, labour mobility, and others. Liberalization of border measures such as tariffs, which are the main focus of the GATT/WTO, is not adequate in providing a level playing field to both domestic and foreign firms. It is necessary to go deeper beyond border measures and establish rules governing domestic markets such as competition policy, which the GATT/WTO cannot provide.

A third development is that Japan and some other East Asian economies have sought to rely on the external pressure that FTAs can generate as a means of promoting deregulation and structural reform of their economies. Since the 1997–98 Asian financial crisis, domestic economic reforms in East Asian economies have slowed considerably. In these economies, FTAs are viewed as providing an opportunity to break out of this stalemate. In the past, Japan had made use of international frameworks such as GATT, OECD and external pressure (especially from the United States) to reform its industries, institutions and policies through trade liberalization. Indeed, structural reform contributed significantly to improving the competitiveness of Japan's manufacturing sector. However, in the latter half of the 1990s, liberalization was becoming more difficult under the WTO framework because of the slow progress in trade liberalization. Faced with a lack of external pressure, notably from the WTO's multilateral trade negotiations, East Asian countries such as Japan and Korea became interested in FTAs as a policy option to promote structural reform. Those countries came to view FTAs in a positive light because they found that the EU and NAFTA were instrumental to structural reforms in the member countries.

Finally, there has been the intensifying rivalry between China and Japan for economic and political leadership in East Asia. Both China and Japan manage FTAs as a means of conducting regional policy, in particular, of protecting their economic and security interests and influence in Southeast Asia. This strategy has made the two countries choose to strengthen their relationships with other East Asian countries through FTAs. ASEAN and Korea themselves have also come to use FTAs as a vehicle of maintaining their economic influences in East Asia.

ECONOMIC EFFECTS OF FTAs

Many of the FTAs in East Asia have not been in existence long enough to provide the necessary information needed for a rigorous empirical examination of the effects of FTAs. In analysing the impacts of FTAs in East Asia, two types of CGE models are used.[1] One is the GTAP model and the other is the Michigan model. The GTAP model has been modified to incorporate a variety of features such as international capital mobility and investment dynamics. The Michigan model incorporates scale economies and imperfect competition.

According to Schiff and Winters (2003), for FTAs involving developing countries, trade creation is substantial while trade diversion is either non-existent or small. In contrast, for FTAs involving developed countries such as the EU and the EFTA, trade diversion is sizeable. They attribute this to the differences in their trade policies vis-à-vis non-FTA members: with regard to non-FTA members, developing countries substantially liberalize their trade regimes after joining FTAs, whereas developed countries do not, as their protection levels are lower to begin with. Schiff and Winters (2003) interpret the results for developing countries as implying that it was non-discriminatory trade liberalization rather than the FTA itself that contributed to trade expansion.

Schiff and Winters (2003) also conducted simulation analyses using computable general equilibrium models to show that there are potential dynamic gains from FTAs. They caution, however, that the gains cannot be expected automatically from tariff reduction alone, and that it is important to lower barriers of entry to the market through measures such as FDI liberalization to increase the benefit from joining an FTA.

Scollay and Gibert (2001) obtained positive impacts on world trade for all FTAs they examined (29 combinations of members) in terms of a GTAP model, indicating that trade creation associated with FTAs is greater than trade diversion. They also found that the volume of trade of non-members declines as a result of FTAs, implying that there is bloc discrimination against non-members. For an ASEAN+3 FTA, they found that the export value of the members increases by 20.34 per cent, while that of non-members declines by 0.65 per cent, resulting in an increase in total world export value of 4.14 per cent. According to the authors, the larger FTAs (in terms of membership) would lead to a larger increase in global trade: global trade liberalization would increase world export values by as much as 23.23 per cent.

Table 5.2 shows the results of three CGE model simulations. Urata and Kiyota (2003) undertake a standard application of a GTAP model with perfect competition and constant returns to scale, while Kawasaki (2003) incorporates some 'dynamic' effects including capital accumulation and the increase in productivity resulting from trade liberalization. In addition, Kawasaki (2003) allows international capital movement. Kiyota (2004) uses the Michigan model. According to the three studies, emerging economies in Southeast Asia and China gain a great deal more in terms of the increase in GDP from joining an East Asian FTA than other economies in Northeast Asia such as Korea and Taiwan. In particular, Thailand and Vietnam would be the largest beneficiaries of an East Asian FTA.[2]

An FTA will induce capital inflows from both within and outside the region as it improves trade rules. As trade, investment and economic growth interact to produce dynamic synergies, concluding an FTA could bring about an outcome much more extensive than that of trade creation and diversion. Baldwin and Venables (1995) assert that trade liberalization produces investment incentives in addition to the static

Table 5.2   Impact of FTAs on GDP (%) (CGE model simulations)

FTA members	East Asia [a]	East Asia [b]	East Asia + Australia/ New Zealand [c]
	Urata–Kiyota	*Kawasaki*	*Kiyota*
Australia/New Zealand	−0.23	–	0.1
China	1.27	3.68	2.9
Hong Kong	1.41	–	2.4
Japan	0.05	0.79	1.0
Korea	1.71	–	3.4
Taiwan	1.51	–	3.4
Indonesia	5.61	4.08	1.8
Malaysia	2.83	10.79	5.7
Philippines	2.02	4.67	3.7
Singapore	2.26	5.66	8.1
Thailand	15.90	27.16	6.1
Vietnam	8.42	19.65	–
Other Asia	−0.31	–	0.0
United States	−0.06	–	0.0
EU	−0.01	–	0.0

Notes: The figures indicate the per cent change from the base.
a   ASEAN+3, Hong Kong and Taiwan.
b   ASEAN, China and Japan.
c   ASEAN+3, Hong Kong and Taiwan (excluding Vietnam).

Sources: Urata and Kiyota (2003), Kawasaki (2003) and Kiyota (2004).

effects, which they call the 'capital accumulation effects'.[3] Capital accumulation is the result of increased domestic savings and investments, and inflows of FDI. The investment incentives could constitute an important part of the economic effects of an FTA.

This section estimates effects of FTAs on trade liberalization and capital accumulation using a modified GTAP model.[4] In this analysis, eight hypothetical FTAs in East Asia have been constructed for simulation purposes. They are: FTAs between China and Japan, China and Korea, and Japan and Korea; and an FTA involving the three Northeast Asian economies (CJK: China, Japan, Korea); three FTAs between AFTA (ASEAN Free Trade Area) on the one hand and China, Japan and Korea on the other; and an East Asian FTA including all East Asian economies. For each hypothetical FTA, effects of trade liberalization (TL) and capital accumulation (CA) are estimated. Trade liberalization refers to tariff elimination among the member countries in the GTAP database published in 2002, which is used to estimate the effective tariff rates of East Asian countries. Recent FTAs are comprehensive in that they include services, investments, trade rules on intellectual property rights, dispute settlement mechanisms and exclusion of anti-dumping rules. However, it is difficult to quantify the degree of improvement in trade rules for simulation. This paper chooses to focus on the effects of tariff elimination, which is the most important element of an FTA.

Table 5.3 presents effects of the eight hypothetical FTAs on each regional GDP. It shows that, while the eight FTAs bring economic benefits to all member countries, non-members will suffer a loss. For example, if Japan and Korea conclude an FTA, the GDP of the two countries would increase, but those of non-member countries— ASEAN and the Rest of World (ROW)—could decrease. Although the effects of TL alone are moderate, introducing those of capital accumulation (CA) increases overall economic benefits substantially. The economic effects of TL of a China–Korea FTA would increase the GDP of the two partners by 0.12 per cent and 0.76 per cent respectively. When the effects of CA are added, the increases amount to 0.45 per cent and 1.76 per cent respectively.

Similarly, when ASEAN and China conclude an FTA, the resulting trade liberalization will increase ASEAN's GDP by 0.23 per cent, and by 2.08 per cent when the effect of CA is added. In Northeast Asian FTAs, Korea is expected to gain relatively more from a CJK FTA than from a bilateral FTA with either China or Japan, as it can benefit from capital accumulation resulting from trade liberalization. As far as Japan

Table 5.3   Impact of FTAs on regional GDP in East Asia (%)

| | FTAs in Northeast Asia | | | | | | | |
| | China–Japan FTA | | China–Korea FTA | | Japan–Korea FTA | | CJK FTA | |
	TL	TL&CA	TL	TL&CA	TL	TL&CA	TL	TL&CA
China	0.27	1.11	0.12	0.45	−0.01	−0.03	0.34	1.29
Japan	0.05	0.12	−0.00	−0.04	0.01	0.04	0.06	0.13
Korea	−0.05	−0.26	0.76	1.76	0.22	0.92	0.94	2.45
ASEAN	−0.03	−0.36	−0.02	−0.19	−0.01	−0.08	−0.06	−0.59
ROW	−0.00	−0.06	−0.00	−0.06	−0.00	−0.02	−0.01	−0.12

| | FTAs in East Asia | | | | | | | |
| | ASEAN–China FTA | | ASEAN–Japan FTA | | ASEAN–Korea FTA | | East Asian FTA | |
	TL	TL&CA	TL	TL&CA	TL	TL&CA	TL	TL&CA
China	0.076	0.441	−0.02	−0.12	−0.01	−0.07	0.36	1.39
Japan	−0.007	−0.076	0.04	0.09	−0.01	−0.05	0.10	0.17
Korea	−0.025	−0.177	−0.04	−0.20	0.13	0.65	1.01	2.84
ASEAN	0.229	2.077	0.43	3.19	0.41	2.17	0.73	4.00
ROW	−0.004	−0.075	−0.01	−0.05	−0.00	−0.04	−0.02	−0.22

Source: Cheong (2005a).

and Korea are concerned, China is a more suitable FTA partner than they are to each other.

Economic effects of an FTA would in theory increase as the number of its member countries expands. As Table 5.3 shows, an East Asian FTA will bring more economic benefits to all members compared to a CJK FTA, but the difference between the two is relatively small. For example, China can expect a GDP increase of 0.34–1.29 per cent in a CJK FTA compared to an increase of 0.36–1.39 per cent in an East Asian FTA. This small difference is attributed to the fact that the economic size and volume of trade of ASEAN are relatively small. ASEAN's aggregate GDP is only about one-tenth of Northeast Asia's. For the same reason, Northeast Asian countries can expect smaller benefits from a bilateral FTA with ASEAN than from bilateral FTAs with each other. These results do not mean that a larger FTA like an East Asian one is not necessarily preferable to a smaller CJK FTA. The larger an FTA, the more economic benefits it will generate.

Suppose Korea establishes an FTA with ASEAN to avoid possible discrimination and negative effects from exclusion in response to the conclusion of the ASEAN–China FTA or an ASEAN–Japan FTA. Together with the CJK FTA, this addition will create a web of four FTAs in East Asia. Since the rules of origin differ in different FTAs, they would produce the spaghetti bowl effect and thus increase trade-related costs. A single-layer FTA such as an East Asian one would minimize the protective effects of FTA members' preferential rules of origin and also create a more competitive environment, which would generate dynamic synergy effects of economic integration. Since the simulation model of this study cannot capture these effects, the economic effects of an East Asian FTA as reported in Table 5.3 are likely to be underestimated. East Asia will be better off with a region-wide FTA.

The CGE model used in this study cannot analyse the behaviour of investors as it is a static one, but it can indirectly estimate the impact of an FTA on regional capital accumulation, using the method of Francois, McDonald and Nordstorm (1997). As shown in Table 5.4, China gains more from a bilateral FTA with Japan than with Korea in terms of capital accumulation. China finds Korea a more desirable partner than ASEAN as far as the increase in GDP is concerned, but the other way around in terms of capital accumulation. For Korea, an FTA with China is preferable to one with Japan. Given those conflicting impacts of FTAs on different regions, a region-wide FTA such as an East Asian FTA would be preferable to a network of bilateral or sub-regional FTAs. An interesting result, though not unexpected, is that Japan is not affected by any East Asian FTAs regardless of its participation, though it suffers from a decrease in capital accumulation when excluded. This result follows from the fact that Japan is the second largest open economy.

The magnitude of the impacts of FTAs would vary from member to member. In general, impacts would be large for a country with high trade dependency and/or high import protection. For example, Thailand, which has relatively high trade dependency and high import tariff protections, gains more from joining an FTA, whereas Japan, which has a low trade dependency and low tariff protections except for a few agricultural products, cannot expect a large benefit.

Table 5.4   Impact of FTAs in East Asia on regional capital stock (%)

| | FTAs in Northeast Asia | | | | | | | |
| | China–Japan FTA | | China–Korea FTA | | Japan–Korea FTA | | CJK FTA | |
	TL	TL&CA	TL	TL&CA	TL	TL&CA	TL	TL&CA
China	0.02	0.21	0.01	0.08	0.00	–0.01	0.02	0.24
Japan	0.00	0.02	0.00	–0.01	0.00	0.01	0.00	0.02
Korea	0.00	–0.05	0.02	0.23	0.01	0.16	0.03	0.36
ASEAN	0.00	–0.06	0.00	–0.03	0.00	–0.01	–0.01	–0.10
ROW	0.00	–0.01	0.00	–0.01	0.00	0.00	0.00	–0.03

| | FTAs in East Asia | | | | | | | |
| | ASEAN–China FTA | | ASEAN–Japan FTA | | ASEAN–Korea FTA | | East Asian FTA | |
	TL	TL&CA	TL	TL&CA	TL	TL&CA	TL	TL&CA
China	0.01	0.09	0.00	–0.02	0.00	–0.01	0.02	0.26
Japan	0.00	–0.02	0.00	0.01	0.00	–0.01	0.00	0.02
Korea	0.00	–0.04	0.00	–0.04	0.01	0.12	0.03	0.43
ASEAN	0.02	0.33	0.03	0.49	0.02	0.31	0.03	0.58
ROW	0.00	–0.02	0.00	–0.01	0.00	–0.01	0.00	–0.05

Source: Cheong (2005a).

MARKET ACCESS IN EAST ASIAN FTAs

Recently, most East Asian countries have begun to promote FTAs, which implies that those countries have been facing strong domestic opposition against trade liberalization, and may have concluded FTAs with the exclusion of substantial numbers of tariff lines from trade liberalization.

The quality of FTAs can be evaluated in terms of several criteria, the most important being the degree of market access. Market access is determined in general by the coverage of tariff reduction, elimination of non-tariff barriers (NTBs), stringency of the rules of origin (ROO) and harmonization of trade rules. Some of these elements such as harmonization of trade rules cannot be easily quantified, but the coverage of tariff elimination and simplicity of the ROO can be measured. This section assesses the quality of FTAs in terms of these two criteria as shown in Table 5.5, where FTAs are classified into four categories depending on their coverage of tariff elimination and complexity of their ROOs.

Table 5.6 summarizes the coverage of tariff elimination in major FTAs in the Western Hemisphere and East Asia. NAFTA, ANZCERTA, AFTA and the ASEAN–China FTA have a broad range of tariff elimination. AFTA plans to impose low internal tariff rates of 0–5 per cent on sensitive items instead of eliminating them

Table 5.5   Effects of tariff elimination and stringency of ROO on trade

Coverage of tariff elimination	Stringency of ROO	
	Less	More
Wide	High impact	Low impact
Narrow	Low impact	Limited impact

Table 5.6   Tariff elimination in FTAs

	Coverage of tariff elimination	Remarks
ANZCERTA	Complete	Gradual liberalization (1983, 1988)
NAFTA	3% (HS8) of agriculture excluded	Quota for textiles is specified
EU–Mexico	EU: 35.2% (HS8) of agriculture excluded	Mexico: 26.1% exception for agriculture
AFTA	98% of total tariff lines included in liberalization package	Intra-regional trade share: 20–25% Use of CEPT is very low (3%)
ASEAN–China FTA	Around 98% of tariff lines liberalized	Extremely sensitive items excluded
JSFTA	58% of agricultural HS (6) excluded	Agriculture with positive tariffs excluded
KCFTA	30% of agricultural HS (6) excluded	Additional liberalization will be discussed after the DDA

Source: Cheong (2005b).

completely. Other FTAs allow a large number of exceptions including agricultural products, as in the FTAs concluded by Japan and Korea.

Different FTAs have quite different specifications for the ROO, although all FTAs studied in this paper employ the regional value content (RVC) ratio in defining the ROO. Many FTAs, including NAFTA, require substantial changes in tariff classification (CTC), making their ROOs highly complex. The ROOs become more complex and stringent when the CTC is combined with the RVC ratio. NAFTA, the EU–Mexico FTA and bilateral FTAs that Japan and Korea have concluded introduce a ROO that stipulates both the CTC and RVC ratio for sensitive items.

As shown in Table 5.7, the ROOs of East Asian FTAs are similar to those of Western FTAs in terms of the CTC, RVC ratio, cumulation[5] and de Minimis. However, AFTA and the ASEAN–China FTA have a very simple and uniform format for the

Table 5.7   Summary of ROO in major FTAs

	NAFTA	EU–Mexico FTA	AFTA	ASEAN–China FTA	Japan–Singapore FTA	Korea–Chile FTA
CTC	Yes	Yes	Not necessary	Not necessary	Yes	Yes
RVC Ratio	50–60%	30–50%	40%	40%	40–60%	30–45%
Cumulation	Yes	Yes	Yes	Yes	Yes	Yes
De Minimis	7%	10%	No mention	No mention	8–10%	8%

Source: Compiled from various sources.

ROO, which is simpler than the one the WTO recommends[6] and which is not found in other RTAs. For example, AFTA and the ASEAN–China FTA do not specify a CTC criterion since they require a 40 per cent RVC ratio. In negotiating FTAs with ASEAN for bilateral FTAs, both Japan and Korea are likely to yield to ASEAN's demand for a simple ROO.

Table 5.8 presents an overall assessment of market access in major FTAs. It shows that ANZCERTA and the ASEAN–China FTA receive high scores (Group I). AFTA can be placed in the same group but with some reservations, given its 0–5 per cent tariff goal instead of complete tariff elimination. NAFTA is inferior to FTAs in Group I because of its complex and restrictive ROO. The Korea–Chile FTA, Japan–Singapore FTA and EU–Mexico FTA are included in Group IV with a relatively narrow coverage of tariff elimination and stringent ROOs. The three FTAs exclude a large number of agricultural items from tariff liberalization on top of introducing a ROO as stringent as that of NAFTA.

Table 5.8   Overall assessment of quality of FTAs

Coverage of tariff elimination	Stringency of ROO	
	Less	*More*
Wide	Group I: ANZCERTA, CA FTA	Group II: NAFTA
Narrow	Group III: AFTA	Group IV: KCFTA, EU–Mexico FTA, JSFTA

CONCLUDING REMARKS

This paper has examined the current progress of FTAs in East Asia that are completed or under negotiation. Many of East Asia's FTAs have been in existence for a relatively short period of time. As a result, they do not throw much light on how discriminatory the existing East Asian FTAs have been or will be, and whether they will collapse into a large single FTA or create a convoluted spaghetti or noodle bowl. Depending on how one interprets the objectives and performance of East Asia's FTAs, one can be either an optimist or a pessimist about the prospects for multilateral trade liberalization in the region.

There is indeed no shortage of arguments suggesting that bilateral FTAs could be complementary to the development of multilateralism and to the extent that they can be concluded quickly to become building blocks for global trade liberalization under the WTO. Bilateral FTAs, it is often pointed out, have other advantages in that they could provide rules in various areas that are not covered by the WTO, such as FDI and labour mobility.

While these advantages may be real, the spread of bilateralism in East Asia could have dangerous consequences. As the simulation studies surveyed above show, the bilateral movement is likely to produce an outcome inferior to a large FTA such as an East Asian FTA or a China–Japan–Korea FTA, because East Asian bilateral FTAs could, among other things, divert more trade from low-cost to high-cost producers. Indeed, if both China and Japan succeed in creating hub-and-spoke networks of bilateral FTAs, then Baldwin (2004) cautions that these networks pose a danger in that the spoke countries could be marginalized both economically and politically. Given this possibility, the potential spoke countries will attempt to join as many FTAs as they can, thereby leading to further proliferation of bilateral FTAs. This development would make East Asia less attractive to foreign direct investment, a situation that Baldwin calls the 'noodle bowl' problem.

China and Japan may be motivated to negotiate bilateral FTAs with other East Asian countries in order to protect and strengthen their political and strategic interests in East Asia. If this were the case, then the proliferation of bilateral FTAs would not necessarily speed up trade liberalization in individual countries. This is because these politically motivated bilateral FTAs could turn into strategic alliances rather than economic unions. Furthermore, there is a concern that some of the bilateral FTAs already concluded, negotiated, or under consideration in East Asia are examples of negotiated protectionism rather than negotiated liberalization, as they tend to leave out politically sensitive sectors, such as agriculture, by making a rather self-serving interpretation of GATT Article XXIV.8.

As countries engaged in negotiating bilateral FTAs in East Asia resort to many provisions for rules of origin to give selective protection to domestic industries as shown in the preceding section, they will strengthen domestic protectionist forces while weakening the domestic pro-liberalization coalition. At the same time, different rules of origin and coverage of imports for liberalization in different bilateral FTAs could create a bewildering spaghetti bowl effect of complex and incompatible agreements, thereby inhibiting a broadening of the geographic scope of integration

(Ravenhill 2004). If this happens, then consolidating a large number of different bilateral FTAs for region-wide trade liberalization will be a Herculean task as it requires standardizing different FTAs into one agreement. It is therefore highly unlikely that an East Asian FTA will emerge by itself as a result of the amalgamation of bilateral FTAs (Cheong 2002). None of East Asia's FTAs makes any mention of a possible extension to other parties. The intensifying rivalry and the growing rift between China and Japan will also make it more difficult to create an East Asian FTA.

In the end, the pros and cons of bilateral FTAs will have to be judged on the basis of their performance. All East Asian countries depend on trade for growth and industrialization, and in knowing that an economically integrated East Asia will offer new investment opportunities and help sustain rapid growth, East Asian policymakers cannot afford to have FTAs degenerate into a convoluted noodle bowl. That is, in light of the consensus among East Asian leaders that the establishment of an East Asian FTA is desirable as it would promote economic prosperity and social and political stability in the region, optimists argue that these separate FTA developments would in the end lead to the formation of an East Asia FTA. So far, however, there is little evidence that supports the optimistic view. The new wave of bilateral FTAs in East Asia is not likely to be supportive of region-wide free trade.

NOTES

This paper is a shortened and revised version of Park, Urata and Cheong (2005), which was presented at the PAFTAD 30 meeting in Honolulu, Hawaii, February 19–21, 2005.

1   It should be noted that CGE models, as other models, suffer from several shortcomings, necessitating caution in interpreting the results. Some of the shortcomings include: specification of behavioural relationships is very simple, possibly missing intricate but important relationships; parameters used in the model are generally not obtained from actual observations but based on educated guesses; sector aggregation is rather broad, masking detailed variations. These problems in CGE models do not condemn such models, but they do imply caveats.

2   Urata and Kiyota (2003) find a disproportionate increase in intra-regional trade compared to extra-regional trade, in their study of an East Asian FTA (ASEAN+3 + Hong Kong + Taiwan). Specifically, the share of intra-East Asia trade in world trade would increase from 11 per cent to 14 per cent, and the share of intra-East Asia exports (imports) in East Asia's total exports (imports) would increase from 44 (50) per cent to 53 (59) per cent. They also report that the trade intensity index would increase from 2.02 to 2.17 as a result of forming an East Asia FTA.

3   Detailed theoretical backgrounds on capital accumulation can be found in Levin and Renelt (1992) and Grossman and Helpman (1995).

4   This section draws on Cheong (2003, 2005a).

5   Cumulation refers to the degree to which inputs (processes and/or materials) wholly or partly originating from one preferential trading partner are allowed to count towards satisfying a ROO governing the processes carried out in another preferential partner. A cumulation rule adds flexibility by allowing inputs originating in two or more parties to a single agreement, or even parties of different agreements, to be counted together to determine origin.

6   According to WTO's Harmonized Non-Preferential Rules of Origin, CTC and/or value content requirements are recommended for most items, which is much stricter than the ROO in the ASEAN–China FTA.

REFERENCES

Baldwin, R.E. (2004) 'The Spoke Trap: Hub-and-Spoke Bilateralism in East Asia', *Korea Institute for International Economic Policy (KIEP) Research Series 04-02*, Seoul: KIEP.

Baldwin, R.E. and A.J. Venables (1995) 'Regional Economic Integration', in G.M. Grossman, and K. Rogoff (eds), *Handbook of International Economics* III, Amsterdam: North-Holland/ Elsevier.

Berg, A. and A. Krueger (2003) 'Trade, Growth, and Poverty: A Selective Survey', *IMF Working Paper No. 03/30*, April.

Cheong, I. (2002) 'East Asian Economic Integration: Recent Development and Policy Implications', *Korea Institute for International Economic Policy (KIEP) Research Series 02-02*, Seoul: KIEP.

———— (2003) 'Korea's FTA Policy: Progress and Prospects' in Y. Kim and C.J. Lee (eds), *Northeast Asian Economic Integration: Prospects for a Northeast Asian FTA*, Seoul: Korea Institute for International Economic Policy.

———— (2005a) 'A Turning Point in an East Asian Regionalism: Recent Development of FTAs' in C.Y. Ahn, R.E. Baldwin and I. Cheong (eds), *East Asian Regionalism: Prospects and Challenges*, Amsterdam: Springer.

———— (2005b) 'Assessing the Quality of FTAs in Terms of Market Access', paper presented at the Pacific Economic Cooperation Council (PECC) Conference, Seoul, 22–25 May.

East Asian Vision Group (EAVG) (2001) *Towards an East Asian Community—Region of Peace, Prosperity and Progress*, Seoul: EAVG Secretariat.

Francois, J.F., B. McDonald, and H. Nordstrom (1997) 'Capital Accumulation in Applied Trade Models' in J.F. Francois and K.A. Reinert (eds), *Applied Methods for Trade Policy Analysis—A Handbook*, London: Cambridge University Press.

Grossman, G.M. and E. Helpman (1995) 'Technology and Trade', *Centre for Economic Policy Research Discussion Paper No. 1134*.

Kawasaki, K. (2003) 'The Impact of Free Trade Agreements in Asia', *REITI Discussion Paper Series 03-E-018*, Tokyo: Research Institute of Economy, Trade, and Industry.

Kiyota, K. (2004) 'The Role of Service Trade Liberalization in Japan's Trade Policies', *Faculty of Business Administration Working Paper 220*, Yokohama National University, December.

Levin, R. and D. Renelt (1992) 'A Sensitivity Analysis of Cross-country Growth Regressions', *The American Economic Review*, 82(4): 942–63.

Park, Y.C., S. Urata and I. Cheong (2005) 'The Political Economy of the Proliferation of FTAs', paper presented at the PAFTAD 30 meeting in Honolulu, Hawaii, 19–21 February.

Ravenhill, J. (2004) 'The Political Economy of the New Asia–Pacific Bilateralism', paper presented to Beijing Forum, 24 August.

Schiff, M. and L.A. Winters (2003) *Regional Integration and Development*, Oxford University Press for the World Bank.

Scollay, R. and J.P. Gibert (2001) *New Regional Trading Arrangements in the Asia Pacific?*, Washington, DC: Institute for International Economics.

Urata, S. and K. Kiyota (2003) 'The Impacts of an East Asia FTA on Foreign Trade in East Asia', *NBER Working Paper 10173*, December.

6 US trade policy towards China: discrimination and its implications

Chad P. Bown and Rachel McCulloch

INTRODUCTION

In a surprisingly short time, the bilateral relationship with China has come to dominate American public and official views on globalization. The list of American grievances is familiar: a burgeoning bilateral trade deficit, currency misalignment, accumulation of US financial assets and various 'unfair' trade practices. These were also staples of the US demonization of Japan in the 1980s, before the seemingly invincible 'Japan Incorporated' began to falter. Now China has replaced Japan as the country with the largest bilateral trade surplus with the United States, and also as the main (though by no means only) object of American dissatisfaction with its trading partners. Just as US bilateral relations with Japan were characterized by a wide range of discriminatory policy initiatives, China is now the object of unprecedented discriminatory treatment in its bilateral relationship with the United States and also as a less-than-equal member of the World Trade Organization since its accession in 2001.

This paper explores several dimensions of US trade policy towards China. We first examine the historical context of US discriminatory trade practices, both as permitted under GATT/WTO rules and through bilateral measures taken outside this framework. We then take a closer look at specific US policy actions towards China: antidumping, WTO accession and free-trade areas negotiated with China's competitors. The next section compares recent US treatment of China with other major instances of US trade policy discrimination, particularly towards Japan. This is followed by consideration of the economic implications of the discriminatory trade policy actions, including their impact on other trading partners, and a conclusion.

US TRADE POLICY DISCRIMINATION IN HISTORICAL PERSPECTIVE

The United States has played a paradoxical role in the development of the post-World War II trading system, championing the principle of non-discrimination in world trade, yet opting for a range of discriminatory policies in its own trade regime. While promoting the most-favoured-nation (MFN) principle in the General Agreement on Tariffs and Trade (GATT), US trade officials also pioneered the use of bilateral trade measures, including voluntary export restraints (VERs) and orderly marketing agreements (OMAs), to protect important domestic industries adversely affected by rapidly growing imports.

These explicitly discriminatory measures, first applied to Japan and later to other newer exporters—mostly in East Asia—to US markets, clearly violated the GATT's MFN principle. Moreover, US officials chose these measures over the non-discriminatory safeguard action permitted under Article XIX of the GATT. Trade discrimination was also fostered through negotiated voluntary import expansions (VIEs) with Japan and other trading partners. Although US trade officials are no longer negotiating targets for Japanese imports, quantitative trade commitments are not entirely a thing of the past—the website of the Office of the United States Trade Representative (USTR) reports a December 2004 agreement with Korea that will guarantee a minimum volume of Korean rice imports from the United States over a ten-year period.[1]

US trade policy discrimination against Japan actually began even before World War II with the negotiation in the 1930s of 'voluntary' restrictions on Japanese exports to the United States of several types of cotton textiles (Metzger 1971: 170–1). Although the imports from Japan were small relative to the US market, they were nonetheless deemed a threat because of rapidly rising volumes concentrated in a few product categories. As with later VERs, these voluntary agreements were stimulated by US threats of unilateral action. But in the early post-war period, with its economy in tatters, Japan hardly appeared to pose a competitive threat to US industries. The United States assisted in the reconstruction of Japan's textile industry and also championed Japan's entry into the GATT in 1955. However, other GATT members had strong reservations, mainly on account of Japan's much lower wages. Fourteen countries accounting for 40 per cent of GATT trade therefore exercised their privilege under Article XXV to refuse to extend MFN treatment to Japan (Dam 1970: 347–8). Although the United States was not among the GATT members that denied Japan MFN treatment, the grudging acceptance into the GATT of Japan, a too-competitive rival in manufactured goods, foreshadowed the harsh conditions of China's WTO accession half a century later. By 1956, bilateral negotiations leading to the post-war VERs on Japanese textile exports to the United States had already begun; Canada, the United Kingdom and the European Economic Community likewise negotiated arrangements intended to discourage 'market disruption' due to imports from Japan (Metzger 1971: 174–5).

Of course, discriminatory trade measures, whether export-restricting or import-increasing, have important external effects on other sectors and countries. What began as Japan's voluntary limits on cotton textile exports to the United States and other importing countries eventually culminated in the global Multi-Fiber Arrangement (MFA), as unrestricted products and later unrestricted exporting countries filled the import gap.[2] The quantitative form of Japan's VERs also promoted product upgrading and may thus have accelerated Japan's transition to more-sophisticated manufactured exports. We discuss these and other externalities associated with discriminatory protection in greater detail below.

Discrimination against Japan and later China has also been implicit in the US application of GATT-consistent laws on unfair trade such as antidumping, as we document in the next two sections. Elastic criteria have made the dumping laws the most popular policy instrument for US industries seeking protection from competing imports, especially imports from transition economies categorized as 'non-market economies'. In recent years, China has become a major target for antidumping action by the United States and worldwide, accounting for nearly one-fifth of all cases in 2002 (Messerlin 2004: Table 6.3). Because dumping margins for China are calculated on a different basis than for most other countries and resulting antidumping duties are usually much larger, this statistic may understate the impact of antidumping action on China's exports to the United States.

Other types of GATT-sanctioned practices offer preferred market access to some countries. The original GATT 'grandfathered' preferential arrangements already in place, most notably British imperial preferences favouring Commonwealth countries (Dam 1970: 14). In response to pressure from potential beneficiaries and the United Nations Conference on Trade and Development (UNCTAD), a GATT waiver in 1971 initiated the Generalized System of Preferences (GSP). Under the GSP, manufactured exports from less-developed countries (LDCs) gained limited preferential access to the markets of the industrialized nations (Pearson 2004: 105). The United States initially opposed the GSP, partly on grounds that it weakened the MFN principle but also from a more practical concern that cheap imports from LDCs would flood US markets. The US version of the system, finally implemented in 1976, excluded 'sensitive' sectors, notably textiles and apparel but also footwear and steel, where competition from LDC exporters was already biting into domestic sales.[3]

Perhaps most important for today's trade environment is the worldwide proliferation of preferential, i.e., discriminatory, trade agreements. Beginning in the mid-1980s, the United States has aggressively promoted 'free trade' agreements (FTAs) with a variety of partners, mostly but not exclusively in the western hemisphere.[4] Although this drive for preferential liberalization arose initially from US frustration with the slow pace of multilateral efforts in the GATT, efforts continued unabated during and even after the Uruguay Round of multilateral negotiations. Such trade agreements were authorized under GATT Article XXIV, which was originally intended to facilitate economic union in Europe but which has emerged as the major loophole in the MFN principle in the World Trade Organization.[5] As of 2002, 250 agreements authorized under Article XXIV had been notified to the GATT or WTO. Of these, 170 remain in force; the WTO estimates that an additional 70 are operational but have not yet been notified.[6] The United States alone has negotiated about a dozen FTAs in addition to the North American Free Trade Agreement (NAFTA) and also participates in a wide variety of looser agreements with specific trading partners (USTR website).

Any country excluded from preferential access is at an obvious disadvantage. Indeed, preferential agreements have become so important a determinant of export success in major markets that mere 'MFN treatment' might now be more accurately described as *least*-favoured-nation status. US trading partners, including the members of the Association of Southeast Asian Nations (ASEAN), are now contemplating FTAs with the United States less to expand market access than to retain their current access (Naya and Plummer 2005).[7] Some analysts view the pressure on excluded countries to negotiate their own FTAs as giving rise to a desirable 'competitive liberalization' process, while others are less optimistic, noting the complex and trade-distorting rules of origin such agreements typically entail as well as the possible inhibiting effect on future multilateral liberalization (Limão 2006). Srinivasan (2004) in fact suggests that China and India, each excluded from most of the important FTAs, should propose repealing GATT Article XXIV and replacing this giant loophole with rules that convert any preferential liberalization among WTO members to MFN liberalization within a stipulated period, such as five years. But since its WTO accession, China has lost no time in negotiating its own FTAs with trading partners in the Pacific region (Antkiewicz and Whalley 2005). Talks are even underway with India, among others.

US TRADE POLICY TOWARDS CHINA: IMPLICIT AND EXPLICIT DISCRIMINATION

In this section of the paper we present data on specific US trade policies that discriminate against China. The discussion is split into two parts. The first two sub-sections focus on *explicitly* discriminatory trade policy, where the result of the US trade policy is to *raise* barriers against Chinese exporters, thus allowing exporters from other countries preferential access to the US market. The third sub-section focuses on *implicitly* discriminatory trade policy, which *lowers* US barriers facing non-Chinese exporters to the detriment of their Chinese competitors.

US use of antidumping against China

Over the last 25 years, the administered protection of antidumping has been the most attractive trade policy instrument for domestic industries seeking insulation from foreign competition. The aggressive use of antidumping was 'pioneered' by the United States but increasingly emulated by many other developed and developing countries.[8] From the perspective of the issues raised in this paper, antidumping is an interesting policy to examine because of the discretionary way it is applied. This discretion, when combined with the political-economy features of administered protection, means that antidumping *can* be a highly discriminatory trade policy action, yet it also has the potential to be imposed on a relatively non-discriminatory basis as well. With this perspective in mind, we examine some of the stylized facts on US use of antidumping against Chinese exporters.

Table 6.1 provides a breakdown of US antidumping activity against its ten most frequently targeted trading partners for two separate periods: 1980–89 and 1990–2003. Not surprisingly, in the more recent period Chinese exporters (a) are the most frequently investigated producers, being named in 91 different antidumping investigations, (b) face a higher likelihood (67 per cent) of having investigations result in duties than other producers, which together leads them to (c) face more antidumping duty actions (61) than producers from any other country, where they finally (d) face the highest level of duties imposed (an average *ad valorem* rate of 127 per cent) of all targeted countries—more than twice as high as the average facing all other countries.[9] These facts suggest that China is 'public enemy number one' in the US antidumping

Table 6.1   US antidumping actions against its ten most frequently investigated trading partners, 1980–2003

a. 1990–2003

Country	Antidumping investigations	Investigations resulting in duties (share of investigations, %)	Only country named in investigation (share of investigations, %)		Mean duty, conditional on duties imposed, % (rank)	Share of US total import market in 1996, %	
1. China	91	61 (67)	41	(45)	127.02	3.5	(8)
2. Japan	53	33 (62)	18	(34)	68.44	14.0	(2)
3. Korea	39	20 (51)	3	(8)	16.65	2.7	(10)
4. Taiwan	30	15 (50)	3	(10)	20.46	3.7	(7)
5. Mexico	26	11 (42)	4	(15)	41.18	10.0	(3)
6. Germany	26	10 (38)	0	(0)	37.60	4.9	(4)
7. India	25	11 (44)	5	(20)	52.89	0.8	(24)
8. Canada	25	6 (24)	11	(44)	25.35	21.0	(1)
9. Brazil	24	12 (50)	2	(8)	76.47	1.2	(16)
10. Italy	19	10 (53)	2	(11)	22.75	2.3	(11)
Other	272	105 (39)	31	(11)	54.55	35.9	
Total	630	294 (47)	120	(19)	64.15	100.0	

b. 1980–89

Country	Antidumping investigations	Investigations resulting in duties (share of investigations, %)	Only country named in investigation (share of investigations, %)		Mean duty, conditional on duties imposed % (rank)	Share of US total import market in 1985, %	
1. Japan	65	41 (63)	28	(43)	50.40	20.1	(2)
2. West Germany	34	11 (32)	6	(18)	34.56	5.7	(3)
3. Italy	30	10 (33)	4	(13)	67.90	2.9	(8)
4. Taiwan	29	12 (41)	12	(42)	29.42	4.6	(6)
5. France	28	10 (36)	4	(13)	23.05	2.6	(10)
6. Korea	27	14 (52)	9	(33)	15.71	3.3	(7)
7. Brazil	25	11 (44)	12	(48)	37.35	2.2	(11)
8. Canada	25	10 (40)	18	(72)	14.78	21.0	(1)
9. United Kingdom	23	4 (17)	3	(13)	30.86	4.6	(5)
10. China	17	12 (71)	9	(53)	44.39	0.7	(22)
Other	181	52 (29)	32	(18)	35.06	32.3	
Total	484	187 (39)	137	(28)	36.81	100.0	

Source: Data compiled by the authors from the *Federal Register*. US import data from Feenstra (2000).

process, even though at the midpoint of the 1990–2003 study period China was still only the *eighth* largest US trading partner—the source of just 3.5 per cent of total US imports in 1996.[10]

Another important finding is the high count and unusually high frequency with which China has been the *only* country named in a particular US antidumping investigation. Over the 1990–2003 period, China was the only country targeted in 45 per cent of the cases in which it was under investigation.[11] Most US antidumping investigations in recent years have considered unfairly traded products from *multiple* foreign countries simultaneously, a trend that has increased since the mid-1980s when a change in the US antidumping law and investigative process allowed the injury determination to be based on 'cumulated' imports from all countries named in an antidumping investigation.[12] Using cumulated imports from more countries increases the likelihood of an affirmative injury determination. Other things being equal, this change could bias the decision of a US petitioning industry toward naming *more* foreign countries in an antidumping investigation, possibly including some for which there is no evidence of dumping, so as to use the cumulated imports from all named countries to increase the likelihood of an affirmative injury determination. Thus, the frequency with which China *alone* is named suggests that there may be something distinctive about imports from China, when compared to US imports from other trading partners.

Given that so many antidumping cases involving China seem 'different' from cases involving other countries, the distinctive features of these cases could perhaps also provide a reason for the higher duties that its firms typically face. To examine this potential explanation, in Table 6.2 we provide summary data on the characteristics of the antidumping investigations that involved China as one of multiple countries being investigated for alleged dumping of the same set of products in the US market. By examining the outcome facing Chinese firms relative to that facing other investigated foreign firms in these multi-country cases, we are able to control for differences in industry characteristics across cases that may also generate differences in the level of antidumping duty imposed across countries. The data for the 1990–2003 period show that the average duty faced by Chinese firms after an affirmative determination was over 80 percentage points higher than the average duty facing all of the other firms from other countries in the multi-country investigations. In the table, we refer to this differential as the 'China premium'.

Returning to Table 6.1, it is also informative to compare the US antidumping policy facing China over the 1990–2003 period with the US antidumping situation facing Japan over the 1980–89 period, during the height of 'Japan-bashing'. Similar to the recent circumstances facing China, in the 1980s Japan was the most targeted exporter in US antidumping actions, targeted nearly twice as often as West Germany, the next most frequently targeted exporting country. Not only were Japanese exporters more frequently investigated than other exporters, but they were also more likely to face affirmative decisions (63 per cent, compared to the average of 39 per cent for other exporters) and thus to have investigations result in antidumping duties.

Table 6.2   China's relative performance in multi-country US antidumping investigations that ended in duties against at least one country

Time period	Mean (median) duty facing China (%)	Mean (median) duty facing all other investigated countries (%)	Mean (median) China premium (%)
1990–2003	117.38	36.41	80.97
(23 multi-country cases involving China)	(118.41)	(32.23)	(84.20)
1980–89	33.94	18.01	15.93
(6 multi-country cases involving China)	(25.65)	(10.81)	(20.24)

Note: Data compiled by the authors from the *Federal Register*. The duty rate used is the final 'all other firms' rate in a US antidumping investigation, which is typically calculated as the trade-weighted average of the firm-specific rates of duty applied in the investigation.

However, Table 6.1 also reveals a notable difference between Japan in the 1980s and China in 1990–2003: Japan was a far more important trading partner in the 1980s than China in the 1990s. Looking at the midpoint of each period, Japan accounted for 20.1 per cent of total US imports in 1985, compared with China's share of just 3.5 per cent in 1996. As a more important trading partner with faster-growing exports (see Table 6.8), we might have expected Japan in the 1980s to have been an even more potent source of trade frictions and potential antidumping investigations than China in the 1990s. Other things being equal, China in the 1990s should have been *less* frequently targeted by US antidumping investigations, compared to Japan in the 1980s. Moreover, Table 6.1 shows that while antidumping duties facing Japanese exporters in the 1980s were higher than the average duties facing firms in other countries, the duties facing Chinese exporters in the 1990s were more than twice as high as the average duties facing all other exporters.[13]

There are a number of potential explanations for differential treatment of China in the antidumping process. One possibility is that Chinese exports are disproportionately concentrated in politically sensitive and/or politically organized sectors in the United States, thus making China more likely to be subject to US antidumping investigations due to the sectoral composition of its exports. However, given the proclivity towards antidumping activity in the steel sector, which alone accounts for nearly 40 per cent of all antidumping cases, when combined with Japan's (net exporter) and China's (net importer) historical global trading position in steel, the sectoral explanation seems highly improbable. Rather, the US antidumping focus on China *despite* its relatively small import share and the sectoral composition of its exports may reflect the greater perceived *threat* that China posed in the 1990s.[14]

As with Japan in the 1980s, China's rapid export growth was a threat not only to US import-competing industries, but also to suppliers in other countries with an established presence in the US market and thus a concern about losing market share to Chinese competitors. A rational response for these exporters is to use the US trade policy process (in this case, antidumping) to obtain preferential access to the US market if they can no longer compete with Chinese firms under conditions of MFN treatment. In the case of antidumping, the preferential access can be obtained either by ensuring that Chinese firms face US antidumping duties that other foreign suppliers do not, or that Chinese firms face much *higher* antidumping duties than the ones imposed on other foreign suppliers in multi-country cases. Prusa (1997, 2001) and Bown (2004) provide empirical evidence that US trade policy has had the effect of protecting not only domestic producers but also non-targeted foreign suppliers. These studies establish that discriminatory application of antidumping duties in the United States has led to substantial *trade diversion*, i.e., increases in US imports in targeted product categories from *non-targeted* foreign suppliers—who thus gained from the US trade policy along with domestic producers. These gains likely came at the expense of exporters first in Japan and then also in China, as they faced higher US antidumping duties than other foreign suppliers (more than twice as high in the case of China).

China's WTO accession and China-specific 'safeguard' laws

A second area of trade policy where China currently faces discriminatory treatment stems from its WTO accession in 2001. The terms of the accession agreement give WTO members the authority to enact 'China safeguards' in the case of surges of imports of products from China. In the GATT/WTO system, safeguards have traditionally been distinct from the 'unfair trade' laws such as antidumping in that users of safeguards do not need to establish that the foreign country or exporting firms have done anything unfair (such as dumping). All that is necessary is for the domestic industry to show that it has been injured or that there is a reasonable threat of injury, and that this injury is associated with an increase in imports.[15] However, at least in principle, safeguard protection is applied to *all* sources of imports, in keeping with its use when injury to the domestic industry is not due to any unfair act of specific foreign suppliers.

Yet there are at least two new safeguards facing China alone. The first, authorized by Section 421 of the US trade law, is applicable to all products imported from China. It is administered in much the same way as the standard, WTO-authorized safeguard law of Section 201. Under both laws, the US International Trade Commission (ITC) is charged with investigating injury, and in the case of an affirmative finding, making a remedy recommendation, which the US president then has the discretion to modify, accept or reject.[16] The second new safeguard facing imports from China, which is administered by the Office of Textiles and Apparel (OTEXA) in the US Department of Commerce, is applicable to all US imports of textile and apparel products from China.

Section 421 China safeguard

The primary way in which the new Section 421 'China safeguard' differs from traditional use of safeguards is the discriminatory nature of the policy. The WTO Agreement on Safeguards requires that US trade restrictions authorized under the standard safeguards law (Section 201) must be applied on a most-favoured-nation (MFN) basis, so as not to discriminate among foreign suppliers. The China safeguards, which are discriminatory both in their consideration and in the potential application of US trade restrictions against exporters from one country only, are thus entirely antithetical to the MFN treatment that the WTO requires for other safeguard protection.

Another important discriminatory element of this safeguard, relative to the standard US Section 201 safeguard requirement for a US industry to receive import protection, is a less stringent requirement to show evidence of injury. Under the China safeguard, if any *other* WTO member uses its China safeguard, the United States can respond to the threat of Chinese exports being 'deflected' to the US market by imposing its own China safeguard without conducting an investigation to establish injury to the US industry.[17]

Table 6.3 describes five ITC investigations of Chinese exporters conducted since 2002 under the China safeguard law. In three of the five cases, the ITC voted that the petitioning US industry was either injured or threatened with injury by Chinese exports and recommended that the US president use a trade remedy such as a tariff or quota to protect the domestic industry. In each case, the president exercised discretion and declined to implement the ITC's trade remedy recommendations, instead stating, for example, in the *Pedestal Actuator* case that

> After considering all relevant aspects of the investigation, I have determined that providing import relief for the US pedestal actuator industry is not in the national economic interest of the United States. In particular, I find that the import relief would have an adverse impact on the United States economy clearly greater than the benefits of such action. (United States 2003)

The pattern of discriminatory restrictions targeting China (relative to other exporters) is likely to evolve further in response to changes in the global trade environment. For example, what would be the US policy response if the Doha Round were to impose additional constraints on the antidumping process? Given the substitutability of alternative policy instruments available to US industries seeking protection from Chinese competition, there is the real possibility that any reduction in the frequency of antidumping cases targeting China would be accompanied by an *increase* in the incidence of China-specific safeguard actions triggered under the new Section 421 of the US trade law—especially if there were also an increase in the president's willingness to impose remedies recommended by the ITC.

The OTEXA China safeguard

While the United States has yet to use the Section 421 'China Safeguard' law to impose new trade restrictions on Chinese imports,[18] the other China-specific safeguard, which pertains only to textiles and apparel, has already resulted in new import restrictions.

Table 6.3   China safeguard investigations by the United States under Section 421

ITC Case no.	Product	Year investigation initiated	Outcome
TA-421-1	Pedestal actuators	2002	Affirmative ITC vote, no remedy imposed
TA-421-2	Steel wire garment hangers	2002	Affirmative ITC vote, no remedy imposed
TA-421-3	Brake drums and rotors	2003	Negative ITC vote
TA-421-4	Ductile iron waterworks fittings	2003	Affirmative ITC vote, no remedy imposed
TA-421-5	Uncovered innerspring units	2004	Negative ITC vote

Source: Information collected by the authors from the *Federal Register*.

The 'China Textile and Apparel Safeguard' is administered through the OTEXA Committee for the Implementation of Textile Agreements (CITA).[19] The investigative process and the ultimate outcome of an OTEXA China safeguard investigation are both much less transparent than for other US trade policies. However, it appears that these investigations typically culminate in bilateral consultations between the OTEXA and the Chinese government. The aim of these consultations is to establish an import limit, frequently through a voluntary restraint by China of its exports to the United States. For example, in bilateral consultations held in December 2003 in response to an earlier *Knit Fabric* (product 222) China textile safeguard investigation, the Chinese government 'agreed to hold its shipments to a level no greater than 7.5 per cent (6 per cent for wool product categories) above the amount entered during the first 12 months of the most recent 14 months preceding the request for consultations' (OTEXA 2003). But this particular application of the safeguard was not sufficient to satisfy the US industry, which requested an additional OTEXA safeguard investigation of Knit Fabric from China in November 2004 as well (Table 6.4).

The most worrisome element of the OTEXA safeguard is the implied US reversion to the 'worst-practice' behaviour of the 1980s, including practices that were supposed to be eliminated with the conclusion of the Uruguay Round negotiations and establishment of the WTO in 1995. This 'safeguard' law is discriminatory in its application (Chinese textiles and apparel only), the investigative process for injury is either non-existent at worst or non-transparent at best, and the outcome often seems to be in the form of 'voluntary' arrangements, such as VERs.

Given the potential for the use of safeguard protection by the United States and other major markets, China imposed export taxes on 148 of its textile products on 1 January 2005, immediately following the end of the MFA. Exports of textile products

Table 6.4   Examples of China textile safeguard investigations by the United States in 2004

OTEXA *category*	*Product under investigation*
349/649	Brassieres and other body-supporting garments
350/650	Dressing gowns and robes
222	Knit fabric
447	Wool trousers
620	Other synthetic filament fabric
301	Combed cotton yarn
352/652	Cotton and man-made fibre underwear
338/339	Men's & boys' and women's & girls' cotton knit shirts and blouses
340/640	Men's & boys' cotton and man-made fibre shirts, not knit
638/639	Men's & boys' and women's & girls' man-made fibre knit shirts and blouses
647/648	Men's & boys' and women's & girls' man-made fibre trousers
347/348	Men's & boys' and women's & girls' cotton trousers

Note: Requests for China Textile Safeguard Action between 8 October and 1 December, 2004, downloaded from the Office of Textile and Apparel's website, <http://otexa.ita.doc.gov/chinare1dec1.pdf>; accessed 9 May 2006.

still surged in the early months of 2005, and in May China raised its taxes on 74 of the same goods (Buckley 2005). Nonetheless, the OTEXA introduced new safeguards, and the European Union threatened to do likewise unless China reduced exports on its own. At the end of May, China reacted by withdrawing its export taxes. These events raise interesting issues concerning the effects of alternative policy measures used to limit imports to a desired level.

Like a US safeguard tariff or quota, an export tax would reduce the volume of Chinese exports to the United States (and also to other markets), thus raising the prices US consumers pay for products imported from China. But under an export tax, the Chinese government collects the revenue. The standard analysis of a US safeguard quota or tariff on apparel imports predicts that it will be welfare-reducing for the economy as a whole, notwithstanding possible gains to competing domestic producers and tax revenue generated. If the trade is instead restricted to the same level by a Chinese export tax, the negative impact on US welfare would be even larger. This is because of the revenue collected by the Chinese. With a safeguard in the form of an import tax on Chinese products, the same revenue would go to the US Treasury; in the case of a safeguard quota, to the recipients of the licences used to regulate imports. The loss to China would likewise be smaller with an export tax than an import tariff or quota.[20]

In the 1970s and 1980s, the United States negotiated VER agreements with Japan and other highly competitive new exporters as a means to limit US imports selectively and thus to avoid disrupting trade with established suppliers. VERs are now prohibited by WTO rules, but China's actions in voluntarily restraining its exports differed from old-style VERs in that all exports, not just exports to a particular market, were being taxed. The export tax revenue could be seen as implicit compensation paid to China by the United States and other importing countries for limiting its own exports. Of course, China was offering to restrain its exports only because its other option was to face import safeguards, and the export taxes were rescinded after safeguards were announced. From the perspective of overall national welfare, both China and the importing countries would be better off under freer trade, i.e., without either an export tax or safeguard protection in the importing countries.

US PTAs with countries that compete with China in the US market

A final example of US trade policy that may have been motivated at least partially by the desire of current suppliers—domestic producers but also established foreign suppliers of US imports—for preferential treatment relative to China is the recent increased willingness of other US trading partners to pursue free trade agreements with the United States. Table 6.5 lists some of the preferential agreements negotiated by the United States since China's WTO accession in 2001. On the part of the United States, most of these agreements entail social or political objectives as much as gains from trade. These include the offer of preferential access to the US market, frequently for products that compete with Chinese exports, in exchange for commitments to enforce labour standards (Cambodia), to combat narcotics trade (ATPDEA), to promote democracy and environmental protection (CAFTA), and to establish better relations in the Middle East post-9/11 (Morocco, Bahrain).[21]

The partner countries in these preferential trade agreements often stand to gain by maintaining existing preference margins or increasing preferential access to the US market in important product categories that compete with Chinese exports. One such example is presented in Table 6.6, which lists each of these countries' textile and apparel exports to the United States, measured both in value terms and as a share of the country's total exports to the US market. For a number of these countries, a substantial share of their total exports to the US market is in textiles and apparel, sectors where China is the largest single US supplier with exports of nearly $15 billion in 2003.

How does trade policy discrimination against China affect the sourcing of US textile and apparel imports? We use Table 6.7 to compare the US import market for textiles and apparel in 2003 with the Japanese and Australian import markets in the same year, as these were two developed countries with relatively liberal market access where textiles and apparel trade based on comparative advantage was more likely to be reflected. Most importantly, neither applied country-specific quotas on trade in textile products. The data suggest that, in a US trade regime without discrimination against China, China would stand to gain considerable market share in the US at the expense of other current import sources. This provides a clear motive for efforts by

Table 6.5   Recent examples of US preferential trade agreements

US agreements since 2001	Description from US Trade Representative
Cambodian Textile Agreement	'increases Cambodia's quota for textile imports by nine per cent … [in exchange for] … Cambodia's progress towards ensuring that working conditions in its garment sector are in "substantial compliance" with internationally recognized labor standards and provisions of Cambodia's labor law.'[a]
Andean Trade Promotion and Drug Eradication Act (ATPDEA) – Colombia, Bolivia, Peru and Ecuador	'… provides the four Andean countries with duty-free access to US markets for approximately 5,600 products. The program expired in December of 2001 and was renewed as part of the Trade Act of 2002 … providing incentives for these four Andean countries to diversify their economies away from narcotics production.'[b]
Dominican Republic – Central American Free Trade Agreement (DR–CAFTA) – Dominican Republic, El Salvador, Honduras, Nicaragua, Guatemala, Costa Rica	'will contribute to the transformation of a region that was consumed in internal strife and border disputes just a decade ago but is now a successful regional economy with flourishing democracies … US is also strengthening ties with the DR-CAFTA countries by entering into an Environmental Cooperation Agreement.'[c]
Morocco Free Trade Agreement	'… this FTA sends a powerful signal that the United States is firmly committed to supporting tolerant, open and more prosperous Muslim societies. I hope other nations in the Middle East and North Africa will closely study the terms of this agreement, and will view it as a model to advance their economic relationships with the United States.'[d]
Bahrain Free Trade Agreement	'Muslim countries can become full participants in the rules-based global trading system, as the United States considers lowering the trade barriers with the poorest Arab nations … Recommendation: A comprehensive US strategy to counter terrorism should include economic policies that encourage development, more open societies, and opportunities for people to improve the lives of their families and to enhance prospects for their children's future. (The 9/11 Commission Report, Pages 378–379)'[e]

Notes
a   USTR press release, 'US–Cambodian Textile Agreement Links Increasing Trade with Improving Workers' Rights', 7 January 2002.
b   ATPA fact sheet from the USTR, 'New Andean Trade Benefits', 25 September 2002.
c   USTR press release, 'Dominican Republic Joins Five Central American Countries in Historic FTA with US', 5 August 2004.
d   USTR press release, 'US and Morocco Conclude Free Trade Agreement', 2 March 2004.
e   USTR press release, 'United States and Bahrain Sign Free Trade Agreement', 14 September 2004.

Source: USTR website, <http://www.ustr.gov/Trade_Agreements/Bilateral/Section_Index.html>; accessed 13 January 2005.

Table 6.6   Preferential trade agreement partners' 2003 textile and apparel exports to the United States, compared with China

Country	Value of 2003 textile and apparel exports to US ($)	2003 textile and apparel exports to US as a share of country's total exports to US (%)
Cambodia	1,252,000,000	99.12
ATPDEA countries		
Colombia	546,100,000	8.61
Bolivia	34,265,892	18.53
Peru	518,900,000	21.48
Ecuador	19,968,924	0.74
CAFTA countries		
Dominican Republic	2,149,000,000	48.23
El Salvador	1,754,000,000	86.90
Honduras	2,576,000,000	77.78
Nicaragua	484,300,000	62.98
Guatemala	1,789,000,000	60.55
Costa Rica	598,500,000	17.84
Morocco	77,214,816	19.49
Bahrain	187,800,000	49.64
China	14,860,000,000	9.80

Note: NAICS product categories 313 (Textiles and Fabrics), 314 (Textile Mill Products) and 315 (Apparel and Accessories).

Source: Data from the ITC *DataWeb* database.

other US trading partners to retain preferential access to the US market through PTA formation or by having the United States impose China-specific import restrictions.

CHINA AS A TARGET

Why has China become the target of discriminatory treatment under US trade policy? To answer this question, it is useful to take a look at the broader political economy of US trade protection. As Krueger (1993) observes, 'Examination of the prevailing pattern of protection in the United States yields the easy conclusion that, whatever is used as a basis for deciding upon the pattern of protection, it is certainly not the criterion of Pareto optimality'. In the case of China, we can identify some 'business as usual' elements, i.e., a US pattern of discriminatory protection that typically targets newer, faster-growing suppliers. But there are also some China-specific considerations

Table 6.7   Sources of US, Australian and Japanese imports of textiles and clothing, 2003

Exporter	Importer		
	United States (%)	*Australia (%)*	*Japan (%)*
China	17.4	49.9	71.7
India	4.3	3.6	1.1
Pakistan	2.7	2.3	0.3
US	–	3.8	2.7
EU12	6.0	9.5	9.1
Canada	4.1	0.4	0.1
New Zealand	0.1	6.9	0.1
Other	65.4	23.6	14.8

Note: (%) of total textile and clothing imports.

Source: Standard International Trade Classification codes 26, 65 and 84. Data from OECD.

that have helped to foster a political environment in which China-bashing, like the earlier Japan-bashing, becomes acceptable or even desirable.

US protection against new entrants that rock the trade boat

US protection is often structured to protect not only domestic producers but also established suppliers of US imports. If protection is motivated by a 'conservative social welfare function' (Corden 1974) that slows down economic change and thus maintains the status quo, it seems that for the United States this welfare function includes the welfare of important established trading partners and allies as well as domestic producers. US multinational firms quite naturally lobby to maintain the market shares of their offshore subsidiaries as well as their domestic production facilities. Likewise, established foreign suppliers who 'know the ropes' in Washington can be effective in gaining preferential access to the US market and thus maintaining their shares as new and highly competitive entrants emerge. A US trade policy goal of protecting established trading partners and the subsidiaries of US multinationals as well as domestic producers can help to explain demonstrated US preference for VERs and antidumping, as well as the use of FTAs that allow preferred partners to maintain or even increase market share.

An inclusive social welfare function is consistent with US protection that targets fast-growing exporters whose growth will otherwise have 'too large' an impact on established market shares—of both domestic producers and traditional suppliers abroad. China's recent export growth has indeed been dramatic. Yet Japan's export growth in the early post-war period was even more dramatic, with an increase of more than 600 per cent between 1949 and 1959 (Dam 1970: 297). And as Table 6.8 shows, China's sustained high rate of export growth is not very different from that of several other successful Asian exporters. These countries have also faced trade policy discrimination from the United States during their periods of rapid export growth.

Table 6.8   Percentage change in export values in constant US dollars

Country	Period	No. of years	Average annual growth rate
Japan	1954–81	27	14.2
Korea	1960–95	35	21.5
Malaysia	1968–96	28	10.2
China	1978–2002	24	11.9
NIEs*	1966	31	13.1

Note: * Newly industrialized economies of Hong Kong SAR, Korea, Singapore, and Taiwan (Province of China).

Source: Prasad and Rumbaugh 2003: 48.

Growth rates do not tell the whole story, especially when growth is, as in the case of China and early post-war Japan, from a very low level. However, the same picture emerges if penetration of the US market is used as a measure of impact and thus potential pressure for protection. China's share of total US merchandise imports was about 11 per cent in 2003, compared with 10 per cent for Japan and 3 per cent for Korea. But both Japan and Korea had larger shares at their peak: Japan's share of US imports reached 22 per cent in 1986, while even Korea, a much smaller economy, accounted for 4.5 per cent of US imports in the late 1980s (Prasad and Rumbaugh 2003: 48). Yet while the total impact of Chinese exports to the US market has not yet reached the level of Japanese exports at the peak of US–Japan trade conflict, protection is a sectoral phenomenon. As with Japan, Chinese exports to the United States are concentrated in a relatively few sectors and thus account for a much larger share of imports for these sectors.

Round up the usual suspects

A few industries stand out as perennial beneficiaries of US protectionism: agriculture, autos, steel and textiles and apparel. Much of the *incidence* of US protection across trading partners, i.e., which countries' exports are restricted, can thus be explained in terms of export mix. As noted above, discriminatory protection against Japanese exports began even before World War II with voluntary restrictions on textiles in the 1930s. China, with its large and fast-growing apparel exports, would thus have been targeted specifically for this reason. The scheduled dismantling of the MFA increased policy pressure to limit China's incursion into established markets.

Moreover, 'non-market' economies are treated differently from market economies in the administration of US trade policy, particularly antidumping policy. The justification in the case of China lies partly in the important role of state-owned enterprises in export activities, a domestic capital market that is guided by government priorities rather than market forces, and a policy-determined exchange rate maintained at a rate generally viewed as low relative to purchasing power parity. Yet the decision whether a particular country should be treated as a market economy is partly political. Under the terms of the 1999 US–China bilateral agreement, key to China's WTO accession, the US Department of Commerce is authorized to continue using the unfavourable non-market-economy designation to evaluate Chinese dumping until 2014—notwithstanding China's actual speed of transition.[22] In contrast, Russia obtained a market economy designation in 2002 (Pearson 2004: 35).

Trade performance and macroeconomic imbalance

In the 1980s, many US policy makers interpreted the huge bilateral trade deficit with Japan as the 'smoking gun'—conclusive proof of Japan's unfair trade practices. The bilateral deficit thus provided an attractive justification for proposed measures to limit Japanese exports to the United States or to expand Japanese imports from the United States. Economists argued, mostly in vain, that the US current account imbalance reflected a domestic macroeconomic imbalance, specifically a large excess of US domestic investment over domestic saving (McCulloch 1988: 312–3). Likewise, the Japanese current-account surplus reflected the large excess of domestic saving over domestic investment. Changes in sectoral trade policies might affect the composition of US–Japan trade flows or even the size of this specific bilateral imbalance, but only macroeconomic changes could reduce the overall current-account imbalances of the two nations.

The recent emergence of a huge bilateral trade deficit with China, as well as the response in the policy community, thus have a somewhat familiar ring. Again, the root of the problem lies in US macroeconomic imbalance, as US domestic saving has plummeted thanks to record fiscal deficits.[23] Again, trade with one country dominates the red ink. But this time around there is also an important difference. Japan in the 1980s had a huge overall current-account surplus and bilateral surpluses with many other trading partners. In contrast, China is a major importer not only of raw materials but also of sophisticated manufactured goods. It has already passed Japan to become the world's third largest *importer*; its bilateral trade balances with most of its East Asian neighbours are negative. Even in trade with the United States, China has become a major importer. Between 2000 and 2003, US exports to China increased 76 per cent while exports to the rest of the world fell 9 per cent (USTR 2004).

One Chinese policy does contribute to a large bilateral trade imbalance with the United States. While the US dollar has fallen against other currencies by as much as a third, China has prevented a similar revaluation vis-à-vis the yuan. As a consequence, the Chinese yuan is now significantly undervalued relative to the dollar, making Chinese goods cheaper in US markets and US goods more expensive in Chinese markets. This undervaluation means that a larger share of the global US current-account deficit shows up in bilateral trade with China. By the same logic, the yuan revaluation that Washington is demanding would reduce the bilateral trade deficit. Because a stronger yuan would mean reduced Chinese purchases of dollar assets, it would also put upward pressure on US interest rates; this in turn would affect US macroeconomic conditions by cutting US consumption and investment expenditures, thus reducing the global deficit.[24]

Intellectual property rights and technology transfer

By the 1980s, Japan was no longer exporting low-end textiles and apparel but had become a major US competitor in some high-technology products. Notwithstanding occasional accusations of industrial espionage, Japanese firms acquired advanced US technologies mainly through licensing agreements with US patent holders. But Japanese direct investments in US high-technology firms were subjected to scrutiny by a special federal agency, and at least one proposed Japanese acquisition of a US semiconductor producer failed to gain approval.

The different types of conflicts seen over decades of trade with Japan are present simultaneously in the case of China. While China remains a highly competitive supplier of low-end simple manufactured goods, it has also made surprisingly rapid progress in more sophisticated production activities. For China, the main intellectual property issues are out-and-out counterfeiting and piracy.[25] As part of its WTO accession agreement, China committed to improve protection of intellectual rights along the lines required by the Uruguay Round agreement on Trade Related Intellectual Property Rights (TRIPs). But while legal arrangements have indeed been improved, enforcement remains lacklustre. In one recent high-profile case, General Motors claimed that the Chinese Chery QQ was a knockoff of its own Chevrolet Spark. And in an echo of policy toward Japan in the 1980s, the Committee on Foreign Investment in the United States reviewed the IBM sale of its personal computer business to the Chinese Lenovo Group.

Trade policies in aid of social objectives

US labour unions, environmental organizations and other non-governmental organizations have increased their advocacy of trade restrictions intended to prevent newer trading partners, mostly less-developed or transition economies, from benefiting from lower costs that are due to lower labour and environmental standards. In April 2004, the AFL–CIO asked President George W. Bush to punish China under Section 301 of the Trade Act of 1974 for gaining unfair advantage in US markets through repression of workers' rights. Under Section 301, violation of internationally recognized labour rights is an unfair trade practice. According to the complaint, China's labour practices resulted in the loss of as many as 727,000 US factory jobs (Greenhouse and Becker 2004). Although the Bush administration rejected the complaint, it has continued to press China on labour issues such as occupational safety and pension rights (Hufbauer and Wong 2004: 12).

China's relatively weak environmental policies and even weaker enforcement of current policies are another source of public pressure on US trade officials to 'do something' about Chinese exports. Like many other developing countries, China has experienced a marked deterioration in environmental quality but at the same time has begun to address the situation through new policies to limit air and water pollution. Yet, as with intellectual property, enforcement effort has lagged behind. Although the costs are borne primarily by China's own residents, some pollutants, such as gaseous mercury from Chinese coal-fired power plants, are already finding their way into the oceans and even into the air breathed by residents of distant countries (Pottinger 2004).

ECONOMIC CONSEQUENCES OF DISCRIMINATORY TREATMENT

In previous sections, we have documented discriminatory policies applied by the United States and other nations to trade with China. In this section we review some likely implications for trade flows, US economic welfare and trade policy developments abroad. Some are familiar from the US experience with discriminatory trade barriers to imports from Japan and other highly competitive Asian exporters.

Trade diversion

Discriminatory US trade policies that limit imports only from China may protect domestic producers, but more often the main effect is to divert import sourcing to the next most competitive supplier, usually another Asian country or a trading partner such as Mexico or Costa Rica with preferred access to the US market. For goods in which China has the world's lowest *opportunity* cost, trade diversion reduces overall economic welfare both in China and in the United States, though it does generate some gains for the 'beneficiaries' of diverted trade, i.e., the countries whose exports to US markets rise as a consequence. Global welfare is reduced to the extent that the affected good is now produced at higher cost.[26]

An additional complication arises when Chinese export restrictions are substituted for US import barriers. Whether exports are controlled through 'voluntary' export restraints or explicit export taxes, this type of trade restriction allows China to appropriate the difference between the good's price in the US market and its cost to Chinese suppliers. This raises the cost to the United States and reduces the loss to Chinese suppliers of the restricted product. Implementation of quantitative export restraints also tends to reduce active competition among suppliers, thus creating additional welfare losses through exercise of market power.

Whatever the specific trade policy, one sure effect is higher cost to US buyers. For goods such as clothing and consumer electronics, Chinese products are often those appealing to lower-income 'Wal-Mart shoppers'—and thus the impact is likely to be regressive. Induced upgrading, discussed below, will also have a regressive impact as the mix of US imports from China shifts toward higher-price goods. But many imports are intermediate goods, purchased by American businesses as inputs for use in their own production activity. Here higher prices harm the competitiveness of US producers and may even speed their exit from US production. As an example, in 1991 US antidumping duties on imported flat-panel displays used in laptop computers raised the costs of US producers relative to their competitors abroad; laptop production accordingly shifted from California and Texas to Japan, Canada, Ireland and Singapore (Irwin 2002: 80).

Quality upgrading

Quantitative limits on Chinese exports are likely to accelerate product upgrading, i.e., a move toward the more sophisticated and higher-priced varieties within a product category. Upgrading is also encouraged by use of a flat-rate (i.e., specific or per-unit) export or import tax but not a trade tax that is levied as a percentage of the good's price. Although product upgrading is part of the normal process of industrial development, trade restrictions tend to raise the speed with which this occurs. Thus, Japan's voluntary restriction of auto exports to the United States accelerated its manufacturers' shift from the small economy cars that had previously constituted the bulk of Japan's sales in the US market to high-end luxury models competing more directly with the products of the US 'big three' auto makers. European producers of smaller cars, who had been losing their share in the US market to Japanese competitors, benefited from trade diversion as they filled the low-end gap in US auto imports left as Japanese firms upgraded their exports. In December 2004, China announced a flat-rate export tax on apparel exports with the explicit objective of promoting the quality upgrading of its export-oriented production. The plan is evidently to cede the low end of the apparel market to other low-wage countries such as Bangladesh.

To the extent that the goal of US trade policy is to preserve the market share of its own producers and to prevent domestic job losses, induced product upgrading may mean that protection can backfire. As Chinese firms climb the 'quality ladder' at an increased pace or even discontinuously (leapfrogging), their products become more directly competitive with the output of firms located in the United States. The case of Japanese autos provides an instructive example. In the auto case, US protection also accelerated Japanese foreign direct investment in the United States. Although this outcome was desired by supporters of the voluntary restraint agreement with Japan, including the United Auto Workers, most of the Japanese 'transplants' are located far from Detroit and are not unionized. Industry employment has been maintained overall, but the VER prevented neither losses to established domestic producers nor displacement of their workers.

Effects on global trade flows

US trade policy toward China can have important spill-over effects on other trade flows, thus creating new trade tensions and the global spread of protectionist pressures. US barriers to imports from China could induce both trade *deflection* and trade *depression*. Trade deflection is the tendency of Chinese exporters to react to a new US trade restriction by shifting sales to other, as yet unrestricted markets, thereby producing import surges in those markets. Trade depression is the reduction in China's *own* imports from the United States as well as other countries, as US trade barriers cause more of China's export-oriented production to be retained domestically.

The deflection of Chinese exports has two noteworthy effects. For countries actively competing with China in the same markets, the resulting surge in deflected Chinese exports is likely to fuel protectionist (anti-China) sentiment, thus increasing resort to antidumping, safeguards or China-specific safeguard measures. Exporters from other countries—including US firms, which are currently the third most targeted globally in antidumping actions—are also likely to be caught up in the protectionist web. On the other hand, some firms and foreign countries benefit from the deflection of Chinese exports. For countries importing intermediate inputs from China, trade deflection means downward pressure on the price of these inputs and a resulting further advantage relative to their US competition; US firms must already pay a higher price for the same inputs due to the direct effects of US protection.

Trade depression means more Chinese output retained at home and thus more domestic pressure in China for import protection. This may lead to an increase in China's own use of antidumping. This type of protection can be structured in a discriminatory manner, again perhaps targeting firms in the United States.

Increased pressure for China to enter preferential trade agreements

China's expanding trade with the rest of the world, together with its frustration with lack of access to the US market, has increased the pressure to negotiate trade agreements with other countries (Antkiewicz and Whalley 2005). As the terms of China's WTO accession have required it to take on more liberalization commitments than many other countries, potential partners will likely have to make significant market-access commitments of their own with respect to China. This could produce an Asian regional trade agreement that excludes the United States, thereby leaving US exporters with 'least favoured nation' status not only in the Chinese market but, perhaps more importantly, in other Asian markets as well.

CONCLUSION

This paper examines recent US policy toward imports from China, highlighting important explicitly and implicitly discriminatory elements. These include the explicitly discriminatory terms of China's WTO accession in 2001 and the administration of antidumping. We compare the recent trade policy treatment of China with earlier trade policy discrimination directed toward Japan. One important difference is that, unlike discriminatory US treatment of Japan in the 1980s, in which 'grey-area' measures such as voluntary export restraints were prominent, most US actions toward China are fully consistent with current WTO rules, including the special terms of China's WTO accession. In examining the underlying reasons for targeting China (and, earlier, Japan), we identify some characteristics of China and Chinese trade that make it more likely to receive special attention. In particular, China's highly competitive garment industry is likely to be targeted simply because this has long been a politically sensitive sector in the United States and also in most other industrialized countries.

Discriminatory restrictions on US trade with China protect competing domestic industries but also non-Chinese foreign suppliers with an established presence in the US market. For the United States, this means other Asian trading partners, but especially countries that have negotiated free trade agreements with the United States. China's rapid development of highly competitive exports industries and its WTO accession in 2001 have increased the payoff to having preferred access to the US market. As with earlier discriminatory actions directed primarily at Japan, and with the Multi-Fiber Arrangement that began with discriminatory action directed at Japan and ended with a global network of managed trade, US trade policy toward China is likely to have complex effects on global trade flows and may produce outcomes far different from those intended. Not surprisingly, discriminatory trade restrictions are costly in terms of overall national and global welfare. Perhaps more surprisingly, they may be ineffective or even counterproductive in protecting production and workers in the affected domestic industries.

NOTES

This paper is a revised version of one prepared for presentation at the PAFTAD 30 conference at the East-West Center in Honolulu, 19–21 February 2005. We are indebted to Peter Drysdale, Peter Petri, Meredith Crowley, and conference participants for helpful discussions and comments, and to Gloria Sheu and Daisuke Nakajima for research assistance. Bown is also indebted to the Brookings Institution for financial support through the 2004–05 Okun–Model Visiting Fellowship in Economic Studies. However, the opinions expressed in this paper are our own and should not be attributed to the Brookings Institution. All remaining errors are our own.

1   In the Uruguay Round, Korea designated rice as a sensitive product. This allowed Korea to postpone liberalizing its restrictions on rice imports and instead commit to importing a specified quantity of rice annually through 2004. The exceptional treatment could be continued for some additional period after 2004, but Korea was required to give individual WTO members the opportunity to negotiate concessions, i.e., specified shares in total Korean imports. In 2004 Korea held such negotiations with the United States and eight other WTO members (USTR 2005). This market-sharing arrangement appears to exclude Vietnam, an internationally competitive rice exporter but not yet a WTO member, from Korea's rice market.

2   Supporters of the Long Term Arrangement in Cotton Textiles included pragmatic non-protectionists who believed that a gradual and 'orderly' increase in the market share of new suppliers among the less-developed countries would likely be beneficial to those suppliers; the argument was that uncontrolled large increases concentrated in a few products were likely to trigger new trade restrictions in the major importing nations (Dam 1970: 300–1).

3   The European Community system, implemented in 1971, included sensitive imports but limited their volume.

4   The Office of the US Trade Representative uses FTA in referring to its bilateral agreements—no doubt adding to public confusion. Elsewhere such agreements are also called preferential trade agreements (PTAs) or—in WTO documents—regional trade agreements (RTAs). The latter terminology seems especially bizarre given such examples as the bilateral US agreements with Israel, Singapore and most recently Australia. So far no one has opted for a more accurate label: discriminatory trade agreement (DTA).

5   The GATT was drawn up prior to pioneering work by Viner (1950) clarifying that such arrangements were not necessarily beneficial in strictly economic terms even for the participants themselves. For those drafting the GATT articles, regional trade liberalization was seen 'as a step toward free trade, partial to be sure but laudable nonetheless' (Dam 1970: 274).

6   See WTO website <http://www.wto.org/english/tratop_e/region_e/region_e.htm>; accessed 14 January 2005.

7   Singapore has already concluded an FTA with the United States. Despite the name, 'modern' FTAs address many non-border issues and thus facilitate foreign direct investment as well as trade (Naya and Plummer 2005). Most US agreements include provisions on enhanced intellectual property protection, labour standards, and environmental protection.

8   Zanardi (2004) presents data indicating that US exporters have also become the target of antidumping as its use has spread beyond the 'traditional' users—United States, Canada, EU, Australia. US exporters are now the third most targeted exporters hit by foreign antidumping actions, trailing only China and Korea. In addition to the traditional users, Brazil, Argentina and Mexico started their intensive use in the 1980s, followed more recently by South Africa and India.

9   The US Department of Commerce is able to use more discretion in calculating Chinese firms' dumping margin in investigations because China is classified as a non-market economy. For non-market economies, the US Department of Commerce often estimates firm costs

using data from a market economy that is judged comparable—for China, this surrogate is typically India. Chinese firms may also be less responsive to administrative requests for information during an investigation, resulting in the US Department of Commerce also relying on the 'Best Information Available' (usually data provided by the petitioners) to calculate a dumping margin. For a discussion of the effect of these factors on the dumping determination in the United States, see Blonigen (2006).

10 As we suggest above, the relevant characteristic of Chinese exports to the United States is their rapid growth. Historically US protection has discriminated against new and rapidly growing competitors, most notably Japan but also the 'newly industrializing economies' of Asia. By 2003, China's share in US merchandise imports had risen to 9.4 per cent, and China was the third largest source of US imports, after Canada and Mexico but ahead of Japan.

11 The only country with a rate comparable to Chinese exporters is Canada. This is likely due to peculiarities of bilateral trade between the US and Canada under the Canada–United States Free Trade Agreement (CUSFTA) and then NAFTA.

12 Hansen and Prusa (1996) evaluate the effects of the cumulation rule on the US antidumping process. They estimate that the rule increased the probability of an affirmative injury determination by 20 to 30 per cent and changed the International Trade Commission's decision (from negative to affirmative) for about one-third of cumulated cases.

13 This is true even after taking into account the upward trend in duties levied in affirmative cases. Blonigen (2006) attributes the upward trend largely to the increased discretion available to the US Department of Commerce in dumping determinations.

14 One contributing explanation is that China was not a GATT participant or WTO member until 2001. Thus, it did not have access to GATT and WTO dispute settlement provisions through which to challenge US-imposed antidumping measures. See, for example, Blonigen and Bown (2003).

15 There are other notable differences between antidumping and safeguards use. In addition to the issue of fair versus unfair trade, the antidumping process is bureaucratic while safeguards in the United States allow for presidential discretion; the injury threshold is higher for safeguard cases; the duration of an imposed safeguard measure is explicitly limited and typically shorter than antidumping; and the use of safeguards can also sometimes require compensation to affected countries, while antidumping does not. See Bown (2002).

16 The International Trade Commission distinguishes between 'global' safeguards, i.e., those authorized under Section 201, and 'special' safeguards, including the China safeguard authorized under Section 421 (<http://usitc.gov/trade_remedy/safeguards/index.htm>; accessed 2 June 2005).

17 See §19 USC 2451a of the US law, 'Action in response to trade diversion'. See also the discussion in Messerlin (2004). Note that we do not refer to this phenomenon as trade diversion here, instead calling it 'trade deflection'. Trade diversion has a well-established meaning in the international trade literature that is distinct from this phenomenon. See Bown and Crowley (forthcoming).

18 Of course, there is also evidence from other laws of administered protection that merely initiating a case can have a dampening effect on trade flows. For the case of antidumping, which has been studied extensively because of relatively good data, see Prusa (1992), Staiger and Wolak (1994) and Bown (2004).

19 For details on the US Department of Commerce's use of the China Textile and Apparel Safeguard, see the OTEXA website <http://www.otexa.ita.doc.gov/Safeguard_intro.htm>; accessed 11 January 2005.

20 With a quota, an amount similar to the tax or tariff revenue goes to the holders of export or import licenses. If exports are restricted by the Chinese government, this 'quota rent' could be captured entirely by China, making the quota case comparable to an export tax in terms of its effects on overall welfare in China and the United States.

21 Based on an analysis of the impact of earlier US PTAs on tariff-binding-reduction negotiations in the Uruguay Round, Limão (2006) concludes that such agreements typically hinder multilateral liberalization.

22 However, US Department of Commerce officials may choose to use local costs. In a 2004 antidumping case, US lawyers representing some Chinese furniture producers successfully argued for the use of local costs, thus obtaining low antidumping margins.

23 Domestic saving is equal to private saving plus the government's budget surplus. Thus, the large fiscal deficit represents a major downward pull on overall US saving.

24 A stronger yuan could be only a partial step toward correction of the US global deficit because China accounts for only a fraction of the global deficit and of foreign official purchases of dollars. See Bown *et al.* (2005).

25 Counterfeiting refers to unauthorized production of trademarked products such as fake designer-label clothing. Piracy refers to unauthorized reproduction of copyrighted material such as CDs or videos as well as unauthorized use of patented technologies.

26 The relevant cost is opportunity cost, i.e., the value of the output foregone in order to produce a particular good. The gains from trade arise mainly from shifting production of any particular good to the place where it can be produced at the lowest opportunity cost, i.e., the country with comparative advantage. Trade flows are, however, based on comparative money costs (competitiveness), which may diverge from opportunity costs for a variety of reasons. For example, a significantly undervalued currency may enable China to export some goods in which it does not have the lowest opportunity cost. The effects of currency undervaluation are similar to those of an across-the-board export subsidy and import tax—beneficial to importers of Chinese products but welfare-reducing overall for both China and the rest of the world.

REFERENCES

Antkiewicz, A. and J. Whalley (2005) 'China's New Regional Trade Agreements', *The World Economy*, 28(10): 1539–57.

Blonigen, B.A. (2006) 'Evolving Discretionary Practices of US Antidumping Activity', *Canadian Journal of Economics*, 37(3): 874–900.

Blonigen, B.A. and C.P. Bown (2003) 'Antidumping and Retaliation Threats', *Journal of International Economics*, 60(2): 249–73.

Bown, C.P. (2002) 'Why are Safeguards under the WTO so Unpopular?', *World Trade Review*, 1(1): 47–62.

—— (2004) 'How Different Are Safeguards from Antidumping? Evidence from US Trade Policies toward Steel', Brandeis University manuscript, July.

Bown, C.P. and M.A. Crowley (forthcoming) 'Trade Deflection and Trade Depression', *Journal of International Economics*.

Bown, C.P., M.A. Crowley, R. McCulloch and D. Nakajima (2005) 'The US Trade Deficit: Made in China?', *Economic Perspectives*, 29(4): 2–18.

Buckley, C. (2005) 'China to End Its Taxes on Textile Exports in Retaliation for US and European Quotas', *The New York Times*, 31 May.

Corden, W.M. (1974) *Trade Policy and Economic Welfare*, Oxford: Oxford University Press.

Dam, K.W. (1970) *The GATT: Law and International Economic Organization*, Chicago: University of Chicago.

Feenstra, R. (2000) 'World Trade Flows, 1980–1997, with Production and Tariff Data', UC-Davis manuscript (and accompanying CD-Rom).

Greenhouse, S. and E. Becker (2004) 'AFL–CIO to Press Bush for Penalties against China', *The New York Times*, 16 March.

Hansen, W.L. and T.J. Prusa (1996) 'Cumulation and ITC Decision-Making: the Sum of the Parts is Greater than the Whole', *Economic Inquiry*, 34: 746–69.

Hufbauer, G.C. and Y. Wong (2004) 'China Bashing 2004', *International Economics Policy Brief PB04-5*, Institute for International Economics, September.

Irwin, D.A. (2002) *Free Trade under Fire*, Princeton: Princeton University Press.

Krueger, A.O. (1993) 'The Political Economy of American Protection in Theory and Practice', in H. Herberg and N.V. Long (eds), *Trade, Welfare, and Economic Policies*, Ann Arbor, MI: University of Michigan Press, 215–36.

Limão, N. (2006) 'Preferential Trade Agreements as Stumbling Blocks for Multilateral Trade Liberalization: Evidence for the US', *American Economic Review*, 96(3): 896–914.

McCulloch, R. (1988) 'United States–Japan Economic Relations', in R.E. Baldwin (ed.), *Trade Policy Issues and Empirical Analysis*, Chicago: University of Chicago Press, 305–30.

Messerlin, P.A. (2004) 'China in the World Trade Organization: Antidumping and Safeguards', *World Bank Economic Review*, 18: 105–30.

Metzger, S.D. (1971) 'Injury and Market Disruption from Imports', in *United States International Economic Policy in an Interdependent World*, Commission on International Trade and Investment Policy, US Government Printing Office, 1: 167–91.

Naya, S. and M.G. Plummer (2005) 'Economics of the Enterprise for Asian Initiative', paper prepared for presentation at the American Economics Association Meeting, Philadelphia, 7–9 January.

OTEXA (2003) 'Committee for the Implementation of Textile Agreements—Announcement of Request for Bilateral Textile Consultations with the Government of the People's Republic of China and the Establishment of an Import Limit for Knit Fabric, Category 222, Produced or Manufactured in the People's Republic of China, December 2003', *Federal Register* 68(248), 29 December.

Pearson, C. (2004) *United States Trade Policy: A work in progress*, Hoboken, NJ: John Wiley and Sons.

Pottinger, M. (2004) 'A Hidden Cost of China's Growth: Mercury Migration', *The Wall Street Journal*, 17 December, A1.

Prasad, E. and T. Rumbaugh (2003) 'Beyond the Great Wall', *Finance and Development*, December, 46–9.

Prusa, T.J. (1992) 'Why are so many Antidumping Petitions Withdrawn?', *Journal of International Economics*, 33(1/2): 1–20.

—— (1997) 'The Trade Effects of US Antidumping Actions', in R.C. Feenstra (ed.), *The Effects of US Trade Protection and Promotion Policies*, Chicago: University of Chicago Press.

—— (2001) 'On the Spread and Impact of Anti-Dumping', *Canadian Journal of Economics*, 34(3): 591–611.

Srinivasan, T.N. (2004) 'China and India: Economic Performance, Competition and Cooperation: An Update', Yale University, February.

Staiger, R.W. and F.A. Wolak (1994) 'Measuring Industry Specific Protection: Antidumping in the United States', *Brookings Papers on Economic Activity: Microeconomics*, 1: 51–103.

United States (2003) 'Presidential Determination on Pedestal Actuator Imports from the People's Republic of China: Memorandum for the United States Trade Representative', 68(14) *Federal Register* 3157, 22 January.

United States Trade Representative (USTR) (2004) 'America's Trade with China', <www.ustr.gov/Document_Library/Fact_Sheets/2004/America's_Trade_with_China.html>; accessed 21 December 2004.

Viner, J. (1950) *The Customs Union Issue*, New York: Carnegie Endowment for International Peace.

Zanardi, M. (2004) 'Antidumping: What are the Numbers to Discuss at Doha?', *The World Economy*, 27(3): 403–33.

7   Does trade lead to a race to the bottom in environmental standards? Another look at the issues

Erlinda M. Medalla and Dorothea C. Lazaro

Economic growth is not a panacea for environmental quality; indeed, it is not even the main issue. What matters is the content of growth—the composition of inputs (including environmental resources) and outputs (including waste products). — Arrow *et al.* (1995)

INTRODUCTION

With no let-up in the pace of globalization and advances in technology, the interrelationship between trade and the environment has become a pressing issue across the globe. Heated discussions abound in various fora involving all sectors: from the streets to civil society, the government, academic and business communities; at the national, bilateral, regional and multilateral levels. It is crucial to understand and address the environmental and sustainability issues that could accompany the escalating trend in trade and globalization.

The issues between trade and environment are found in various areas of concerns. One is in the area of *governance*. The debate here focuses on how international trade has influenced environmental regulations. Has it encouraged a 'race to the bottom' in environmental standards, or 'a race to the top', leading to a convergence of standards at a higher level? Another set of issues relates to *competitiveness*. This is of course linked to the first, with governance affecting competitiveness, and competitiveness issues affecting or influencing the manner of governance. Strict environmental regulation will affect a country's competitive advantage. The question arises whether environmental protection has been more of a disguised form of protectionism. On the other hand, it is also argued that increased trade and growth could eventually lead to better environmental protection. Questions have turned to *North–South issues*, the debate over the disparate implications for the developed and developing countries—whether globalization will lead to 'industrial flight' from the North and the growth of 'pollution havens' (or 'pollution haloes') in the South. Another major concern is with *corporate strategy*, specifically the issues of trans-boundary environmental management and corporate standards applied by transnational corporations (TNCs) in their subsidiaries located in developing countries (Jenkins *et al.* 2002). Finally, we return to the issue of governance—at the global level. What is the state of the global environmental regime that could govern these issues in trade and environment linkages?

This paper aims to contribute further to the discussion on trade and environmental linkages, mainly by looking at some theoretical underpinnings, learning from some findings in the literature, and offering additional empirical evidence in relation to what is happening in the global environment. It is hoped that it will shed light on some of the key questions arising from trade and environmental issues. For example, is there evidence that international trade encourages a 'race to the bottom' in environmental regulations? Are developing countries more likely to export polluting products? Are calls for environmental protection no more than disguised protectionism? What is the state of the global/multilateral regime dealing with trade and environment? Towards this end, the paper has five main sections. The first section looks at some theoretical underpinnings and findings on trade and environment linkage. This is followed by a discussion on the current trade structure of products by pollution-intensity classification between developed and developing countries. The next two sections deal respectively with some observations on environmental regulations and the environment in the multilateral agenda. The concluding section reiterates the need to pursue trade and environment policies in tandem.

TRADE AND ENVIRONMENT LINKAGE: SOME THEORETICAL UNDERPINNINGS AND LITERATURE FINDINGS

The trade and environment linkage has already been the subject of a number of academic discussions and notable empirical analyses. Various works attempt to provide empirical evidence about the nature and impact of these linkages, and, not surprisingly, findings are mixed.[1] Birdsall and Wheeler (1993) found that pollution intensity in developing countries grew fastest when environmental regulations in high-income countries were toughened, suggesting that different environmental standards could create pollution havens. However, five years later Mani and Wheeler (1998) analysed import–export ratios for five heavily polluting industries and indicated that these havens may exist only temporarily, if at all. By regressing measures of environmental regulations (in addition to other control variables) on dirty exports of 24 OECD and non-OECD countries, Wilson *et al.* (2002) found a significant negative linkage in some industries. Conversely, various other studies have found very little or no evidence that differences in environmental regulations across countries are a significant determinant of trade flows.[2]

In these attempts, as well as other existing empirical studies, the data limitation remains a hindrance to making a comprehensive conclusion or even close statistical relationship of both areas.[3] What is certain however is that the debate over the linkages between trade and environment will remain and could become more intense in the future as a result of increased global and regional integration.

Nonetheless, while empirical results from different studies might vary, the basic theoretical hypothesis underlying the policy interrelationship is more definite—*that there should be no conflict between good economic policy and good environmental policy.* A good economic policy should not prevent the adoption and implementation of good environmental policy, and vice versa.[4] Ideally both should be present.

In general, there is a consensus that a relatively open trade policy is good economic policy. Trade theory suggests that for a small country, in the absence of market imperfections (e.g., the case of externalities), the use of trade barriers—whether in the form of tariffs or quantitative restrictions—creates market distortions that reduce overall welfare. However, environmental concerns almost invariably involve externalities that cannot be captured by market forces alone. Therefore, in general, a good environmental policy is one that leads to the internalization of these externalities, whether through command-and-control measures or market-based instruments.

Hence, translating the above-stated basic hypothesis, there should be no conflict between an open trade policy and good environmental policy. A liberal trade policy should not prevent the adoption and implementation of good environmental policy, and vice versa. Ideally, both should be present. This is when goods and resources are properly priced and the market would work more efficiently, leading to optimum welfare.

This does not imply that there are no possible trade-offs between trade and environmental policy. Too-restrictive environmental regulations could unduly penalize real comparative advantage, but lax environmental policy would provide unintended (and unjustified) subsidies. In the real world, there is often a lack in policy or policy administration which could lead to either outcome. In many instances, there is a tendency to mix and match policy tools in an attempt to make up for this deficiency. When nothing is done about the level and quality of environmental protection, there is fear that unrestrained international trade could lead to environmental degradation. In addition, there is worry that competition for trade and investment itself could encourage a 'race to the bottom' in environmental standards, or the creation of pollution havens in developing countries. Conversely, there is the apprehension that environmental protection can be no more than disguised protectionism. These are certainly legitimate considerations that should be addressed.

The question is what is good-enough policy in the first place. What does a good environmental policy imply? Generally, it is one that leads to correct pricing of environmental resources, i.e. one that reflects relative scarcities and value to society. Hence, as in the case of capital and labour, the relative price of environmental resources depends on relative factor endowments. If one country has a lower environmental standard than another, it could simply be a true reflection of the country's absorptive capacity and not necessarily evidence of a 'race to the bottom' or existence of pollution havens. Indeed there is a growing recognition that environmental standards should not necessarily be harmonized across locations, whether nationally or internationally. This is true even across locations where the same conditions apply, since different nations may have different valuations of environmental resources (WTO 1999; see also Dion *et al.* 1997).

Then again, there could be synergy between trade and environmental regulation. Openness to trade could lead to better environmental regulation (this is in addition to the possible positive income effects). Alternatively, good environmental regulation could benefit trade (see below). Hence, more in-depth analysis and empirical evidence is necessary to draw clear conclusions.

Race to the bottom and pollution havens

The 'race to the bottom' hypothesis[5] was initially formulated in the context of local competition for investments and jobs within federal states, where the decentralized environmental responsibilities gave each state independence in setting their environmental standards in line with their priorities (WTO 1999). Most critics argue that increased competition for trade and foreign direct investment could lead to a lowering of environmental standards and regulations (WB 2000). Furthermore, governments that attempt to maintain high standards will see their efforts undermined by the existence of less stringent regulations elsewhere. This will then lead to an overall lowering of environmental standards internationally (Jenkins *et al.* 2002).

Particularly in developing countries, the arguments for the 'race to the bottom' and pollution haven hypotheses lead to the contention that growth in these countries must necessarily be accompanied by severe environmental degradation. Busse (2004) finds some evidence suggesting that the level of environmental regulations is influenced by income level and that the primary effect appears to come via income itself. This more or less supports the environmental Kuznet's curve,[6] which posits that growth harms the environment at low levels of income and helps at high levels (Frankel and Rose 2001).

In the same way, as real income rises, the demand for environmental quality also rises. This translates into environmental progress given the right conditions, effective regulation and externalities, which are largely confined within national borders and therefore amenable to national regulation (Frankel 2003). Recent evidence however suggests that even at the lower-income level, there already exists a more subtle and complex relationship between economic development and environmental protection. It appears that many developing countries are becoming more environmentally aware and have started the fight against pollution at much lower levels of income than that of the rich countries (WB 2000).

In the 1970s, when Japan began to reduce its exports of highly polluting products, the fast growing East Asian 'Tigers'—Korea, Taiwan (China), Singapore and Hong Kong—began to increase their exports of such products. This trend diminished in the 1980s, and a stable pattern emerged with the Tigers importing somewhat more than they exported in the highly polluting sectors. In China, for instance, the share of the five dirtiest industries in total industrial output has fallen, while imports of pollution-intensive products have actually increased (WB 2000).

There is also some evidence of a positive correlation between openness to trade and some measures of environmental quality. Although this may be due to endogeneity of trade rather than causality, trade may indeed have a generally beneficial (although not very significant) effect on certain measures of environmental quality.[7] At the very least, there is no evidence that trade has the detrimental effect on the environment that the 'race to the bottom' theory would lead one to expect (Frankel and Rose 2001). In addition, openness can indeed provide developing countries with both the incentive to adopt, and the access to, new technologies, which may provide a cleaner or greener way of producing the goods concerned. In the case of the companies with foreign market clienteles as well as foreign investors in the offshore countries, their environmental standards are made at par with those of the developed countries. The quality requirements in those markets encourage use of the latest technology, which is typically cleaner than old technologies (WB 2000).

In general, existing studies show positive results on the impact of trade on environmental outcomes and indirectly on the impact on environmental regulation. Is there more direct evidence of a 'race to the bottom' in environmental standards as countries fight to attract foreign capital, and create pollution havens? This hypothesis is analogous to tax havens that apply low rates in order to attract financial capital. It implies a deliberate strategy on the part of host governments to 'undervalue' purposely the environment in order to attract new investment (Jenkins *et al.* 2002). Again, there are some mixed findings.

In the case of China, there is a difference between internally generated and foreign investments. A recent study shows that foreign direct investments (FDIs) originating from Hong Kong, Macao and Taiwan are attracted to provinces with a relative abundance of low-skilled labour and relatively weak environmental controls. In contrast, FDIs from non-Chinese sources are attracted by high levels of skilled labour and high pollution levies. This shows the reverse of the pollution haven hypothesis (Dean *et al.* 2004).

A similar pattern occurred in the trade of pollution-intensive products between North America and Latin America (WB 2000). Particularly for the United States, there appears to be some evidence for the hypothesis that stringency of environmental regulation is a source of comparative disadvantage in dirty industries (Mulatu *et al.* 2004). There are also some findings supporting the 'pollution haven' hypothesis, but the overall evidence is relatively weak and does not survive numerous robustness checks (Smarzynska and Wei 2001). In terms of trade, there is an increasing trend towards cleaner industries among US imports without evidence that pollution-intensive industries have been disproportionately affected by the tariff changes (Ederington *et al.* 2004).

There is also almost no evidence that investors in developing countries are fleeing environmental costs at home. For instance, the pattern of US outbound foreign investment between 1982 and 1994 at least in the case of four developing countries— Côte d'Ivoire, Mexico, Morocco and Venezuela—rejects the hypothesis that investment is skewed toward industries in which the cost of pollution abatement is high (Eskeland and Harrison 1997). In the case of Mexico, however, there is some indication of a 'pollution haven' effect, albeit limited to only a few industries. Depending on the empirical specification, they account for anywhere between 5 and 40 per cent of total FDI and between 5 and 30 per cent of output over the sample period. For other pollutants that are less regulated or come largely from non-industry sources, no systematic relationship between FDI and pollution is detected (Waldkirch and Gopinath 2004).

A more extensive study, however,[8] found no evidence to support the pollution haven hypothesis that industries facing above-average abatement costs with environmental regulations would relocate their activities in pollution havens. The exception is iron and steel products, where a negative and statistically significant link has been established, implying that higher compliance with international treaties and conventions and more stringent regulations, are associated with reduced net exports (Busse 2004).[9] Earlier analysis also did not find likely evidence that the Kyoto Protocol will drive industry to developing countries (Baumert and Kete 2002).

Hence, for the most part, studies find no evidence that the cost of environmental protection has been the determining factor in foreign investment decisions. Environmental regulations do not seem to be the determining factor in international location decisions (WTO 1999): factors such as labour and raw material costs, transparent regulation and protection of property rights are likely to be much more important investment considerations. This is true even for polluting industries. In fact, countries do not become permanent pollution havens, because along with increases in income are increased demands for environmental quality and a better institutional capacity to supply environmental regulation (WB 2000). Furthermore, these polluting industries (including such industries as chemical industries, ferrous and non-ferrous metals, pulp and paper and oil refining) are more likely to conglomerate in capital-abundant developed countries, and to a lesser extent, in economies in transition and newly industrialized countries (WTO 1999).

The case of the global commons

The discussion above becomes more complicated in the case of global commons, where environmental impacts (costs) cross borders. Local environmental problems are best addressed by local environmental regulations: those that are targeted to deal with the specific local conditions. Transboundary and global problems would need collective action from the countries and regions affected. Some trade measures may be called for and some policy harmonization and collective management of common resources may be required. The problem, in various aspects—including policy and implementation—thus becomes much more complex.

In the first place, there needs to be a critical mass of supporters (globally or in the affected region). This presupposes an awareness of costs, which implies, in the absence of more tangible evidence, a strong and clear scientific basis. Otherwise, it would be difficult, if not impossible, to gather commitment and support from the affected countries. Even when there is consensus about the nature and the costs, there is the problem and question about what would be an equitable sharing of responsibilities.

In these lie the major differences between the case of the Montreal Protocol (protection of the ozone layer) for example, and the Kyoto Protocol (on carbon emissions). In the case of the Montreal Protocol, enough scientific evidence has been gathered, and mechanisms have been thrashed out to produce an agreement that was more or less acceptable to all parties. In the case of the Kyoto Protocol, the United States is not a signatory. It chooses to conduct its own scientific research, and it has a problem with developing countries such as India and China, who are among the major carbon polluters but are in effect exempted from the adjustments. This is also relevant with respect to Kyoto party countries, specifically Canada, which is a major source of US energy imports that would entail higher carbon emissions and more difficulty in complying with the Kyoto emission target (see Zhang and Baranzini 2004 for estimates of carbon emissions across selected OECD countries).[10] The issues arising are numerous, including implications on competitiveness, which are very difficult to deal with. First of all, there is the problem of how to decide the initial allocation of permits and emission targets. In connection with this, how are member subsidiaries of non-member multinational companies to be treated? These problems are magnified for neighbouring Kyoto and non-Kyoto parties. Can trade measures be invoked and what are the mechanisms, and consequently, what are the implications for WTO? (See Zhang 2004; Zhang and Assuncao 2004; and Zhang and Baranzani 2004 for more discussion.)

The bottom line is that equitable solutions are extremely difficult to find.

CURRENT TRADE STRUCTURE OF POLLUTION-INTENSIVE PRODUCTS

This section attempts to find further evidence about the impact of trade on the environment. Although there are many environmental indicators, this paper uses pollution index or pollution intensity in the analysis, primarily because of the relatively comprehensive nature of environmental regulations addressing pollution. The other reason is more practical—the availability of comparative data across the countries.

Specifically, this paper looks at the trends in the share of pollution-intensive industries (as most commonly used) for developed and developing countries, and takes as given that all these countries have more or less become more open with the removal of trade barriers around the globe, especially the Asia-Pacific region. There are, of course, other factors that determine the share in exports of these industries, the most important being the level of environmental regulations. However, this is difficult to quantify, and there is little or no available comparative data. Hence, the conclusion we could derive would be limited to a more intuitive interpretation of findings.

Is there evidence that developing countries are more likely to export polluting products?

Table 7.1 shows the structure of exports and imports trade for developing and developed countries (see Table 7.9 for the complete list) by pollution classification.[11] The exports and imports of hazardous and/or pollutive products comprise around 69 per cent of total exports and 68 per cent of total imports. These are highly concentrated in the developed countries. This is to be expected, as developed countries dominate world exports. What is more striking is that it is only in the non-hazardous/non-pollutive exports where the average share of developing countries comes close to that of the developed countries (42 per cent to 55 per cent respectively). Thus, there appears to be no evidence that developing countries are more likely to export polluting products. On the contrary, these results indicate that developing countries are less likely to export polluting products. Indeed, developing countries have a higher

Table 7.1   Average share of trade products, per country group, by pollution classification 1996–2000 (%)

Pollution classification	Country group	Average share	
		Exports	*Imports*
Extremely hazardous/highly pollutive	Developed	61.56	73.34
	Developing	29.36	23.45
Hazardous/highly pollutive	Developed	72.29	66.96
	Developing	19.79	28.82
Non-hazardous/highly pollutive	Developed	72.99	82.05
	Developing	24.45	14.96
Extremely hazardous/pollutive	Developed	77.76	63.93
	Developing	18.87	31.79
Hazardous/pollutive	Developed	80.69	82.44
	Developing	16.76	30.86
Non-hazardous/pollutive	Developed	78.19	74.27
	Developing	19.58	21.47
Hazardous/non-pollutive	Developed	83.58	73.29
	Developing	13.44	22.57
Non-hazardous/non-pollutive	Developed	54.63	76.87
	Developing	42.10	21.51

Notes

1   Country classification is from the Philippine Environment Management Bureau (EMB), based on Medalla (2001).

2   Shares of developed and developing countries may not add to up to 100%, since trade data of least-developed countries (LDCs) are not classified as developing countries.

Source: PC–TAS (SITC).

revealed comparative advantage index (RCA) for these non-pollutive and non-hazardous exports at around two, compared to that of around 0.7 for developed countries. Developed countries have a higher RCA index on pollutive products than developing countries, although not by as much (1.02 versus 0.91). Table 7.2 shows the RCA index per specific product classification.

Table 7.3 provides additional information on the share of the product group by pollution classification for developed and developing countries. Consistent with their revealed comparative advantage, developed countries export a larger share of pollutive industries at around 71 per cent of their total exports, compared to around 57 per cent for developing countries. In contrast, developed countries export a smaller share of non-pollutive industries at around 9 per cent, compared to around 16 per cent for developing countries.

Table 7.2   Revealed comparative advantage index

Pollution classification	Country group	RCA index	
		1996	*2000*
Extremely hazardous/highly pollutive	Developed	0.82	0.78
	Developing	1.37	1.44
Hazardous/highly pollutive	Developed	0.97	0.98
	Developing	0.91	0.90
Non-hazardous/highly pollutive	Developed	0.97	1.00
	Developing	1.15	1.08
Extremely hazardous/pollutive	Developed	1.03	1.05
	Developing	0.90	0.88
Hazardous/pollutive	Developed	1.08	1.08
	Developing	0.77	0.81
Non-hazardous/pollutive	Developed	1.04	1.09
	Developing	0.93	0.81
All pollutive	**Developed**	**1.02**	**1.03**
	Developing	**0.91**	**0.93**
All non-pollutive			
Hazardous/non-pollutive	Developed	1.12	1.13
	Developing	0.59	0.63
Non-hazardous/non-pollutive	Developed	0.74	0.74
	Developing	2.00	1.84

Notes
1   Country classification is from the Philippine Environment Management Bureau (EMB), based on Medalla (2001).
2   Total export is the sum of developed and developing countries' exports. This excludes data from least-developed countries (LDCs).

Source: PC–TAS (SITC).

Trade performance of selected pollution-intensive products

The analysis above combines industries under the major categories of pollution classification. For a better picture of exports of pollution-intensive products, more specific sectors are examined below. Pollution-intensive industries are defined as industries characterized by high levels of toxic release after efforts have been made to control the pollution and/or high levels of pollution abatement costs, compared with other industries (Jenkins *et al.* 2002).[12] Accordingly, the pollution-intensive industries selected include those with above-average pollution abatement costs as a percentage of total costs. Table 7.4 shows the industries and corresponding Standard Industrial Trade Classification (SITC) trade categories with the highest abatement costs (calculated by Low (1992) for US industries with at least 1.8 per cent).

Table 7.3   Share of product group by pollution classification in total exports, per country group (1996–2000)

Pollution classification	1996		1997		1998		1999		2000		Average
	US$ billion	Share %	US$ billion	Share %	US$ billion	Share %	US$ billion	Share %	US$ billion	Share %	Share %
Total exports											
World											
Developed	3,318	100	3,412	100	3,407	100	3,462	100	3,713	100	100
Developing	983	100	1,067	100	1,024	100	1,107	100	1,349	100	100
All pollutive											
World	**3,044**		**3,155**		**3,131**		**3,208**		**3,522**		
Developed	**2,368**	**71**	**2,426**	**71**	**2,436**	**72**	**2,466**	**71**	**2,604**	**70**	71
Developing	**562**	**57**	**608**	**57**	**576**	**56**	**624**	**56**	**770**	**57**	56.6
All hazardous											
World	1,873		1,952		1,980		2,002		2,142		
Developed	1,516	46	1,563	46	1,589	47	1,590	46	1,649	44	45.8
Developing	302	31	328	31	325	32	344	31	415	31	31.2
Extremely hazardous											
World	611		628		573		614		770		
Developed	415	13	423	12	404	12	415	12	481	13	12.4
Developing	150	15	158	15	131	13	160	14	230	17	14.8
All non-pollutive											
World	**470**		**491**		**484**		**478**		**508**		
Developed	**302**	**9**	**308**	**9**	**300**	**9**	**297**	**9**	**308**	**8**	8.8
Developing	**154**	**16**	**168**	**16**	**168**	**16**	**164**	**15**	**183**	**14**	15.4

Notes
1   Country classification is from the Philippine Environment Management Bureau (EMB), based on Medalla (2001).
2   Shares of developed and developing countries may not add to up to 100%, since trade data of least-developed countries (LDCs) are not classified as developing countries.

Source: PC–TAS (SITC).

The findings are generally the same. Figures 7.1–7.5 show that, over the past decade, exports and imports of pollution-intensive products have been dominated by developed countries. A much larger share of these products is exported by developed countries. Similarly, imports of these products are concentrated in the developed countries. The general pattern is that developing countries import more than they export of these pollution-intensive products, with the exception of minerals, both non-metallic and non-ferrous. Indeed, the data seem to reject the assertion that polluting industries have migrated from developed to developing countries, although there are of course exceptions.

Table 7.4   Classification of pollution-intensive industries

Industry	SITC No.	Description
Industrial chemicals	51	Organic chemicals
	52	Inorganic chemicals
	562	Manufactured fertilizers
	59	Other chemical material and products
Paper and pulp	251	Pulp and waste paper
	641	Paper and paperboard
	642	Articles of cut paper and board
Non-metallic minerals	66	Non-metallic mineral manufactures
Iron and steel	67	Iron and steel
Non-ferrous metals	681	Silver and platinum
	682	Copper
	683	Nickel
	685	Lead
	686	Zinc
	687	Tin
	689	Other non-ferrous base metals

Notes: SITC Rev. 3. Selection of industries based on Low's (1992) classifications.
Source: Busse (2004).

For almost all of these industries, the shares for developed countries did not change significantly during the last decade. However, the share in trade of pollution-intensive products from 1991 to 2000 grew somewhat for developing countries. Nevertheless, the share is much higher for imports compared to exports (see Table 7.5). This again follows the revealed comparative advantage index to the country groups. Although relative RCA index is increasing in favour of developing countries, developed countries generally have a higher RCA index in the industry-levels with the exception of iron and steel,[13] and non-ferrous metals (see Table 7.6).

Is there evidence of international competition in attracting polluting industries?

The evidence based on the pollution intensity of trade does not support the perception that developing countries are gaining a comparative advantage in pollution-intensive production because of lax environmental regulations. The tendency, at least in the last decade, is rather that developed countries are dominating in polluting industries, which suggests that classical factors of comparative advantages predominate over differential environmental standards. This can be explained by the fact that polluting industries are typically very capital intensive, and abatement costs usually represent only a small percentage of production costs (WTO 1999).

Figures 7.1–7.5   Trade structure of pollution-intensive products

Figure 7.1 Industrial chemicals   *Figure 7.2* Iron and steel

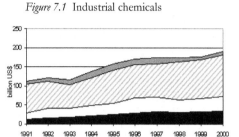

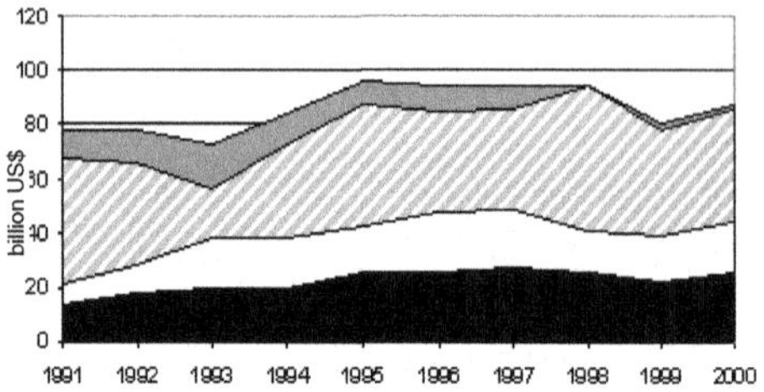

Figure 7.3 Pulp and paper 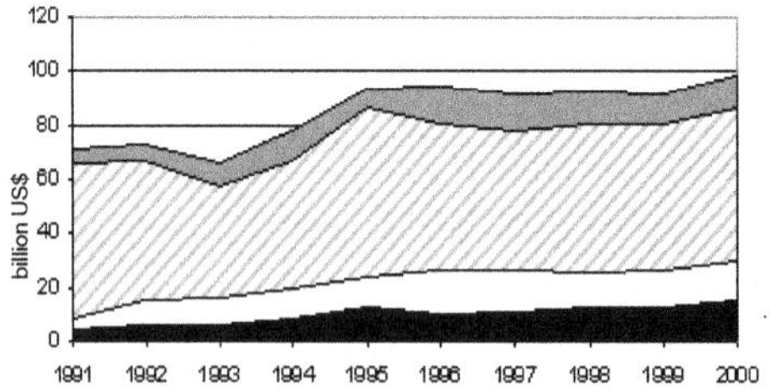   *Figure 7.4* Non-metallic minerals

Figure 7.5   Non-ferrous minerals

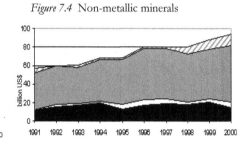

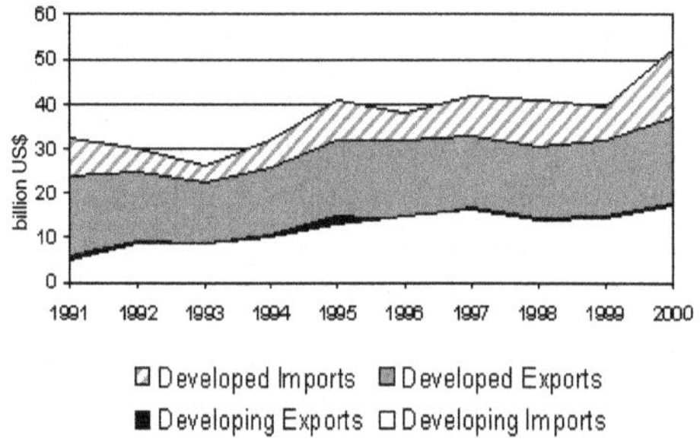

☐ Developed Imports   ▨ Developed Exports
■ Developing Exports   ☐ Developing Imports

Source: PC–TAS (SITC).

Table 7.5   Trade share of selected pollution-intensity products, per country group 1991–
2000 (%)

Reporter	1991		1994		1997		2000	
	Exports	*Imports*	*Exports*	*Imports*	*Exports*	*Imports*	*Exports*	*Imports*
Industrial chemicals								
Developed	90.65	78.39	86.77	71.68	81.41	67.19	81.74	69.47
Developing	9.35	21.61	13.23	28.32	14.85	29.88	14.74	27.84
Iron and steel								
Developed	85.03	76.29	80.73	65.66	69.88	60.93	69.86	62.58
Developing	14.97	23.71	19.27	34.34	20.25	34.86	20.42	32.03
Non-ferrous metals								
Developed	79.81	86.74	70.62	75.63	60.02	70.77	62.16	73.80
Developing	20.19	13.26	29.38	24.37	30.43	27.35	29.07	24.35
Non-metallic metals								
Developed	82.05	82.02	76.77	75.94	78.68	74.94	81.62	79.77
Developing	17.95	17.98	23.23	24.06	18.23	22.22	14.88	17.43
Paper and pulp								
Developed	95.19	88.21	90.62	78.04	86.69	71.32	83.61	71.24
Developing	4.81	11.79	9.38	21.96	10.45	24.52	12.97	24.64
Total								
Developed	87.94	81.13	83.04	72.55	77.40	68.13	77.89	70.59
Developing	12.06	18.87	16.96	27.45	17.24	28.57	16.90	26.02

Note: For 1991–94, share is computed from the sum of developed and developing countries. For 1997–
2000, share may not tally because actual world trade data are used.

Source: PC–TAS (SITC).

SOME OBSERVATIONS ON ENVIRONMENTAL REGULATIONS AND INTERNATIONAL TRADE

The potential impacts of trade and trade policy on the environment are well recognized. The effects are reflected at several levels, mainly in terms of scale, structure, product, technology and regulation (see Box 7.1) The effects may be positive or negative. Indeed, studies have shown that the impact of trade liberalization on the environment is generally positive, especially if it is accompanied by effective environmental policies. As trade liberalization improves the efficient allocation of resources, promotes economic growth and increases general welfare, it increasingly acts as a positive agent, which could provide resources for environmental improvement.

At the same time, environmental regulation would also have effects on trade, both positive and negative. The most common negative implication of a national environmental regulation would be increased costs (from complying with environmental regulations) as well as market access restrictions or limitations.

Table 7.6   Revealed comparative advantage per product classification

Reporter	1991	2000
Industrial chemicals		
Developed	1.08	1.00
Developing	0.59	0.98
Iron and steel		
Developed	1.01	0.92
Developing	0.95	1.45
Non-ferrous metals		
Developed	0.95	0.81
Developing	1.28	2.04
Non-metallic minerals		
Developed	0.97	1.00
Developing	1.14	0.99
Paper and pulp		
Developed	1.13	1.03
Developing	0.31	0.86

Notes: Classification based on Low (1992). Total trade is the sum of developed and developing countries exports.

Source: PC–TAS (SITC).

Box 7.1   Five main environmental effects of trade liberalization

• *Scale effects* are associated with the overall level of economic activity resulting from trade liberalization. Positive scale effects may result from higher economic growth particularly when appropriate environmental policies are present. Negative scale effects may occur when higher economic growth brings increased pollution and faster draw-down of resources due to the absence of appropriate environmental policies.

• *Structural effects* are associated with changes in the patterns of economic activity resulting from trade liberalization. Positive structural effects may result when trade liberalization promotes an efficient allocation of resources and efficient patterns of consumption. Negative structural effects may occur when appropriate environmental policies do not accompany changes in patterns of economic activity.

• *Product effects* are associated with trade in specific products that can enhance or harm the environment. Positive product effects may result from increased trade in goods which are environmentally beneficial, such as energy-efficient machinery, while negative product effects may result from increased trade in goods that are environmentally sensitive, such as hazardous wastes.

• *Technology effects* are associated with changes in the way products are made depending on the technology used. Positive technology effects may result when the output of pollution per unit of economic product is reduced.

• *Regulatory effects* are associated with the legal and policy effects of trade liberalization on environmental regulations, standards and other measures.

Source: OECD 1994/1995 from Aldaba and Cororaton (2001).

Nevertheless, good environmental regulation could also have a positive impact on trade. An increased burden of environmental taxation would generally spur innovation in order to be competitive. A restrictive environmental policy affects economic growth through two channels of transmission that operate in opposite directions: the first channel lowers the marginal impact of innovation on productivity growth; the second channel spurs innovation. The latter requires some research and development initiatives for reduction of pollution intensity (Ricci 2004).

Trade consideration has also become apparent in the growing development of environmental policy, which even to some extent makes use of market instruments. While pollution control policies are currently enforced using the traditional 'command and control' principle, a paradigm shift to a market-based approach is gaining acceptance, and policy instruments are already being put in place. Examples of market-based instruments (MBIs) include pollution charges, environmental subsidies, deposit-refund systems and tradable permits. In the best of all worlds, governments would use proper environmental polices to 'internalize' the full environmental costs of production and consumption—the 'polluter pays' principle (see Box 7.2).

Table 7.7 shows the summary of environmental laws/regulations of selected developing countries within the APEC region. Environmental concern remains one of the top priorities in the overall planning of developing countries. Laws appear to be adequate in these countries, belying fears of a trend towards a race to the bottom in environmental regulations (future studies could look into the standards use, whether low or high, and the extent of implementation and/or enforcements of these laws).

Even where there is a lack of environmental law, community and civil society involvement appears to be of increasing influence in pushing for environmental concerns. In Indonesia, the price of pollution is determined by the intersection of *plant level* demand and a *local environmental* supply function, enforced by community

---

Box 7.2   Differentiating government environmental regulation approaches

'Command and control' principle
In a 'command and control regime', the government enforces regulatory measures and permit requirements to control activities that cause environmental pollution.

Environmental quality standards prescribe the allowable and acceptable level of pollutants, with fines and penalties for non-compliance. Policies are now shifting from this dominant approach to more market-based instruments for economic and technical arguments.

'Polluter pays' principle
The 'polluter pays' principle aims at ensuring that the costs of environmental control fall in the first place on the polluters, thereby ensuring that market forces take these costs into account and that resources are allocated according to production and consumption.

Source: PIDS website: <http://www.pids.gov.ph>

Table 7.7   Existing environmental regulations of selected (APEC) developing countries

| Country | National policy on environment | EIA | Agency | Existing legislations/ Government regulations | | | | |
				Air pollution	Ambient air standards/ Emission standards	Water pollution	Hazardous waste
Chile	Seven Principles: Basic Law for the Environment (1994)	Environmental Impact Assessment System described	National Commission on the Environment (CONAMA)	Supreme Decree 4 regulating stationary sources; Supreme Decree 185 regulating SO_2, arsenic, and particles from large sources; Supreme Decree 211 regulating vehicular sources	Resolution No. 1215, Ministry of Health, SD 59, SD 185	Water Code, Mining Code	Sanitary Code; Municipal Ordinance, Law No. 3133 (1916)
China	Environmental planning in the Ninth Five years (namely the 2010 long-term planning)	National laws and regulations related with EIA; managing ordinances on protecting environments of construction projects	State Environmental Resource Committee (SERC); State Environmental Protection Administration (SEPA)	The prevention and cure law of the People's Republic of China on air pollution (amended), adopted by the National People's Congress on 29 April 2000	Air environment quality standard GB 3095–1982 promulgated by the State Environmental Protection Administration (SEPA). Ambient air quality standard GB 3095–1996 promulgated by SEPA	Law of the People's Republic of China on prevention and cure of Water Pollution (amended), promulgated by the National People's Congress in May 1996	Hazardous and Toxic Waste Management
Indonesia	Indonesia Agenda 21 (1997)	Various activities required EIA	Ministry of Environment (MenLH); Environmental Impact Management Agency (BAPEDAL)	Standard Air Pollution Index; Blue Sky Program	Emission Standards for motorized vehicles	Water Pollution Control	
Malaysia	National Environmental Action Plan (NEAP); Local Agenda 21 for Malaysia (2002)	Environmental Quality (Prescribed Activities) (Environmental Impact Assessment) Order, 1987	Department of Environment, Ministry of Science, Technology and Environment (MOSTE)	Environmental Quality (Clean Air) Regulations, 1978; Environmental Quality (Control of Lead Concentration in Motor Gasoline) Regulations, 1985; Motor Vehicle (Control of Smoke and Gas Emission) Rules, 1978	Environmental Quality (Control of Lead Concentration in Motor Gasoline) Regulations, 1985	Environmental Quality (Sewage and Industrial Effluents) Regulations, 1979	Environmental Quality (Prescribed Premises) (Scheduled Wastes Treatment and and Disposal Facilities) Order, 1989
Mexico	Programa del Medio Ambiente (Environment Program) 1995–2000	Regulation for the implementation of General Law for Ecological Equilibrium and Environmental Protection	Ministry of Environment, Natural Resources and Fishery	Regulation on Environmental Impact Regulation on Prevention and Management of Pollution from Vehicles in the Federal District and Metropolitan	Mexican Official Standards (NOM)	National Water Resource Law	General Law for Ecological Equilibrium and Environmental Protection Regulation on Hazardous Waste, Mexican Official

				Area			Standards (NOM)
				Summary Offences Act; Environment Act 2000	Environment Planning Act	Water Resource Act	Environment Contaminant Act
Papua New Guinea	Managing Papua New Guinea's Unique Environment Strategic Directions 1996–98	EIA is essentially a preventive process. EIA and resource planning are together a total approach to environmental management	Department of Environment and Conservation (DEC)	Summary Offences Act; Environment Act 2000	Environment Planning Act	Water Resource Act	Environment Contaminant Act
Peru	Environmental Code and Natural Resources	Environmental Protection Standards for Industry – Supreme Decree No. 011-97-ITIBCI, 5 January 1997	There is no governmental office exclusively in charge of environmental management	Environmental Code and Natural Resources (Legislative Decree No. 613); Electricity Regulation (Supreme Decree No. 29-94-EM); Hydrocarbon Regulation (Supreme Decree No. 046-93-EM); Mining Regulation (Supreme Decree No. 016-93-EM)	Environmental Code and Natural Resources (Legislative Decree No. 613)	Environmental Code and Natural Resources (Legislative Decree No. 613); Mining Regulation (Supreme Decree No. 016-93-EM); Environmental Protection from Mining (Supreme Decree No. 016-93-EM)	Environmental Protection Standards for Industry (Supreme Decree No. 011-97-ITIBCI, 5 January 1997); Regulations for Environmental Protection from Mining Activities (Supreme Decree No. 016-93-EM, enacted, 1 May 1993)
Philippines	National Action Plan for Sustainable Development, Philippine Agenda 21 (PA21) 1996; Medium-Term Development Plan	Environmental Impact Statement System of PD 1586. The System requires proponents of environmentally critical projects (ECPs) in environmentally critical areas (ECAs) to secure an Environmental Clearance Certificate (ECC) prior to construction	Department of Natural Resources and Environment – Environment Management Bureau	RA No. 8749 – Philippine Clean Air Act of 1999; PD 984 – Pollution Control Law	PD 1152 – Establishing Air Quality to Protect Public Health and Damage to Living Things and Property; PD 1181 – Air Pollution from Motor Vehicles DAO 14 and 14-A of 1993	PD 1067, Water Code of the Philippines (1976); PD 984, Pollution Control Law	RA 6969, Toxic Substances and Hazardous and Nuclear Wastes Control Act of 1990
Thailand	Policy and Prospective Plan for Enhancement and Conservation of National Environmental Quality, BE 2543–2559 (1997–2016)	Office of Environmental Policy and Planning announces regulations (on EIA Expert qualification and EIA licensing) of Sections 19 and 28 of the Enhancement and Conservation of National Environmental Quality Act (NEQA), 1975, which was supplemented by the 2nd NEQA, 1988, the Ministry of Science, Technology and Environment (MOSTE)	National Environmental Board; Office of Environmental Policy and Planning, MOSTE	National Environmental Quality Act, 1992	Notification of the National Environmental Board, No. 10, 1995; Notification of the Ministry of Industry	National Environmental Quality Act, 1992	National Environmental Quality Act, 1992; Hazardous Substances Act, 1992

Source: JICA Country Profile on Environment, 1999–2000, various reports.

pressure or informal regulation. The results also suggest that the price of pollution is higher when plants are particularly visible, and is far lower in poorer, less-educated communities. Although these results cannot be generalized, it can nevertheless be shown that environmental considerations are embedded and promoted through community–factory interactions (Pargal and Wheller 1995).[14]

Even if no regulations are imposed, whether formally or informally, there are at least some firm-level efforts to control pollution if only to create a good reputation, especially to environmentally conscious (export) markets, as well as to reduce the risk of legal liabilities, should a major environmental accident occur.

The rapid adoption of voluntary environmental management standards (ISO 14000) promulgated by the International Organization for Standardization (ISO) has prompted many corporations to assume greater environmental responsibilities. In addition the financial community sees to it that firms do not have a poor environmental profile (WTO 1999).

ENVIRONMENT IN THE MULTILATERAL TRADE AGENDA

Countries act individually through their national policies and implementation to solve environmental problems. However, because of the linkage between trade and environment, environmental effects and issues spill across borders. In addition, there are cases of global commons as previously noted. Hence, there is a need for multilateral institutions.

When the international trading system was reconstructed after World War II, the environmental consequence of economic integration was not a primary concern.[15] Nevertheless, if environmental issues had a low priority during the first four decades

---

Box 7.3   The green provisions in the WTO

Examples of provisions in the WTO agreements dealing with environmental issues are as follows:

• *GATT Article 20*: policies affecting trade in goods for protecting human, animal or plant life or health are exempt from normal GATT disciplines under certain conditions.

• *Technical Barriers to Trade* (i.e. product and industrial standards), and *Sanitary and Phytosanitary Measures* (animal and plant health and hygiene): explicit recognition of environmental objectives.

• *Agriculture*: environmental programmes exempt from cuts in subsidies.

• *Subsidies and Countervail*: allows subsidies, up to 20 per cent of firms' costs, for adapting to new environmental laws.

• *Intellectual property*: governments can refuse to issue patents that threaten human, animal or plant life or health, or risk serious damage to the environment (TRIPs Article 27).

• *GATS Article 14*: policies affecting trade in services for protecting human, animal or plant life or health are exempt from normal GATS disciplines under certain conditions.

of the GATT, they came back with a vengeance in the early 1990s. The starting point of the current debate was a series of contentious environmentally related trade disputes, especially the 'tuna–dolphin' dispute between Mexico and the United States.[16] With the formation of the WTO in 1995, environmental issues, as they relate to trade, are now firmly anchored in the multilateral trading system (see Box 7.3). The Doha Round will be the first WTO round to deal with environmental concerns as an official issue (WTO 1999). Whether or not to include the environmental agenda in the already organized and structured multilateral WTO has become a relevant and controversial question.

Recurring issues

Are calls for environmental protection a disguised form of protectionism?

While trade measures are rarely, if ever, the first-best policy for addressing environmental problems, governments have found trade measures a useful mechanism for encouraging participation in and enforcement of multilateral environmental agreements in some instances, and for attempting to modify the behaviour of foreign governments in others. At present, the WTO has the burden of resolving the relationship between environmental regulation and trade in the middle of a highly controversial trade battle on the subject of genetically modified organisms between the European Union and the United States (Busse 2004).

Moreover, as among the member-states, the WTO has become the focal point for environmental disputes (see Box 7.4), in spite of the fact that environmental issues, with the exception of trade-related aspects, are by and large outside its mandate. This is owing primarily to the fact that the WTO, compared to other international institutions, has a well-structured and formal arbitration body backed by trade sanctions as the ultimate enforcement tool (WTO 1999).

Contrary to the general impression that WTO Panel rulings have interfered with the ability of individual countries to pursue environmental goals, recent rulings have in fact confirmed otherwise: countries can enact environmental measures even if they affect trade and even if they concern others' Processes and Production Methods (PPMs), as long as the measures do not discriminate among producer countries (Frankel 2003).

Is there a conflict between development and commonly proposed global environmental measures?

Negotiations in multilateral trade agreements need to be characterized by more balanced and equitable participation of developed and developing countries (IISD 2000). The development of the environmental agenda in trade negotiations would depend on the interest and motivations of each member-state and hence the need to examine the driving forces behind it. For instance, the aim of the European Union in securing agreement to include environment is to legitimize trade sanctions to impose environmental policies *extraterritorially*. This reflects the disposition of the EU's institutions of government to prefer centralized command and control rather than the free-market policies and the *subsidiarity* principle as a means of improving the

Box 7.4   A disguised restriction on international trade? A note from WTO dispute settlement decisions

The question of whether a measure constitutes a disguised restriction on international trade has been studied by several panels and Appellate Body reports, and in particular detail by the panel in the *EC–Asbestos case*. Three criteria have been progressively introduced in order to determine whether a measure is a disguised restriction on international trade: (i) the publicity test; (ii) the consideration of whether the application of a measure also amounts to arbitrary or unjustifiable discrimination; and (iii) the examination of 'the design, architecture and revealing structure' of the measure at issue.

(i) In the *US–Canadian Tuna* case, the panel adopted a literal interpretation of the concept of 'disguised restriction on international trade' only based on a publicity test. It felt that 'the United States' action should not be considered to be a disguised restriction on international trade, noting that the United States' prohibition of imports of tuna and tuna products from Canada had been taken as a trade measure and publicly announced as such'.

In the *US–Gasoline* case, the Appellate Body considered, however, that it was 'clear that *concealed* or *unannounced* restriction or discrimination in international trade does *not* exhaust the meaning of "disguised restriction"'. The panel in the *EC–Asbestos* case interpreted this sentence as implying that a measure that was not published would not satisfy the requirements of the second proposition of the introductory clause of Article XX. The panel noted that the French decree applies unequivocally to international trade, since as far as asbestos is concerned, both importation and exportation are prohibited. In this sense, the criteria developed in the *US–Canadian Tuna* (1982) and in *US–Automotive Springs* cases have already been satisfied. The panel further observed that this remark also suggests that the expression 'disguised restriction on international trade' covers other requirements than the sole publicity test.

(ii) In the *US–Gasoline* case, the Appellate Body also considered that the kinds of considerations pertinent in deciding whether the application of a particular measure amounts to 'arbitrary or unjustifiable discrimination' may also be taken into account in determining the presence of a 'disguised restriction on international trade':

> 'Arbitrary discrimination', 'unjustifiable discrimination' and 'disguised restriction' on international trade may, accordingly, be read side-by-side; they impart meaning to one another. It is clear to us that 'disguised restriction' includes disguised *discrimination* in international trade ... We consider that 'disguised restriction', whatever else it covers, may properly be read as embracing restrictions amounting to arbitrary or unjustifiable discrimination in international trade taken under the guise of a measure formally within the terms of an exception listed in Article XX.

(iii) Another requirement was taken into account by the Appellate Body in *US–Shrimp* and by the panel in the *EC–Asbestos* case. In *EC–Asbestos*, after finding that the measure at issue met the publicity criterion, the panel examined as an additional requirement the 'design, architecture and revealing structure' of the measure, as it had already been introduced in *Japan–Alcoholic Beverages* in order to discern the protective application of a measure. The panel then concluded that '[a]s far as the design, architecture and revealing structure of the Decree are concerned, we find nothing that might lead us to conclude that the Decree has protectionist objectives'. Similarly in the *US–Shrimp* case, the panel demonstrated that the measure at issue did not constitute a disguised restriction on international trade by examining the 'design, architecture and revealing structure' of the measure.

Note: Footnotes omitted for brevity.
Source: WTO (2002).

environment. This brings about the fear of a weakening of the WTO's free-market structures in the pursuit of a still poor environmental policy (Oxley 2002).

Although economists generally recognize four fundamental principles when pondering the negotiation of a set of multilateral standards to restrain government action on the environmental issues,[17] it is presumed that only in the first principle will the WTO necessarily become involved, as any direct impact on trade favours (or implicates) an agreement at the multilateral level. In particular, a meaningful trade dispute resolution for environmental issues is very difficult to implement (Maskus 2002).

However, the need for a multilateral trade environmental standard does not necessarily entail harmonization of all environmental standards in general. In fact, there is a growing consensus that environmental standards should not necessarily be harmonized across locations, whether nationally or internationally. In addition, although national standards (as defined by laws and regulations) are uniform, their implementation is a function of local authorities in cooperation with the community. The 'price of pollution' in each area is determined by the way national standards are monitored and enforced. Ignoring the trade-offs taking place locally could undermine and render ineffective national regulatory and policy reform (Dion *et al.* 1997).

In sum, local pollution problems are arguably best addressed by standards targeted to the specifics of the local conditions. The case is different for transboundary and global problems where there would be a need for some policy harmonization and collective management of common resources (WTO 1999). This is where the linkages of conflict in jurisdiction come in as a defining issue.

The WTO and MEAs conflict

There are approximately 200 multilateral environmental agreements (MEAs) in place today. Only about 20 of these contain trade provisions. For example, the Montreal Protocol for the protection of the ozone layer applies restrictions on the production, consumption, and export of aerosols containing chlorofluorocarbons (CFCs). The Basel Convention, which controls trade or transportation of hazardous waste across international borders, and the Convention on International Trade in Endangered Species (CITES) are other multilateral environmental agreements containing trade provisions (see Table 7.10 for a list of MEAs with trade implications).

Although the WTO has always held sustainable development to be a principle of trade liberalization, it has had to face a rising number of MEAs that often conflict with WTO principles. Several significant MEAs provide that parties are obliged to use trade bans to enforce the environmental objectives of the treaties, and are even required to ban trade with countries that are not parties to the MEAs. However, the WTO does not permit any member to impose its own policies extraterritorially under the threat of trade bans (the MEAs say one country will not trade with another unless it applies that country's policies and standards), and it does not permit members of the WTO to discriminate against other countries in their trade policies (Oxley 2002). So also in the case of MEAs, the proliferation of amendments, protocols or annexes to various MEAs not only keeps the Party–non-Party nexus alive, but also might make it more subtle and confusing (Hoffman 2003).

Another important issue is the concern of developing countries. The prevailing discussions on environmental issues have so far been largely focused on the need to accommodate *trade measures* pursuant to multilateral environmental agreements (MEAs) as well as *eco-labelling* based on non-product related PPMs (see Box 7.5). 'Developing country issues', such as safeguarding and further improving market access, controlling the export of domestically prohibited goods, and promoting technology transfer have been pushed to the side. Thus, while in developed countries there is pressure to accommodate the use of trade measures for environmental purposes within the framework of WTO rules, it appears that there is no concomitant effort to actually control exports of environmentally harmful products and obsolete technologies to developing countries. Overall, there seems to be a lack of balance in the discussions on trade and environment and this has led developing countries to adopt defensive postures in international debates (Jha and Vossenaar 1999).

Box 7.5   How the WTO relates to environmental agreements

At Doha, members agreed to launch negotiations on the linkage between trade and environment. However, these negotiations are circumscribed to four issues: the need to clarify the relationship between existing WTO rules and specific trade obligations set out in multilateral environmental agreements (MEAs); the exchange of information between the WTO and MEA secretariats; the criteria for granting observer status to other international organizations; and the liberalization of trade in environmental goods and services.

How do WTO rules apply to WTO members that have also signed environmental agreements outside the WTO? Suppose a WTO member government puts into place a trade measure to protect its environment that is provided for in an environmental agreement it has signed. Should it fear being challenged in the WTO dispute settlement procedure? The new negotiations aim to clarify the relationship between trade measures taken under the environmental agreements and WTO rules.

Should the focus be on actual obligations, or broader principles? Some members advocate identifying individual 'specific trade obligations' that the WTO should examine. Others prefer a more general approach that would look at the principles governing the relationship between the WTO and the environmental agreements, and how the environmental agreements' trade measures might be accommodated in the WTO. For example, some advocate the principle that there should be no 'hierarchical' relationship between the two legal regimes—neither the WTO, nor the environmental agreements should be dominant.

In the meantime, proposals to grant observer status in the WTO to other international governmental organizations are currently blocked for political reasons. In the Trade and Environment Committee's special sessions, eight requests are pending, including four from multilateral environmental agreements. The negotiations aim at developing criteria for allowing these organizations to be observers in the WTO.

Source: Abridged from WTO Briefing Notes on Trade and Environment <http://www.wto.org>

Perceived solution

Apart from WTO provisions or MEAs, probably the best way to address environmental issues is to remove obstacles to incomplete markets. The vast majority of environmental degradation can be attributed to situations in which environmental resources are not properly valued, leading to so-called positive or negative externalities. Above all, these arise due to inefficient property rights systems, imperfect or asymmetric information and government failure, where government policy focuses more on special interest groups than on the general public (Busse 2004).

Technical cooperation is also the key to achieving the objectives of these existing multilateral agreements. This should start with the integration of tested-environmental programmes, say from developed countries to developing countries, at a gradual rate that would not be hurtful in the adjustment of the industries. Coordination can be had among the donors–government–private sector and civil society groups (Audley and Ulmer 2003).

Developing countries also lack capacity to build credible certification bodies, with the result that their firms often encounter problems in certifying compliance with international standards. Enforcing environmental standards and norms and monitoring them is also an enormous problem for developing countries and thus requires the continued assistance from developed countries (Jha and Vossenaar 1999).

Other prospects

Advent of environmental goods

During the more recent decades, environmental goods have found a growing niche in the market. In a recent study, Bora and Teh (2004) estimated that in 2002, total exports of environmental goods reached about $238.4 billion (using the OECD defined list or $215.3 billion using the APEC defined list), representing between 3.6 and 4.0 per cent of world exports. From 1990 to 2002, trade in environmental goods grew more than twice as fast (14 per cent) as total merchandise trade (6 per cent). In terms of shares, developed countries make up 79 per cent of environmental goods exports, developing countries about 20 per cent, and LDCs less than one per cent. Developed countries make up 60 per cent of environmental goods imports, developed countries 39 per cent and LDCs less than one per cent (see Figure 7.6).[18]

Bora and Teh (2004) investigated the impact of the environmental goods trade. Their results show a statistically significant, negative correlation between trade in environmental goods and environmental resources used. It appears that countries which trade more environmental goods have less pollution or consume energy more efficiently. Bora and Teh argue that the factors fuelling this dynamism include the greater awareness of the value of the environment and concern about pollution as well as institutionalization of environmental protection in countries around the globe. However, as a precaution in analysing the trend in the industry, there is the risk of primarily focusing trade liberalization on products integrated in 'end of pipe' equipment (Drouet 2004).

What remains a problem is that there is no clear agreement among WTO members on the definitions and coverage of environmental goods, despite reference to the

Figure 7.6   Growth of environmental goods trade, 1990–2002

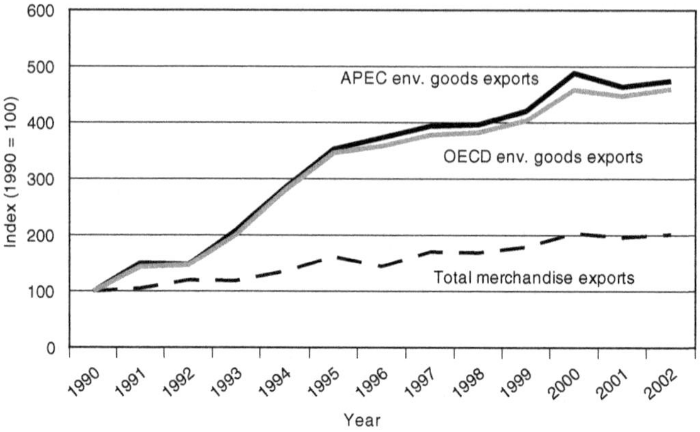

Source: Bora and Teh (2004).

OECD's definition of the environment industry as 'activities which produce goods and services to measure, prevent, limit, or minimise or correct environmental damage to water, air and soil, as well as problems related to waste, noise and ecosystems' (Sugathan 2004).

Environmental service

Environmental services cover one segment of the environmental industry. Trade in environmental services appears to be relatively free of restrictions in comparison with other service sectors. The current GATS classification of environmental services fails to account for the present regulatory reality and for how business operates in this sector. A new possible classification of the sector would therefore need to address the issue of the so-called 'non-core' environmental services or services with 'dual use'.

Nearly 50 member countries of the WTO have made commitments on environmental services in the context of GATS, but they include those that are the major players in the international markets. The majority of commitments (around 20) have been made by developed and East European countries. Only two commitments are scheduled by countries from the Asian region, and two from Latin America. The remaining commitments have been made by countries from Africa. Notably, no limitations on foreign investment have been included in the specific commitments (Butkeviciene 2004).

Eco-labelling

Another approach that has been discussed to address environmental degradation of individual firms or countries is eco-labelling schemes. An eco-label is a form of legally protected label that is applied to (or certification awarded to) a product or service, warranting that it complies with certain pre-determined environmental and (sometimes) social criteria. Eco-labels are policy instruments that attempt to communicate distinctions in similar products based on their relative environmental impact (Naumann 2001).

There are a number of national and private eco-labelling schemes in existence worldwide (see Table 7.8) Most eco-labelling schemes were developed in the early 1990s, and new product categories are being added continuously.

Product labelling requires that (imported) goods be correctly distinguished by labels that state, for instance, that the product has been produced without, or with very little, environmental degradation. Consumers in industrial countries might be ready to pay a higher price for improved standards. This approach could also lessen concerns about low standards expressed by trade unions (in high-income countries) and non-governmental organizations, and could provide an incentive for firms in the exporting nations to upgrade their standards without binding rules. In particular the voluntary participation of all parties involved is the most appealing argument for labelling, as it allows the willingness-to-pay rule to decide the level of harmonization of environmental standards and avoids internationally binding trade restrictions (Busse 2004).

Notwithstanding these clear advantages, there are also important problems involved with labelling. First, due to the likely premium on commodities with higher standards, labelling might create incentives for private firms to overstate the standards by which they abide. Second, it might be doubtful whether eco-labelling for iron and steel

Table 7.8   National eco-labelling programmes

Country/group	*Name of eco-labelling programme*
Australia	Environmental Choice
Austria	Austrian Eco-Label
Canada	Environmental Choice Programme
Croatia	Environmentally Friendly
European Union	European Flower
France	NF-Environment
Germany	Blue Angel
India	Ecomark
Japan	Eco Mark
Netherlands	Stichting Milieukeur
Nordic Countries	Nordic Swan
Korean Rep.	Ecomark
Singapore	Green Label Singapore
Sweden	Good Environmental Choice
Thailand	Thai Green Label
United States	Green Seal

Source: Naumann (2001).

Table 7.9   List of developed and developing countries

Developed	Developing	
Australia	Algeria	Kenya
Austria	Argentina	Korean Rep.
Belgium	Armenia	Kuwait
Belgium–Lux	Azerbaijan	Kyrgyzstan
Canada	Bahrain	Macau
Denmark	Bangladesh	Madagascar
Finland	Barbados	Malaysia
France	Benin	Maldives
Germany	Bhutan	Mali
Greece	Bolivia	Mauritius
Iceland	Brazil	Mexico
Ireland	Brunei	Morocco
Israel	Burundi	Mozambique
Italy	Cameroon	Nepal
Japan	Chile	Nicaragua
Malta	China	Niger
Netherlands	Colombia	Nigeria
New Zealand	Comoros	Oman
Norway	Costa Rica	Pakistan
Portugal	Côte D'Ivoire	Panama
S. Afr. Cus. Un	Croatia	Papua New Guinea
South Africa	Cyprus	Paraguay
Spain	Dominica	Peru
Sweden	Dominican Rep.	Philippines
Switz. Liecht	Ecuador	Qatar
UK	Egypt	Senegal
USA, Pr, Usvi	El Salvador	Singapore
	Ethiopia	Slovenia
	Gambia	Sri Lanka
	Georgia	Sudan
	Ghana	Suriname
	Grenada	Syria
	Guatemala	Tajikistan
	Guinea	Tanzania
	Haiti	Thailand
	Honduras	Trinidad & Tobago
	Hong Kong	Tunisia
	India	Turkey
	Indonesia	Turkmenistan
	Iran	Uganda
	Jamaica	Uruguay
	Jordan	Venezuela
	Kazakstan	Yugoslavia
		Zimbabwe

products is an appropriate way to deal with the negative linkages between environmental regulations and comparative advantage (Busse 2004).

One important enquiry is the implications of eco-labelling for developing countries. There is a concern that eco-labels are complex schemes developed by national authorities to limit foreign competition as the labelling of product groups often favours domestic products over foreign products and is not always compatible with many of the products in developing countries. To many developing countries, the current debate involving eco-labelling represents another form of industrialized countries' blocking out of developing country exports. Developing countries fear that stricter product standards relating to environmental criteria are increasingly being used as a trade barrier for their exports, and that these environment-based restrictions are used as an indirect means of protecting 'northern' industries (Naumann 2001).

In the medium to long-term, eco-labelling may thus have important consequences for market access in foreign countries where eco-labelling standards are well developed and have captured significant market share. Countries thus have the option of developing their own eco-labels, or their industries can focus on obtaining foreign eco-labels that are relevant in their current (or future) export markets (Naumann 2001).

TRADE AND ENVIRONMENT POLICIES IN TANDEM: THE WAY FORWARD

We return to our fundamental hypothesis: there is no inherent conflict between adopting an open trade policy and good environmental policy. Indeed, it is ideal to have both.[19] The conflict arises as a result of the failure of political institutions to address environmental problems, especially those of a global nature which require a concerted effort to solve them (WTO 1999). It is not trade *per se* which would lead to the 'race to bottom' in the environmental regulations. It is more the lack of awareness or prioritization of the environment as well as the laxity and incapability in the implementation of existing mechanisms that would have detrimental effects on the environment, no matter what kind of trade policy regime exists. Then again, as pointed out earlier, openness to trade could even be positively related to environmental quality. Developing countries may even be able to achieve higher levels of environmental performance long before they reach the income levels of the industrialized countries.

This is not to say that there are no trade-offs between trade and environment. Too few and lax environmental regulations could bring about false comparative advantage, while too stringent regulations could erode real comparative advantage. There are no perfect policies, but these should at least be guided by sound principles.

There should be efforts to reduce the cost of environmental regulations through special adjustment provisions as well as infrastructural support. There is a strong need for trade-related capacity building not only for environmental protection but also to support sustainable development as a whole. Moreover, any environmental policy or capability-building programme should reflect a country's absorptive capacity. It is only in this case that general welfare is optimized.

Table 7.10   MEAs with trade implications

MEA	Date in force	Eligible signatories	No. of signatories	Products affected
Wildlife preservation	01 May 1942	Americas National parks	22	Migratory birds
Whaling convention	10 Nov 1948	All countries	49	Whales
Bird protection	03 May 1950	All countries	15	Birds and bird eggs
Plant protection	18 Apr 1951	Europe, Mediterranean	34	Plants
Plant protection	02 Jul 1956	SE Asia, Pacific	24	Plants, containers, soil, etc.
Quarantine of plants	19 Oct 1960	All Countries	8	Plants and weeds
Atlantic tuna/ICCAT	21 Mar 1969	All Countries	28	Tuna and tuna-like fish
Natural resources	16 Jun 1969	Africa	43	Soil water, flora and fauna resources
Animal transport	20 Feb 1971	Europe	22	Animals
Benelux birds	01 Jul 1972	Benelux	3	Birds
CITES	01 Jul 1975	All countries	152	Plants, animals threatened by trade
Polar bears	26 May 1976	Arctic countries	5	Polar bears
Atlantic fish	01 Jan 1979	All countries	19	Fish
Vicuna convention	19 Mar 1982	Andes	4	Vicuna
CCAMLR	07 Apr 1982	All countries	27	Antarctic marine living resources
Tropical timber	01 Apr 1985	All countries	54	Non-coniferous tropical woods
Montreal ozone Protocol	01 Jan 1989	All countries	175	Controlled substances that deplete ozone layer
Drift nets	17 May 1991	All countries	15	Marine living resources
Basel convention	05 May 1992	All countries	147	Hazardous waste production
Biological diversity/ CBD	29 Dec 1993	All countries	168	Conservation of biological diversity
Climate change	21 Mar 1994	All countries	176	Six greenhouse gasses
Bluefin tuna	20 May 1994	Australia, Japan, NZ	3	Bluefin tuna

Source: Annex 15, International Trade Centre (2004).

Aside from formal regulations, informal regulatory mechanisms coupled with local community education would prove to be effective and beneficial. Community pressure is one effective source of compliance and cooperation.

Finally, trade measures are seldom the *first best* policy tools to achieve environmental objectives, be it in the multilateral or regional context. What could be done is to promote a 'race to the top' like the so-called 'California Effect',[20] such that companies would be willing to meet the country's higher standards not only to avoid losing the hold on the market but such that they could also easily meet the standards in the international arena.

NOTES

An earlier version of this paper was presented during the 30th Pacific Trade and Development Conference *'Does Trade Deliver What It Promises? Assessing the Critique of Globalization'*, 19–21 February 2005, Honolulu, Hawaii. The authors wish to thank Dr Zhong Xiang Zhang for useful comments and suggestions on an earlier draft.

1 See Busse (2004).
2 These include, for example, Tobey (1990), Low and Yeats (1992), Van Beers and Van den Bergh (1997), Jänicke *et al.* (1997), Xu (2000), Xu and Song (2000), Harris *et al.* (2002), Grether and De Melo (2003), Kahn (2003).
3 An example is the lack of adequate and comprehensive data on the stringency of regulations across countries. To address this, multilateral initiatives and environmental data collection activities are currently being conducted by OECD, EUROSTAT, Blue Plan Medstat, European Environment Agency, World Conservation Union, WHO and other organizations from various MEAs or conventions.
4 Of course, good environmental policy is basically good economic policy as well, especially with regard to the use of market-based instruments. However, to aid in the discussion for this paper, we separate environment policy from other economic policy areas.
5 A less extreme version of this 'race to the bottom' hypothesis is the 'stuck-in-the-mud' hypothesis, that competition, while not necessarily leading to a reduction in environmental standards, does discourage governments from raising standards—sometimes also referred to as the 'chilling' effect of globalization on environmental regulation.
6 The environmental Kuznet's curve refers to the predicted relationship whereby environmental quality first deteriorates and then improves as per capita income levels rise.
7 Favourable 'gains from trade' effects dominate for measures of air and water pollution such as SO_2 concentrations (Frankel 2003).
8 This study, based on a Hecksher–Ohlin model, used a comprehensive new database for environmental regulations across 119 countries and five high-polluting industries.
9 High-income countries, where environmental regulations are usually more stringent in comparison to those of middle or low-income countries, have experienced a considerable decline in the export–import ratio of iron and steel products since the late 1970s.
10 Estimates of OECD countries' (total energy-intensive industries) cost increases from a tax of \$100/tonne of carbon as a percentage of production value are as follows: Australia (5.2); Canada (4.1); USA (2.8); Germany (1.6); UK (1.6); France (1.4); Italy (1.4); Belgium (1.3); Japan (1.2). Source: Zhang and Baranzini (2004).
11 Based on Philippine Environmental Management Bureau classification. Actual pollution intensity of each product may differ from one country to another.

12   The most common approach identifies pollution-intensive industries as those industries which have a relatively high share of pollution abatement costs in total costs, or relative to their turnover. Another approach considers the volume of pollution generated by an industry per dollar of output or value added, or per person employed.

13   These are the same findings as in Busse (2004).

14   Evidence from developing countries suggests that local communities can sometimes exert effective pressure on firms to clean up their act even without the backing of formal regulations and laws.

15   Only indirect references to the environment were included in the exception clause of GATT 1947, Article XX, which allows countries to sidestep the normal trading rules if necessary to protect human, animal, or plant life or health, or to conserve exhaustible natural resources, provided that such measures do not discriminate between sources of imports or constitute a disguised restriction on international trade.

16   Although the ruling in this case was never adopted by the GATT Council, and hence is not legally binding on the parties, it was viewed by the environmental community as a threat to environmental policy-making in general, and the use of trade measures to support environmental objectives in particular, including the legal status of trade provisions in multilateral environmental agreements (MEAs).

17   (1) The issue is clearly trade related such that trade flows are distorted; (2) there are international externalities, such as environmental spill-overs, involved that limit the attainment of global optimality, and multilateral rules are an appropriate way to internalize those externalities; (3) in the case of no multilateral rules, national governments would choose sub-optimal policies that result in insufficient regulations or a 'race to the bottom' on regulations; and (4) any damages from not complying with international regulations can be assessed in financial terms and, thus, allow the dispute settlement to function.

18   Western Europe alone accounted for almost half the environmental goods exports and is a net exporter whether the APEC or OECD definition is used. Asia is the second largest trader of environmental goods and is a net importer whether the APEC or OECD definition is used. North America is a net exporter only if the APEC definition is used. All the other regions are net importers of environmental goods, whichever definition is used.

19   They are integral to a good overall economic policy.

20   After the passage of the US 1970 Clean Air Act Amendments, California repeatedly adopted stricter emissions standards than other US states. Instead of a flight of investment and jobs from California, however, other states began adopting similar, tougher emissions standards. A self-reinforcing 'race to the top' was thus put in place in which California helped lift standards throughout the US. Vogel (1995) attributes this largely to the 'lure of green markets' (WB 2000).

REFERENCES

Aldaba, R.A.M. and C.B. Cororaton (2001) 'Trade Liberalization and Pollution: Evidence from the Philippines', *PIDS Discussion Paper Series No. 2001–25*.

Arrow, K., B. Bolin, R. Constanza, P. Dasgupta, C. Folke, C.S. Holling, B-O. Jansson, S. Levin, K-G. Maler, C. Perrings, D. Pimentel (1995) 'Economic Growth, Carrying Capacity, and the Environment', *Science*, 268 (28 April): 520–21.

Audley, J. and V. Ulmer (2003) 'Strengthening Linkages between US Trade Policy and Environmental Capacity Building', *Carnegie Endowment Working Papers 40*: July.

Baumert, K. and N. Kete (2002) 'Will the Kyoto Protocol Drive Industry to Developing Countries? Earth Trends', World Resources Institute. Available at <http://earthtrends.wri.org/pdf_library/features/cli_fea_carbon.pdf>; accessed 20 June 2006.

Birdsall, N. and D. Wheeler (1993) 'Trade Policy and Industrial Pollution in Latin America: Where are the Pollution Havens?', *Journal of Environment and Development*, 2(1): 137–49.

Bora, B. and R. Teh (2004) 'Tariffs and Trade in Environmental Goods', *WTO Workshop on Environmental Goods*: Para 31 (iii) of the DDA, Geneva, 11 October.

Busse, M. (2004) 'Trade, Environmental Regulations and the World Trade Organization: New Empirical Evidence', *World Bank Policy Research Working Paper 3361*, July. Available at <http://www-wds.worldbank.org/servlet/WDSContentServer/WDSP/IB/2004/07/30/000009486_20040730113356/Rendered/PDF/3361wpstrade.pdf>; accessed 20 June 2006.

Butkeviciene, J. (2004) 'GATS Negotiations and Issues for Consideration in the Area of Environmental Services from a Development Perspective', *UNEP–UNCTAD CBTF–Singapore Workshop*, May.

Dean, J., M.E. Lovely and H. Wang (2004) 'Are Foreign Investors Attracted to Weak Environmental Regulations? Evaluating the Evidence from China', *World Bank USITC Working Paper 2004-01-B*, May.

Dion, C., P. Lanoie and B. Laplante (1997) 'Monitoring Environmental Standards: Do Local Conditions Matter?', *Policy Research Working Papers*. World Bank.

Drouet, D. (2004) 'Trends in Environmental Goods Industry', *WTO Workshop on Environmental Goods*. Para 31 (iii) of the DDA, Geneva, 11 October.

Ederington, J., A. Levinson and J. Minier (2004) 'Trade Liberalization and Pollution Havens', *Advances in Economic Analysis & Policy*, 4(2): Article 6. Available at <http://www.bepress.com/bejeap/advances/vol4/iss2/art6>; accessed 20 June 2006.

Eskeland, G.S. and A.E. Harrison (1997) 'Moving to Greener Pastures? Multinationals and the Pollution Haven Hypothesis', *Policy Research Working Papers*. World Bank, January.

Frankel, J. (2003) 'The Environment and Globalization', *NBER Working Paper 10090*, November.

Frankel, J. and A. Rose (2001) 'Is Trade Good or Bad for the Environment? Sorting out the Causality,' *NBER Working Paper Series 9201*, September.

Grether, J-M. and J. de Melo (2003) 'Globalization and Dirty Industries: Do Pollution Havens Matter?' *NBER Working Paper Series 9776*, June.

Harris, M., L. Konya and L. Matyas (2002) 'Modelling the Impact of Environmental Regulations on Bilateral Trade Flows: OECD, 1990–96', *World Economy*, 25(3): 387–405.

Hoffman, U. (2003) 'Article 1: Specific Trade Obligations in Multilateral Environmental Agreements and their Relationship with the Rules of the Multilateral Trading System—a Developing Country Perspective', *UNCTAD Trade and Environment Review*. Available at <http://r0.unctad.org/trade_env/test1/publications/TER2003eversion/Lead1.htm>; accessed 13 July 2006.

International Institute for Sustainable Development (IISD) (2000) *Environment and Trade: A Handbook*. Available at <http://www.iisd.org/pdf/envirotrade_handbook.pdf >; accessed 1 July, 2006.

Jänicke, M., M. Binder and H. Mönch (1997) ' "Dirty Industries": Patterns of Change in Industrial Countries', *Environmental and Resource Economics*, 9(4): 467–91.

Jenkins, R., J. Barton, A. Bartzokas, J. Hesselberg, H.M. Knutsen (2002) *Environmental Regulation in the New Global Economy: the Impact on Industry and Competitiveness*, Cheltenham: Elgar.

Jha, V. and R. Vossenaar (1999) 'Breaking the Deadlock: a Positive Agenda on Trade, Environment and Development?' in G.P. Sampson and W.B. Chambers (eds), *Trade, Environment, and the Millennium*, Tokyo: United Nations University Press, 65–95.

Kahn, M. (2003) 'The Geography of U.S. Pollution Intensive Trade: Evidence from 1958 to 1994', *Regional Science and Urban Economics*, 33(4): 383–400.

Low, P. (1992) 'Trade Measures and Environmental Quality: the Implications for Mexico's Exports', in P. Low (ed.), *International Trade and the Environment*, Washington DC: World Bank, 105–20.

Low, P. and A. Yeats (1992) 'Do Dirty Industries Migrate?' in P. Low (ed.), *International Trade and the Environment*, Washington DC: World Bank, 89–103.

Mani, M. and D. Wheeler (1998), 'In Search of Pollution Havens? Dirty Industry in the World Economy, 1960–1995', *Journal of Environment and Development*, 7(3): 215–47.

Maskus, K. (2002) 'Regulatory Standards in the WTO: Comparing Intellectual Property Rights with Competition Policy, Environmental Protection, and Core Labor Standards', *World Trade Review*, 1(2): 135–52.

Medalla, E. (2001) 'Environmental Impact of Trade Policy Reforms on Pollution Intensity', *Philippine Journal of Development*, Number 52, 28(2), Second Semester, 167–203.

Mulatu, A., R.J.G.M. Florax and C. Withagen (2004) 'Environmental Regulation and International Trade: Empirical Results for Germany, the Netherlands and the US, 1977–1992', *Contributions to Economic Analysis & Policy*, 3(2): Article 5. Available at <http://www.bepress.com/bejeap/contributions/vol3/iss2/art5>; accessed 20 June 2006.

Naumann, E. (2001) 'Eco-Labelling: Overview and Implications for Developing Countries', *DPRU Policy Brief 01/P19*, October.

Oxley, A. (2002) 'The WTO Doha Development Round: the Threat to International Business of the Spread of Environmental Trade Sanctions', Australian APEC Study Centre. Available at <http://www.apec.org.au/docs/oxley2002a.pdf>; accessed 20 June 2006.

Pargal, S. and D. Wheller (1995) 'Informal Regulation of Industrial Pollution in Developing Countries: Evidence from Indonesia', *Policy Research Working Papers*. World Bank.

Ricci, F. (2004) 'Environmental Policy and Growth when Inputs are Differentiated in Pollution Intensity'. Available at < http://www.u-cergy.fr/IMG/2004-23Ricci.pdf>; accessed 20 June 2006.

Smarzynska, B. and S-J. Wei (2001) 'Pollution Havens and Foreign Direct Investment: Dirty Secret or Popular Myth?', *NBER Working Paper No. 8465*.

Sugathan, M. (2004) 'Environmental Goods and Services negotiations: Challenges and opportunities', *WTO Workshop on Environmental Goods*. Para 31 (iii) of the DDA, Geneva, 11 October.

Tobey, J. (1990) 'The Effects of Domestic Environmental Policies on Patterns of World Trade: an Empirical Test', *Kyklos*, 43(2): 191–209.

Van Beers, C. and J. van den Bergh (1997), 'An Empirical Multi-Country Analysis of the Impact of Environmental Regulations on Foreign Trade Flows', *Kyklos*, 50(1): 29–46.

Vogel, D. (1995). *Trading Up: Consumer and Environmental Regulation in a Global Economy*, Cambridge: Harvard University Press.

Waldkirch, A. and M. Gopinath (2004) 'Pollution Haven or Hythe? New Evidence from Mexico', *Oregon State University Working Paper 2004–07*. Available at <http://oregonstate.edu/dept/econ/pdf/mexpollution.pdf>; accessed 1 July, 2006.

Wilson, J., T. Otsuki and M. Sewadeh (2002), 'Dirty Exports and Environmental Regulation: Do Standards Matter to Trade?' *World Bank Policy Research Working Paper 2806*.

World Bank (WB) (2000) 'Is Globalization Causing a "Race to the Bottom" in Environmental Standards?', *World Bank Briefing Papers* Part 4. April. Available at <http://www1.worldbank.org/economicpolicy/globalization/documents/AssessingGlobalizationP4.pdf>; accessed 1 July, 2006.

World Trade Organization (WTO) (1999) *Trade and Environment. Special Studies No. 4*. Available at <http://www.wto.org/english/tratop_e/envir_e/environment.pdf>; accessed 1 July, 2006.

—— (2002) 'Committee on Trade and Environment. GATT/WTO Dispute Settlement Practice Relating to GATT Article Xx, Paragraphs (B), (D) And (G) Note By The Secretariat WT/CTE/W/203', 8 March.

Xu, X. (2000), 'International Trade and Environmental Regulation: Time Series Evidence and Cross Section Test', *Environmental and Resource Economics*, 17(3): 233–57.

Xu, X. and L. Song (2000), 'Regional Cooperation and the Environment: Do "Dirty" Industries Migrate?', *Weltwirtschaftliches Archiv*, 136(1): 137–57.

Zhang, Z.X. (2004) 'Open Trade with the United States without Compromising Canada's Ability to Comply with its Kyoto Target', *Journal of World Trade*, 38(1): 155–82.

Zhang, Z.X. and L. Assuncao (2004) 'Domestic Climate Policies and the WTO', *The World Economy*, 37(3): 359–86.

Zhang, Z.X. and A. Baranzini (2004) 'What Do we Know about Carbon Taxes? An Inquiry into their Impacts on Competitiveness and Distribution of Income', *Energy Policy*, 32: 507–18.

8 What's new about outsourcing?

Justin Yifu Lin and Ying-Yi Tsai

INTRODUCTION

The past two decades have seen a spectacular growth in outsourcing activities in the world economy. Several studies have documented this trend and provided important implications for trade (see, for example, Abraham and Taylor 1996; Campa and Goldberg 1997; Hummels, Rapoport and Yi 1998; Feenstra and Hanson 1999). Although it is not at all a new phenomenon (Domberger 1998), outsourcing has become a buzzword to characterize the world economy as one of closer integration of trade but greater disintegration of production (Feenstra 1998).

Sometimes outsourcing is used to refer to a firm's use of outside contractors to complement their production of end commodity in selected labour-intensive sectors, specifically, apparel, textiles, garments and footwear; but usually the term refers to the relocation of service functions to locations remote to the corporation's home country. More generally, it implies significant changes in the structure of the economy, with the implication, *inter alia*, that outsourcing may represent a form of trade different from traditional types. This suggests that the global scope and pattern of outsourcing activity may rest on theoretical foundations that go beyond those offered by the principle of comparative advantage, and may require the development of policy measures directed towards the alleviation of anxiety over job losses while keeping away government interventions that would interfere with efficient trade.

In contrast to most studies of outsourcing which examine wage and employment effects, we focus here on policy issues closely associated with outsourcing in the trade arena, and address the following questions: what policy implication for technology transfer does outsourcing provide; how does the nature of intellectual property protection vary with and without outsourcing; does an expedited transfer of technology to the developing countries, a flow facilitated by outsourcing, pose any threat to economic vitality in the developed economies?

Our analysis begins by exploring the meaning of 'outsourcing', and the factors that drive its development. Of principal interest is a better understanding of what exactly social scientists mean by 'outsourcing', and its implications for trade in light of the heavy volume of global intra-industry trade in intermediate goods. We argue that variations in market environments may explain the growing outsourcing trend. We then consider outsourcing experiences in the semiconductor industry, as it features not only a rapidly changing environment induced by technological innovation but also a close intra-industry partnership between major name-brand producers and contract manufacturers in the Asia-Pacific region. We also touch upon the implications for employment of outsourcing in industries facing highly volatile market demand. Our goal is to understand how growth of outsourcing impinges upon the use of labour and the progress of global technological innovation through learning-by-doing. After all, it is an important task of any theory of trade to explain the links between technological progress and growth of outsourcing, on the one hand, and between market conditions and innovations, on the other. We conclude with policy implications for technology transfer and property rights in the outsourcing partnership, as well as the implications for trade relations between developed and developing economies in the Asia-Pacific region.

LITERATURE REVIEW

The meaning of outsourcing

Outsourcing is said to arise when a firm decides to purchase intermediate inputs from an outside supplier either at home or in a foreign country, instead of keeping the production of the input within the firm's boundaries. When a firm purchases the input in the home country, it engages in domestic outsourcing, and when it purchases input from abroad, it undertakes foreign outsourcing, or arm's-length trade (Antras and Helpman 2004). Some terms have been used to refer to the remarkable increase in the way firms organize production on a global scale, others are used to characterize the disintegration of production process in the world economy. Jones and Kierzkowski (1990: 31), for instance, used 'fragmentation' to describe the changes of an integrated production system into one with separated production blocks connected by service links. Krugman (1995) used the term 'slicing the value chain' to characterize the growing disintegration of the production process. Hummels, Rapoport and Yi (1998) characterized production as a 'value chain' and use the term 'vertical specialization' to describe the specialization of a country in particular segments of the chain of production. Arndt (1997) used 'intra-product specialization' to describe the disintegration of the production process. Venables (1999) examined the consequences of falling transport costs for intermediate goods, and showed that fragmentation does not necessarily lead to increased trade volumes, or to international convergence of factor prices, and that its effects depend on the relative factor intensity of different stages of the production process. And Baily and Farrell (2004) took a business perspective in the use of 'offshoring', a term they reserved for the relocation of non-core jobs away from the corporation's home country, and explored its implications for the controversy over job losses in the United States.

One way of considering the meaning of outsourcing is to examine the context in which outsourcing occurs. Shy and Stenbacka (2003: 207) provided a good example: they offered an intra-industry analysis of differentiated oligopolists using their designs of organizational production modes as strategic instruments. In this context, they defined outsourcing to mean that a 'firm buys the input instead of carrying out the production of the input at its own facility which is endowed with an identical technology'.

Van Mieghem (1999), using the framework of a competitive stochastic investment game with recourse, defined 'outsourcing' as the special case where the contractor has no in-house production capability and is dependent on the subcontractor for the entire supply of a product. He further differentiated outsourcing from subcontracting, and defined 'subcontracting' as the situation in which the contractor 'procures an item or service that is normally capable of economic production in the contractor's own facilities and that requires the contractor to make specifications available to the subcontractor' (954, citing Day 1956).

Labour impact of outsourcing

Labour-market effects have been at the heart of the debate over rising outsourcing activities. Feenstra's observation (1998: 310) that 'the rising integration of world markets has brought with it a disintegration of the production process, in which manufacturing or services activities done abroad are combined with those performed at home' raises the possibility that market integration means job losses and depressed wages for developed countries. Drezner (2004) argued that the outsourcing issue became important in the United States 'when a [US] presidential election year [2004] coincided with an uncertain economy'. Fears about the effect of trade on jobs and wages are rampant not just in the United States but also in Europe and Japan, while protectionist sentiments are rising across a wide spectrum of countries.

Many studies have examined the enormous US trade deficit and concluded that a flood of imported goods from China and the offshoring of services to India are to blame for the loss of US jobs. Between 2000 and 2004, the US manufacturing sector lost 2.85 million jobs (US Bureau of Labor Statistics 2004), and many US journalists have argued that outsourcing is the prime culprit. Lou Dobbs, a well-known news anchor for CNN, has prominently featured the issue of outsourcing on his program, arguing that it is 'a clear call to our business and political leaders that our (the United States') trade policies simply are not working' (Dobbs 2004).

In fact, much attention has been directed toward the relations between wage inequality, job losses and outsourcing activities. For instance, Abraham and Taylor (1996) studied a firm's decision to contract out for business support services; tested a cost-saving hypothesis for outsourcing, i.e., 'contracting out may be a way for high-wage organizations to take advantage of low market wage rates for certain types of low-skill work' (396); and concluded that 'high-wage establishments cannot easily pay low wages … on their own payrolls' (417). Campa and Goldberg (1997) measured outsourcing by the imported intermediate inputs for various industries for Canada, Japan, the United Kingdom and the United States, and showed that there was a doubling of the share of imported inputs between 1975 and 1996 for all manufacturing in the United States and a large increase in foreign outsourcing in the United Kingdom. Feenstra and Hanson (1999) estimated the relative impact of trade versus technology on US wages over the period 1979–90 and found that both foreign outsourcing (of intermediate inputs) and expenditures on computers have played a role in the increase of the relative wage for non-production workers. Similarly, Feenstra (1998) measured all imported intermediate or final goods that American firms produce or sell under their brand names; compared different measures of foreign outsourcing; and showed that they have all increased since the 1970s.

Nonetheless, Baily and Lawrence (2004) argued that it is the interplay among weak market demand, rapid productivity growth, and the strength of the dollar that has been causing job losses in the United States since 2000. They demonstrated that outsourcing need not be the culprit for job losses in the United States, at least since 2001. In their study of the extent of job dislocation due to offshoring in the manufacturing and service sectors over the period 2000–2003, they showed that only about 314,000 US manufacturing jobs—11 per cent of the total decline in manufacturing jobs—were lost as a result of trade. They further showed that service sector offshoring destroyed even fewer jobs. Bernard, Jensen and Schott (2004: 2) showed that 'not all US manufacturing industries have attracted the same degree of low-wage country import competition over the past thirty years'; that 'low-wage country competition creates winners as well as losers in terms of employment growth and output'; and that 'industries consistent with US competitive advantage ... will continue to outperform. Even within industries that face high levels of low-wage competition, some firms will survive and thrive by adjusting their mix of products'.

The above findings suggest, therefore, that whether outsourcing causes job losses or not remains an issue for further investigation; and that the nature of outsourcing and the mechanism through which it affects employment and wages requires a much more thorough examination before one can judge the role it plays in particular economies.

The changing nature of trade under outsourcing

Traditional trade theory suggests that comparative advantage determines the direction of trade, or alternatively, differences in skill and resources explain international specialization. Hence, if two countries engage in trade, each country will export commodities whose factor content reflects the underlying differences in relative endowments of factors of production. The Heckscher–Ohlin model provides a theory of international trade based on factor proportions; it predicts that relative abundance of production factors determines production in each country and, thus, the pattern of trade. Ethier (1982) also emphasized net trade in factor services and suggested that economies of scale make international specialization inevitable.

Although specialization seems to be able to offer a technology-driven source of the growing trend for manufacturing or services activities done outside the firm's boundaries, economies of scale may provide an explanation of the rising offshoring activities in sectors with substantial technology intensity. Nonetheless, we argue that theories focused on how comparative advantage, specialization and scale economies can produce outsourcing essentially ignore some critical dimensions of the phenomenon, and that outsourcing provides an avenue for absorption of technological expertise from the outsourcing firm in the developed economies. This becomes more apparent when issues of competition and technological progress come into play.

Simply look at some of the success stories of economic development in Asia. Many entrepreneurs in Hong Kong learned their businesses as production workers, serving effectively as apprentices to foreign managers. The locals subsequently used this knowledge to establish their own enterprises. In Taiwan, entry into several leading-edge industries, such as electronics, semiconductors and digital television, depended upon substantial foreign outsourcing and expertise from the United States and Japan. Similarly, foreign outsourcing in China from the United States and some European countries has been important in facilitating the flow of knowledge about advanced manufacturing techniques.

These examples imply that some important aspects of outsourcing—including network effects, market structure and technological progress—still beg for more detailed analyses.[1] Indeed, Helpman and Krugman (1985) demonstrated that the issue of market structure must be carefully considered, as trade flows often seem to reflect arbitrary or temporary advantages resulting from technological progress and/or economies of scale.

Further, the cause of outsourcing and the mechanism by which it relates to speedy technological progress in the developed countries and economic growth in the less developed countries, as well as other undesirable effects, are also obviously important questions. Lin, Tsai and Wu (2004), for instance, offered an explanation of outsourcing based upon demand uncertainty. Considering how rapid technological progress is producing volatile market environment in many industries, they show that outsourcing can be Pareto-improving. In the presence of future demand uncertainty, the possibility of using outside resources implies that a firm can more effectively allocate its resources by exploiting the flexibility that emerges from outsourcing. Therefore, uncertainty can play an important role in a firm's outsourcing decision, in addition to concerns over transaction costs (Coase 1937; McAfee and McMillan 1988), scale economies (Cachon and Harker 2002) and specialization (Pisano, 1990).

A NEW DIMENSION OF OUTSOURCING

In contrast to the landscape characterized by outsourcing production of the Barbie Doll, a star product of Mattel Inc., and Nike sportswear,[2] other industries present very different pictures, that is, the line of demarcation between what can be done in-house and what should be outsourced is becoming less clear.

Consider production of the pacemaker, an implant widely used to stabilize heartbeats (Deutsch 2004). Engineers at Medtronic, which is located in Minneapolis, Minnesota, designed the original monitor for CareLink, a home-use wireless gadget that can receive data transmitted from the pacemaker. For its next model, the work of designing a new monitor will be contracted to other companies at home rather than abroad. Similar examples of design outsourcing abound. Honeywell contracts with IBM for the design of many of the core processors used in its fighter jet. Boeing Commercial Aircraft also contracted out the design of the wing structure and fuselage on the Boeing 7E7. General Motors Shanghai has contracted out the design of the interior of a high-end car sold in China to Visteon, an automotive supplier based in Michigan and listed in the NYSE offering integrated systems in chassis, driveline, electronics, audio, exteriors and interiors.

Are the outsourcing activities by Medtronic and General Motors (GM) different in any sense from those by Mattel and Nike? We argue that interactions between innovation, market demand and technological progress can, in many instances, provide insights into understanding outsourcing in different industries. Indeed, while Mattel and Nike both use a large number of subcontractors abroad and generate a significant share of merchandise value-added in the home country, the contracting out of design works allows Medtronic and GM to push forward rapidly new varieties of their products in response to fast-changing market environments. In their development of new products, brand-name producers such as Medtronic and GM can take advantage of the outside opportunities by outsourcing to specialists and leveraging on the other firms' technologies. As a result, the brand-name producers can use their in-house resources fully, avoid the time-consuming product development process and even reduce some costly fixed investment (Lin, Tsai and Wu 2005).

To put the changing nature of trade with outsourcing in perspective, we use the semiconductors industry as an example. There are several reasons for choosing this industry as an example of the importance of scale economies, rapid innovation and demand uncertainty to explain outsourcing. First, it is a rapidly expanding industry whose products permeate the production structures of electronics systems, which, in turn, influence virtually every activity in the manufacturing and service sectors. Figure 8.1 shows the steady growth of semiconductor (SC) content in the electronics market since 1990.

Second, in the semiconductors industry, economies of scale prevail in each individual production segment at the firm level, while overall growth in product quality is subject to Moore's Law.[3] This implies that fluctuations in national income could strongly influence growth in the semiconductors industry. Figure 8.2 displays revenue growth of the semiconductors industry relative to the global GDP, and clearly shows a positive correlation with fluctuations in global GDP.

Figure 8.1   Growth of semiconductor (SC) content in the electronics system

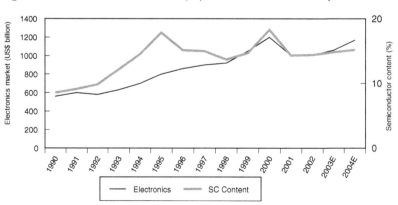

Sources: Morgan Stanley Research, World Semiconductor Trade Statistics (WSTS), and Dataquest.

Figure 8.2   Cycle of the semiconductor industry

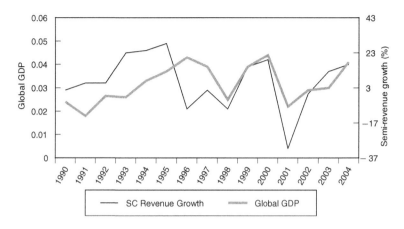

Sources: Morgan Stanley Research, World Semiconductor Trade Statistics (WSTS).

Third, vertical disintegration in the semiconductors industry has been distinct and quite dramatic, especially over the past 20 years. The increasing specialization of the world's largest electronics producers such as IBM, the growth of fabless companies and the emergence of foundry businesses in Asia provide evidence for this phenomenon.[4]

Fourth, according to surveys conducted by the Fabless Semiconductor Association (FSA), intra-industry outsourcing generated 15 per cent of the industry's revenue in 2002, and this figure is expected to rise further to 34 per cent in 2010 (Edelstone, 2003). The FSA survey also reported that nearly 84 per cent of global fabless companies use four Asian foundries specializing in the processing and manufacturing of silicon wafers.[5] With these four foundry partners in the vertical-related production alliances, fabless companies focus on the design, development and marketing of their products. Global revenues for fabless company revenue have grown steadily on an average of 40 per cent since 2003, totalling $8.3 billion.

Overall, rapid technological innovation and close intra-industry linkages have driven the growth of the semiconductors industry. The production of chips requires several competencies in each individual segment in the value chain, including circuit design, verification, wafer processing, assembly, testing and product distribution. This implies, therefore, that chip production depends essentially upon large fixed investments, innovation, and the ability to acquire technology.

Figure 8.3 illustrates the production segments for a functioning chip. In the front-end segments of chip design and wafer processing, huge investments in R&D for both product and process innovation are essential for successful new invention, and in the back-end segments of assembly and testing, fixed-asset investment is important for product delivery. Thus, differences in technological specialization, capability of engaging in costly fixed investment and the market volatility can drive decisions on global production locations for different fragments of the production process.

Figure 8.3 IDM *vs.* fabless business model

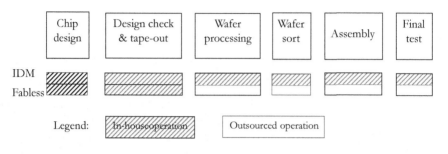

Source: International Technology Roadmap for Semiconductor (ITRS, 2002).

As technology progresses and the level of manufacturing complexity rises, companies typically need to invest a significant amount of capital expenditure to attain and retain those manufacturing capabilities. The extreme capital intensity and the cyclical nature of the industry have made such high levels of continued investment unsustainable for most companies, especially during economic downturns. Consequently, firms in the semiconductors industry begin partially to outsource manufacturing steps. This is evident from the division of chip design and manufacturing competencies into separate businesses, with many fabless companies providing their designs to the specialized, manufacturing-oriented foundries. With this change, the focus for chip-design companies shifted more towards product marketing, increasing the ability of these companies to leverage the value chain for the end user. The function of research and development (R&D) split into two domains: the manufacturing R&D, which the foundries assumed, and the product development R&D, which the fabless companies assumed.

The aforementioned development gives rise to three business models: the integrated device manufacturer (IDM) mode, the fabless model and the hybrid model with which companies in the semiconductors industry are characterized.[6] Essentially, the IDMs internalize the entire chip production supply chain, while fabless companies retain in-house chip design and outsource other functions. The third model (not shown in Figure 8.3), the hybrid model, allows a company to use selectively wafer foundry services from other IDMs or foundries or both.

Given the different business models, it is evident that the development of specialized foundry businesses has been a major success story for some Asian economies. For instance, foundries in Taiwan offer an attractive processing cost option by providing basic wafer-processing services with customized process modules to accommodate distinctive processing requirements of different customers. This is because they are able to aggregate demand from multiple customers, to achieve economies of scale needed to operate a multibillion-dollar wafer fab optimally and dampen the rising costs of capital. Indeed, foundries invest heavily in the wafer fabrication facility, market available capacity to the IDMs, and pursue more product varieties to amortize their fixed-development costs. Moreover, foundries must also invest in process innovation in addition to capital investment. As a result, the ability to benefit from the increased scale and focus derived from a captive and well-funded customer base has enabled the foundries to support concentrated investments in process R&D and to narrow or even exceed the technology lead that most IDMs previously maintained. Alternatively, the level of manufacturing complexity demands that foundries keep up with frontier technology in order to secure contracts from the fabless and/or the IDMs. The IDMs, on the other hand, by contracting with the foundries, can take advantage of excess capacity that the foundry may have in the high season, while internalizing legacy processes in-house. The IDMs also use foundries for advanced process development, and transfer the process back to their fabs as needed, so that at the high season, the IDMs can be 'fab-lite' while retaining their vertically integrated structure.

Figure 8.4 illustrates the worldwide semiconductor capital expenditure by geographical location. It shows that the Asian semiconductor companies engaging in the back-end activities of wafer fabrication, chip test and assembly have made major investments in production facilities.

Figure 8.4   Worldwide semiconductor capital spending by region

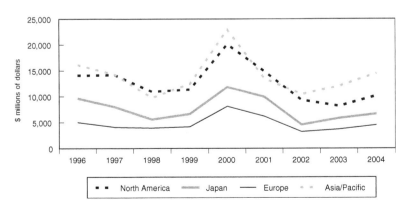

Source: Gartner Dataquest, Inc. <www.gartnerdataquest.com>.

POLICY IMPLICATIONS

While most early works have focused on the link between outsourcing and labour costs (e.g. Feenstra and Hanson 1996; Feenstra 1998), three important messages emerge from the development of outsourcing activities in the technology sector. First, variations in market demand associated with technological innovation play a crucial role in determining the direction of vertical specialization. Second, the interaction of technology progress and market size with increasing returns helps to shape intra-industry trade within the broader context of globalization. And third, outsourcing opens up an avenue for technology accumulation, which facilitates technological progress and market competition.

Technological progress, market volatility and employment

Many studies have attempted to explain the observed contracting behaviour based upon volatile output demand, wage and benefit cost savings, and the availability of outside contractors' specialized skills (Abraham and Taylor 1996); rapid technological changes, increased risk and the search for flexibility (Deavers 1997) and demand uncertainty (Van Mieghem 1999; Lin, Tsai and Wu 2005). Although outsourcing can arise due to many other causes (e.g., Gonzalez-Diaz, Arrunada and Fernandez 2000), the rapid technological progress underlying volatile market environments has, indeed, facilitated the choice of outsourcing across industries: firms can improve upon production efficiency by contracting out some production processes to specialized suppliers and focusing on fewer activities.

Although job losses have been regarded as an immediate impact on the outsourcing firm's home country, industry-specific characteristics ought to be examined before economists draw conclusions on whether outsourcing leads to job losses. The basic idea is that labour—a variable input—serves as the only device that can be implemented in response to a changing market once a firm's fixed-asset investment is conducted. The use of labour depends crucially upon its marginal revenue product, which varies across industries. Thus, industry-specific characteristics should be taken into account while evaluating the employment impacts of outsourcing (Lin, Tsai and Wu 2004; Tsai and Wu 2005). Therefore, we should not assess the proximate cause of the increased outsourcing activities without taking into account the effects of technological progress, market volatility and industry-specific characteristics.

Outsourcing, demand uncertainty and fixed-asset investment

The decision of firms to source production outside their boundaries will most certainly have an impact on in-house fixed-asset investment, and is expected to have different effects on the allocation of resources for research activities, particularly in the presence of uncertainty (Abel *et al.* 1996; Caballero 1991; Dixit and Pindyck 1994; Pindyck 1988, 1993). In a volatile market environment with rapid technological progress, a firm must decide whether to invest now or postpone the decision until later. This decision has the same structure as a financial call option (McDonald and Siegel 1986; Van Mieghem 1999). Waiting allows additional information about market demand to be gathered at the cost of losing the discounted payoff during the waiting period. Outsourcing provides an opportunity to balance a trade-off between a capacity shortage, when demand unexpectedly surges, and excess capacity otherwise. Consider a brand-producing firm facing uncertain market demand with irreversible and non-easily expandable capital investment: outsourcing can represent a trade-off between costly and irreversible fixed investment associated with a lower marginal cost of in-house production and the flexibility of avoiding such a fixed investment at the cost of paying the supplier a premium relative to the in-house marginal cost. Thus, should the firm be able to adjust, amid a volatile market environment, its use of labour *ex post* its capital investment, the demand for labour will fall when its contribution to overall firm profit is low; and name-brand producers will outsource more when the level of demand uncertainty increases. In fact, Van Meighem (1999) studied the capacity investment problems of the manufacturer and subcontractor. He showed (955) that 'optimal manufacturer and supplier capacity levels are imperfectly substituted with respect to capacity costs and contribution margins', and that 'manufacturers will indeed subcontract more when the level of market uncertainty increases and when markets are more negatively correlated'.[7]

Outsourcing, technology diffusion and intellectual property protection

Since the 1990s, there has been a wave of massive 'manufacture outsourcing' from such major brand-name producers as Hewlett-Packard, Motorola, and IBM. The ability of these corporations constantly to provide new products has depended on an extensive system of outsourcing to the newly industrialized economies, namely South Korea, Taiwan, Hong Kong and Singapore. Compatibility of technology expertise between the supplier and the purchaser certainly plays an important role in defining the buyer–supplier relationship. Nevertheless, the diffusion of technology through outsourcing contracts and its implications for intellectual property protection cannot be neglected while studying the buyer–supplier relationship in a broader context of production networks. Indeed, leading firms invest significant resources to develop technology libraries for use either in numerous products or in fewer and sometimes single products (Dell and Fredman, 1999). Although the costs of product development could be amortized over product varieties, the decision to invest scarce resources for library development exposes the research firm to high risk, not only in terms of prospects for marketability but also in competition threat through spill-overs.

Furthermore, contracting out more work necessitates relying on suppliers to do some of the design work, as the expertise that comes from learning-by-doing moves from the brand-name buyer to the supplier. Increasing the amount of outsourcing work means relying on subcontractors to discover cost-reducing and quality-improving innovations, activities that formerly were controlled within the buyer's own firm. The purchasing firm can give the subcontractor incentives to innovate by promising to favour it over other potential suppliers when the contract is renewed, so that the incumbent supplier knows that it mostly likely will benefit from its own improvement over a longer period than just the term of the current contract (Laffont and Tirole 1988).

Much attention in the theoretical literature of industrial organization has been devoted to the trade-off between incentives and risk sharing (Holmstrom and Milgrom 1987). The supplier must be given incentives to hold down production costs. The contract that does this best specifies a fixed price, but a fixed-price contract pushes all risk associated with unforeseeable and unpreventable cost fluctuations onto the supplier. Under such circumstances, the fixed-price contract is not in the supplier's interest, despite providing full incentives to perform. It is, therefore, not surprising that, once having acquired technological expertise through learning-by-doing, the supplier can pose a competitive threat to the purchaser. This is particularly the case in an open economy with extensive outsourcing. Subcontractors operating in low-cost countries will gain the capability to compete via their accumulation of product-specific information. When this expertise is combined with their country's low wages, they can often capture market share and quasi-rents by underpricing rivals in more technologically advanced countries. Moreover, the governments of nations with little indigenous R&D activity have incentives to be lax in their enforcement of intellectual property protection in this type of contracting environment. Hence, outsourcing has played a major role in the transfer of technology to newly industrializing countries, and intra-industry trade with certain types of partners may increase an innovating country's exposure to the risk of outsourcing.

According to a 2002 market survey by Dataquest, the worldwide intellectual property market grew 10 per cent in 2002, while the semiconductor market grew only 1 per cent. The top 20 companies accounted for about 84 per cent of all intellectual property revenues in the industry, suggesting that the industry is highly fragmented (Tully, Hirst and Heidarson 2003). Indeed, this is evident from the semiconductor experiences of high concentration in a few Asian foundries of wafer fabrication for global IDMs and fabless companies, and substantial growth of the fabless semiconductor companies as a result of intellectual property outsourcing from at least 1995 (Fabless Semiconductor Association 2005).

OUTSOURCING AND ITS IMPLICATIONS FOR ASIA-PACIFIC ECONOMIES

Over the past two decades, outsourcing has been progressively more dispersed in international production networks across countries, with emerging economies in the Asia-Pacific region spectacularly increasing their shares in world exports and, at the same time, experiencing industrial upgrading from labour-intensive activities to the manufacture of such capital-intensive goods as electronic and telecommunication parts and components. In the wake of the worldwide production fragmentation emerging from massive international outsourcing, there are stronger production networks between the purchasing firms (or multinational corporations)—mainly based in the United States, Japan, and in some European countries—and their suppliers in East Asia, as Hong Kong, Singapore, South Korea and Taiwan are deepening their division of labour with other emerging Asian Pacific economies.

Without doubt, economies in the Asia-Pacific region have been deeply involved in outsourcing since at least the 1980s, when many leading manufacturers established assembly operations in the region, lured by government investment incentives and the availability of skilled, low-cost labour.[8] The Asia-Pacific region later became the most important worldwide production base for telecommunications equipment, electronics and semiconductors by successfully upgrading its capabilities from the manufacturing activities in labour- to capital- and even technology-intensive products, i.e., from mere assembly of imported inputs to a more value-added form of exporting known as original equipment manufacturing (OEM). In fact, in the late 1980s and early 1990s, leading firms in the technology sector began to outsource their circuit board and product-level assembly to smaller firms in Asia, with Hong Kong, Singapore and Taiwan being notable early centres.[9] This trend suggests that economies in the Asia-Pacific region have long been an important manufacturing location for the most standardized and price sensitive electronics products. Nevertheless, most new capacity in Asia is now being established in China, where capital was relatively scarce, at least, in the 1980s and the supply of skilled labour was also fairly limited.

What implications for the further development of Asia-Pacific economies can we possibly draw from the changing pattern of trade as well as the geographical location of centres for outsourcing activities? First, competitive advantage should play a key factor while defining the paths of development. In a strong system of global production networks, the increasing trade between the US and the Asia-Pacific economies, and even that within the Asia-Pacific region, had enabled the centre of gravity for the production of labour-intensive goods to be moved away from the first-tier newly industrialized economies such as South Korea and Taiwan to Indonesia, Malaysia, the Philippines, Thailand and even China. This implies that the growing importance of trade in parts over trade in final (or end) products, at least in the manufacturing sector, had constituted *prima facie* evidence of a growing interdependence of countries through outsourcing. Second, more infrastructure and policy incentives ought to be provided if the Asia-Pacific economies are to sustain the continuing progress of technology and industrial upgrading. The economic success in countries such as Singapore, South Korea, Taiwan and China demonstrates that these Asia-Pacific economies had not only exploited the country differences within the region but also effectively used the opportunity to learn, via outsourcing, the imported technology and upgrade their home industrial capabilities. Third, stronger government support in raising the quality of the work force towards technology- or skill-intensive activities should be encouraged, as the global production practices move towards more outsourcing. In fact, as these economies develop, the Asia-Pacific countries shift from labour-intensive manufacturing to higher-value areas, notably marketing, product design, and the manufacture of sophisticated intermediate goods. Taiwan's textile and apparel industry, for example, has moved most garment production to China and other lower-cost locations, but at the same time major exports of Taiwan have become electronic products. Similarly, the emergence of China as a source country of telecommunications parts also suggests that the country is taking over from Singapore, South Korea and Taiwan the role of producer of labour-intensive products. These facts suggest that the investments in human capital for a trained, skilled labour force actually help these Asia-Pacific economies not only in building up the production capacities but also in securing a strategic position within the global production networks.

NOTES

An earlier version of this paper was presented at the Pacific Asia Free Trade and Development 30th Conference held on 19–21 February 2005, at the East-West Center, Honolulu, Hawaii.

1 We acknowledge the contribution of important works on these topics, including explanations for outsourcing (Abraham and Taylor 1996; Deavers 1997); the firm's decision of what to outsource and when to outsource (Grossman and Helpman 2003); and trade structure and the role of multinational companies (Antras 2003; Antras and Helpman 2004).
2 See Feenstra (1998).
3 Gordon Moore, co-founder of Intel, predicted that there would be a doubling in the number of transistors manufactured on a single piece of silicon every two years. Moore's Law essentially implies that rapid technological progress in the semiconductor industry brings about increased chip functionality at lower costs.
4 Venables (1999) studies implications for trade of the changing production structure in the electronics industry.
5 See <http://www.fsa.org/resources/fablessfacts/profile.asp>; accessed 10 May 2006.
6 Scherer and Ross (2000: 531) used the term 'tapered integration' to characterize the hybrid business model. Kerschbamer *et al.* (2002) investigate a firm's investment choices under different scenarios of full integration (equivalent to the IDM business model), non-integration (the fabless model) and tapered integration (the hybrid model).
7 Van Mieghem (1999) differentiated subcontracting from outsourcing. Essentially, subcontracting involves in-house production capability (including facilities) while outsourcing does not.
8 See Yeats (1998), who elaborated on this point across many industries ranging from electrical machinery, machine tools, chemicals, and synthetic fibres to aircraft and auto parts.
9 See Sturgeon (2003).

REFERENCES

Abel, A.B., A.K. Dixit, J.C. Eberly and R.S. Pindyck (1996) 'Options, the Value of Capital, and Investment', *Quarterly Journal of Economics*, 111(3): 753–77.

Abraham, K.G. and S.K. Taylor (1996) 'Firms' Use of Outside Contractors: Theory and Evidence', *Journal of Labor Economics*, 14: 394–424.

Antras, P. (2003) 'Firms, Contracts, and Trade Structure', *Quarterly Journal of Economics*, 118: 1375–418.

Antras, P. and E. Helpman (2004) 'Global Sourcing', *Journal of Political Economy*, 112: 552–80.

Arndt, S.W. (1997) 'Globalization and the Open Economy', *North American Journal of Economics & Finance*, 8(1): 71–9.

Baily, M.N. and D. Farrell (2004) 'Exploding the Myths of Offshoring', *The McKinsey Quarterly*, Web Exclusive, July, available at <http://www.mckinseyquarterly.com/article_print.aspx?L2=2&L3=38ar=1453>; accessed 10 May 2006.

Baily, M.N. and R. Lawrence (2004) 'What Happened to the Great US Job Machine? The Role of Trade and Offshoring', *Brookings Paper on Economic Activity*, 2: 211–48.

Bernard, A.B., J.B. Jensen and P.K. Schott (2004) 'Facing the Dragon: Prospects for US Manufacturers in the Coming Decade', Tuck School of Business: Dartmouth University, available at <http://mba.tuck.dartmouth.edu/pages/faculty/andrew.bernard/facingthedragon.htm>; accessed 1 August 2006.

Caballero, R. (1991) 'On the Sign of the Investment–Uncertainty Relationship', *American Economic Review*, 81(1): 279–88.

Cachon, G.P. and P.T. Harker (2002) 'Competition and Outsourcing with Scale Economies', *Management Science*, 48: 1314–33.

Campa, J. and L. Goldberg (1997) 'The Evolving External Orientation of Manufacturing Industries: Evidence from Four Countries', *Federal Reserve Bank of New York Economic Policy Review*, 4: 79–99.

Coase, R.H. (1937) 'The Nature of the Firm', *Economica*, 4: 386–405.

Day, J.S. (1956) *Subcontracting Policy in the Airframe Industry*, Boston: Harvard University.

Deavers, K.L. (1997) 'Outsourcing: a Corporate Competitiveness Strategy, not a Search for Low Wages', *Journal of Labor Research*, 18: 503–19.

Dell, M. and C. Fredman (1999) *Direct from Dell: Strategies that Revolutionized an Industry*, New York: Harper Business.

Deutsch, C.H. (2004) 'Companies, Focusing on Brands, are Outsourcing some Design Work', *New York Times* (30 December): Section C, Page 1, Column 2.

Dixit, A.K. and R.S. Pindyck (1994) *Investment under Uncertainty*, Princeton: Princeton University Press.

Dobbs, L. (2004) 'A Home Advantage for US Corporations', CNN: 27 August.

Domberger, S. (1998) *The Contracting Organization: A Strategic Guide to Outsourcing*, New York: Oxford University Press.

Drezner, D.W. (2004) 'The Outsourcing Bogeyman', *Foreign Affairs*, 83(3): 22–34.

Edelstone, M. (2003) 'Morgan Stanley Research Report: Semiconductors', available at <http://www.morganstanley.com>.

Ethier, W.J. (1982) 'National and Iinternational Returns to Scale in the Modern Theory of International Trade', *American Economic Review*, 72(3): 389–405.

Fabless Semiconductor Association (FSA) (2005) 'Publications—Outsourcing Trends', available at <http://www.fsa.org/publications/outsourcingtrends/index.asp>; accessed 10 May 2006.

Feenstra, R.C. (1998) 'Integration of Trade and Disintegration of Production in the Global Economy', *Journal of Economic Perspectives*, 12: 31–50.

Feenstra, R.C. and G.H. Hanson (1996) 'Globalization, Outsourcing, and Wage Inequality', *American Economic Review Papers and Proceedings*, 86: 240–5.

—— (1999) 'The Impact of Outsourcing and High-technology Capital on Wages: Estimates for the United States, 1979–1990', *Quarterly Journal of Economics*, 114(3): 907–40.

Gonzalez-Diaz, M., B. Arrunada and A. Fernandez (2000) 'Causes of Subcontracting: Evidence from Panel Data on Construction Firms', *Journal of Economic Behavior and Organization*, 42: 167–87.

Grossman, G. and E. Helpman (2003) 'Outsourcing versus FDI in Industry Equilibrium', *Journal of the European Economic Association*, 1: 317–27.

Helpman, E. and P.R. Krugman (1985) *Market Structure and Foreign Trade*, Cambridge: MIT Press.

Holmstrom, B. and P. Milgrom (1987) 'Aggregation and Linearity in the Provision of Intertemporal Incentives', *Econometrica*, 55: 303–28.

Hummels, D., D. Rapoport and K. Yi (1998) 'Vertical Specialization and the Changing Nature of World Trade', *Federal Reserve Bank of New York Economic Policy Review*, June: 79–99.

International Technology Roadmap for Semiconductors (ITRS) (2002), available at <http://public.itrs.net/Files/2002Update/2002Update.htm>; accessed 10 May 2006.

Jones, R.W. and H. Kierzkowski (1990) 'The Role of Services in Production and International Trade: a Theoretical Framework,' in R.W. Jones and A.O. Krueger (eds), *The Political Economy of International Trade: Essays in Honor of Robert E. Baldwin*, Oxford: Basil Blackwell, 31–48.

Kerschbamer, R., N. Maderner and Y. Tournas (2002) 'Idiosyncratic Investments, Outside Opportunities and the Boundaries of the Firm', *International Journal of Industrial Organization*, 20: 1119–41.

Krugman, P. (1995) 'Growing World Trade: Causes and Consequences', *Brookings Paper on Economic Activity*, 1: 327–77.

Laffont, J-J., and J. Tirole (1988) 'Repeated Auctions of Incentive Contracts, Investment, and Bidding Parity, with an Application to Takeovers', *Rand Journal of Economics*, 19: 516–37.

Lin, J.Y., Y. Tsai and C-T. Wu (2004) 'Optimal Capital Investment, Uncertainty and Outsourcing', *China Economic Quarterly*, 4: 119–38.

—— (2005) *Choice of Semiconductor Network Structure under Demand Uncertainty*, National University of Kaohsiung, mimeo.

McAfee, P. and J. McMillan (1988) 'Search Mechanisms', *Journal of Economic Theory*, 44: 99–123.

McDonald, R.L. and D.R. Siegel (1986) 'The Value of Waiting to Invest', *Quarterly Journal of Economics*, 101: 707–28.

Pindyck, R.S. (1988) 'Irreversible Investment, Capacity Choice, and the Value of the Firm', *American Economic Review*, 78(5): 969–85.

—— (1993) 'A Note on Competitive Investment under Uncertainty', *American Economic Review*, 83(1): 273–77.

Pisano, G.P. (1990) 'The R&D Boundaries of the Firm: an Empirical Analysis', *Administrative Science Quarterly*, 35: 153–76.

Scherer, F.M. and D. Ross (2000) *Industrial Market Structure and Economic Performance*, 3rd edn, Chicago: Rand McNally.

Shy, O. and R. Stenbacka (2003) 'Strategic Outsourcing', *Journal of Economic Behavior and Organization*, 50: 203–34.

Sturgeon, T.J. (2003) 'Exploring the Risks of Value Chain Modularity: Electronics Outsourcing during the Industry Cycle of 1992–2002', *MIT Industrial Performance Center Working Paper Series 03-003*.

Tsai, Y. and C. Wu (2005) 'Demand Uncertainty and the Choices of Business Model in the Semiconductor Industry', *Seoul Journal of Economics*, 18(4): 303–24.

Tully, J., C. Hirst and C. Heidarson (2003) 'Semiconductor Intellectual Property Market: Worldwide, 2002', Gartner Dataquest, 7 May, available from <http://www.gartner.com>; accessed 16 August 2006.

US Bureau of Labor Statistics (2004) *Employment Survey Statistics*, July.

Van Mieghem, J. (1999) 'Coordinating Investment, Production and Subcontracting', *Management Science*, 45: 954–71.

Venables, A.J. (1999) 'Fragmentation and Multinational Production', *European Economic Review*, 43: 935–45.

World Semiconductor Trade Statistics (WSTS), available at <http://www.wsts.org/plain/content/view/full/1224>; accessed 10 May 2006.

Yeats, A.J. (1998) 'Just How Big is Global Production Sharing?', *Policy Research Working Paper 1871*, Washington: The World Bank.

9 Have developing countries gained from the marriage between trade agreements and intellectual property rights?

Sumner J. La Croix and Denise Eby Konan

INTRODUCTION

In 1995, the new WTO Agreement included an extensive set of rules governing Trade-Related Intellectual Property Rights (TRIPs). TRIPs established minimum standards for copyright, patent, trademark, trade secrets and geographical indications; specified public and private methods to enforce these rights; and provided developing countries with additional time to meet these goals. During the ensuing ten years, governments, international institutions and individuals have increasingly questioned whether developing countries are gaining from the marriage of trade agreements and intellectual property law. This paper uses historical, theoretical and empirical methods to explore whether developing countries have gained from the incorporation of IPR standards into the WTO framework.

Our analysis begins by examining the nineteenth-century development of the emerging economic power, the United States, and the role that intellectual property rights (IPR) played in its development. We find that the United States provided strong patent protection to domestic and foreign innovators, but no copyright protection for foreign authors during much of the nineteenth century. We note that many of the IPR policies adopted by the United States in the nineteenth century are now prohibited by TRIPs rules requiring equal treatment of foreign and domestic copyright holders. We then show how changes in the structure of US industries over the course of the last 125 years have induced major changes in US IPR policy. After extensive bilateral pressure on both developed and developing countries during the 1980s and 1990s, the United States joined the European Union in pushing for the incorporation of minimum IPR standards—TRIPs—in the 1995 WTO treaty.

We also provide an overview of the major TRIPs provisions and then examine in more detail the major developments in international IPR law since TRIPs. The main developments are: (1) the United States and the European Union continue to press for the establishment of IPRs in 'new' fields of intellectual innovations, including genetically modified plants and animals, computer software, business methods, and chip designs; (2) the United States and the European Union strengthen their copyright and patent protection in a number of product categories along numerous dimensions and initiate efforts to negotiate so-called 'free trade area' (FTA) agreements with developed and developing countries that require trading partners to strengthen their IPR laws and enforcement; (3) the United States and the European Union join the World Copyright Treaty (WCT) which prohibits de-encryption devices, breaking encryptions, and distributing copyrighted products using channels not allowed by their owners; and (4) the resistance of developing countries in Asia and elsewhere to the legal innovations identified above.

We examine recent theoretical literature on global IPR harmonization to determine whether IPR patent harmonization should be expected to generate increases in global welfare. Our review focuses on the two-country model developed by Gene Grossman and Edwin Lai (2004), as this model generates a pattern of patent harmonization that is broadly consistent with the pattern established in TRIPs. Grossman and Lai found that patent harmonization should lead to an increase in the strength of patent protection in both developed and developing countries, and an increase in world welfare if developing countries are provided with compensation for the increased flow of rent transfers to developed countries that occurs under the harmonized patent system.

We also consider how the internet and digitization of copyrighted works have affected copyright piracy within and across countries. Digitization has reduced the cost of copying most copyrighted material and requires changes in copyright law if these works are to be optimally protected. The Internet has facilitated both national and international piracy of copyrighted digitized works. As knowledge-intensive services become a bigger component of GDP, copyright law is assuming a more prominent role in GDP growth. We consider whether the combination of the Internet and digitization require changes in national copyright laws and the TRIPs Agreement.

A brief conclusion finds that the creation of intellectual property in new types of inventions is necessary, but that the scope, depth, and enforcement of IPRs is likely to differ across countries according to their economic and political institutions, their per capita income, and their capability to engage in and disseminate the fruits of R&D.

ARE STRONG IPRs NECESSARY FOR DEVELOPMENT? THE CASE OF THE UNITED STATES

Are IPRs necessary for economic development? Evenson and Westphal (1995), and Maskus (2000) have correctly argued that a simple package of intellectual property rights is likely to enhance GDP growth rates even in very low-income countries. Helpman (1993), La Croix and Konan (2002) and Srinivasan (2000), among others, have argued that excessive protection can lead to a transfer of rents to developed countries, restrain consumer access to new goods and make it more costly for nascent R&D efforts to develop new products that will find a market in the home country or foreign countries.

One way to consider the question is to look to history and examine the interaction between IPRs and economic growth for the countries that industrialized during the nineteenth century—today's developed countries. Khan and Sokoloff (2001: 235) observed that the system of patent rights established in Britain had numerous features that 'reflected its origins in royal privilege'. Several officials needed to approve the patent application; high fees were charged to file a patent application; access to the patent's design was restricted until its expiration; patents could be obtained on technologies discovered by a third party outside Britain, and the patent had to be used inside Britain ('working requirements') to remain in force. Britain was not alone in allowing foreign discoveries to be patented by a British third party without the consent of the original discoverer; other countries, including France and the Netherlands, also allowed the patenting of pirated technologies. These provisions meant that domestic intellectual property laws in Europe's leading countries actually encouraged the pirating of foreign technologies during the first half of the nineteenth century.

Khan and Sokoloff (1998) found that the framers of the US Constitution and the legislators in the first sessions of the US Congress were familiar with British precedent, and consciously innovated when they considered intellectual property. The Constitution specifically provides the US Congress with the power '[t]o promote the Progress of Science and useful Arts, by securing for limited Times to Authors and Inventors the exclusive Right to their respective Writings and Discoveries'.[1] In its first session, the US Congress passed a revolutionary patent law that provided for low application fees, impersonal patent examination, grants only to the original discoverer and disclosure of the invention's specification upon issuance of the patent.[2] Kahn and Sokoloff argued that easy access to the US patent law, speedy judicial remedy of disputes over patents, and access to large, new markets led to three important results: there was a surge in the per capita patenting rate over the course of the nineteenth century, with an increase of 1,500 per cent recorded between the 1840s and the 1870s; a larger percentage of inventors was more likely to specialize in inventive activity (Lamoreaux and Sokoloff 1996, 1999); and the well-defined patent rights and specialization in inventive activity spurred the development of sophisticated technology markets in the mid-nineteenth century. Patent agents and lawyers not only facilitated the filing of patent applications, but also acted to match potential buyers and sellers of patented technologies and to match potential investors with the inventors of new technologies.

The response to the highly productive American system differed across countries. In 1852, the leading political and economic power—Great Britain—strengthened its patent laws to bring them more into accordance with American practices. Two small countries reacted very differently. The Netherlands eliminated its patent system in 1869 and did not restore it until 1912, and Switzerland radically weakened its patent law in 1850 and did not restore effective patent rights until 1907 (Schiff 1971).[3]

Numerous scholars (Griliches 1994; Mowery 1983, 1995; Lamoreaux and Sokoloff 1999) have discussed the long-term decline in patenting rates by US residents which began in the late nineteenth century and did not reverse course until the early 1980s. While some of the change may have been due to the increased prevalence of research activities within large corporations, Lamoreaux and Sokoloff (1999, 2003) also speculated that a series of federal court rulings between 1890 and 1920 reducing the scope of patent claims and establishing clearer rights in the use of other forms of contract and property law to protect inventions had the effect of reducing the expected value of a patent. This led firms to choose other, more effective instruments (trade secrets, restrictive covenants, rights to employee patents) to establish rights to their inventions. The long-term trend in patent protection in the United States is surprising:

strong patent rights during the nineteenth century, weaker patent rights from early twentieth century to the 1980s, and stronger patent rights covering a larger spectrum of inventions since the early 1980s.

At the 1883 Paris Conference on international patent rights, there was conflict between the United States, which favoured a patent system with reciprocal rights (providing incentives to countries with weaker patent systems to upgrade) and few exemptions, while Great Britain and France wanted a weaker system with national treatment (providing few incentives to countries with weaker systems to upgrade) and compulsory licensing. The final agreement was a blow to US interests, as it adopted national rather than reciprocal treatment as the required standard for patent law.

US copyright law followed a very different course. The first US copyright law (enacted in May 1790) 'secured the copies of maps, charts, and books to the authors and proprietors of such copies' after registering their copyright, depositing the copy, notifying the public, and paying a nominal fee. Judicial decisions and legislative amendments changed the copyright law substantially during the nineteenth century, with US courts weakening protection by recognizing the doctrines of fair use, first sale, and work for hire, and expanding protection by increasing copyright terms, extending copyright protection to new products such as photographs, lithographs and records, and providing protection to derivative products, such as translations and performances.

A major contrast between American and European copyright laws at the beginning of the nineteenth century was that American law did not provide protection for foreign copyright, while copyright laws in Great Britain and France did: both countries recognized foreign copyrights (subject to reciprocity and home publication) early in the nineteenth century and granted national rights to foreigners by mid-century. Their copyright stances are consistent with their respective positions as the suppliers of literary and non-fiction works to millions of French- and English-speaking residents in current and former colonies. It is unsurprising that France was the leader in this drive, as France was more likely than Great Britain to remain a net supplier of literary and non-fiction works to its numerous small colonies given the respective sizes of the home and colony markets. By contrast, government officials in Great Britain surely recognized that it would become a net importer of copyrighted material as population and income in its former colonies, particularly the United States, surpassed that of Great Britain.

Between 1820 and 1890, American and European authors regularly lobbied the US Congress to change this provision and were opposed by US publishers. An 1841 convention between Great Britain and the United States providing for recognition of foreign copyrights was not even considered by the US Senate. In 1883 the US government turned down an invitation to attend a conference in Berne organized to consider international harmonization of copyright law, and refused to sign the 1886 Berne Convention. Khan and Sokoloff (2001) assert that the growth of the American literary sector in the late nineteenth century may have increased the demand for American books in foreign countries sufficiently to induce a change in the wealth-maximizing US policy. Thus, as the US switched from being a net importer to being a net exporter of copyrighted goods, Congress responded in 1891 by amending the US copyright law to recognize foreign copyrights.[4]

The US recognition of foreign copyrights was not retroactive, i.e., work already in the public domain remained there. From the perspective of wealth maximization, this is understandable as the stock of valuable prior work was predominately that of British authors. Establishing copyright in the already existing stock of books could increase neither the quality nor quantity available to the US public—and it prevented the payment of royalties to popular British authors.

BILATERAL PRESSURE, TRIPs AND THE WORLD COPYRIGHT TREATY

The schizophrenic attitude of the US towards intellectual property rights (strong on patents, weak on copyrights) changed as the structure of the US economy changed after World War II. With the growth of the computer software industry and the rise of large export markets for US films, television programmes, video games and phonograms, the United States began to run trade surpluses in copyrighted goods even as its overall balance of trade account deteriorated. Siwek (2004) shows that the size of copyrighted industries (as a percentage of gross domestic product) and their export share has continued to expand over the last 15 years.

Intellectual property rights (IPRs) have been a contentious issue for the United States and developing countries for the last 25 years. In the early 1980s, the US Trade Representative (USTR) found that many developing countries—the ASEAN countries prominent among them—had weak intellectual property laws or failed to take adequate measures to enforce them. The USTR threatened countries with the loss of their Generalized System of Preferences (GSP) status and other trade-related benefits if they did not take action to strengthen IPR laws and increase enforcement activities. Between 1985 and 1995, numerous Asian countries, in response to US pressure and the changing structure of their own economies, strengthened their IPR laws and increased enforcement. The TRIPs provisions of the 1995 WTO Treaty represent a significant step on the road to IPR convergence by both developed and developing countries, as they committed all GATT signatories to establishing IPRs that meet specified minimum standards (see Table 9.1).

TRIPs was intended to harmonize national systems of IPRs as well as to broaden and strengthen the legal rights provided to owners of intellectual property (Zhutshi 1998). It forced many middle-income and developing countries to make extensive changes to their IPR laws in the mid-1990s and to spend additional resources on IPR enforcement activities. More surprising is that the United States and Europe also had to enact significant upgrades to their IPR laws to conform to TRIPs.[5]

There have been several significant events regarding intellectual property rights over the last decade since the creation of the TRIPs agreement. Among these are two World Intellectual Property Organization (WIPO) treaties, the Doha Declaration on the TRIPs Agreement and Public Health, significant upgrades of copyright laws in developed countries, and the negotiations on the harmonization of substantive patent law, geographical indications and the protection of traditional knowledge.

Table 9.1   Major features of the TRIPs agreement

1. GATT members must apply the principle of national treatment to all foreign IPR owners (Articles 1(3), 3).

2. All GATT members must comply with the central provisions of four conventions:
   a. Paris Convention (Article 2(1))
   b. Berne Convention (Article 9(1)) without moral rights provisions
   c. Rome Convention (Article 14)
   d. Washington Treaty (Article 35) with the modification that compulsory licenses of integrated circuit technology are prohibited.

3. GATT members cannot exclude certain classes of products from being patented (with limited exceptions specified in TRIPs); pharmaceuticals cannot be excluded from product or process patents (Article 27(1)).

4. Countries must protect patents for 20 years from date of application (Article 28).

5. Patent holders no longer have an obligation to work their patent locally if they supply the market's demand for the good with imports (Article 28).

6. Pharmaceutical products in the pipeline, i.e., which were developed earlier and are just now completing safety and efficacy procedures to come to market, must receive at least five years of protection (Articles 70(8), (9)).

7. GATT members must adopt either a patent system or a *sui generis* system for protecting plant varieties (Article 27).

8. The detailed enforcement procedures specified in the GATT must be incorporated into each member's national laws (Article 41).

9. GATT members must adopt stricter enforcement measures, including border controls, to prevent imports of counterfeit goods (Articles 51–60).

10. TRIPs eliminates compulsory licensing of trademarks as well as local linkage requirements (Articles 15–24). Marks may be assigned with or without the transfer of the business to which the trademark belongs.

11. TRIPs requires copyright protection of computer programs (Article 10(1) and data bases (10(2)). All computer programs must receive at least 50 years of protection (Article 12).

12. TRIPs requires all GATT members to protect trade secrets (Article 39).

13. GATT members must protect original industrial designs for at least 10 years (Article 26).

14. TRIPs requires that authors and their successors in title have the right to authorize or prohibit the commercial rental to the public of originals or copies of their copyright works (Article 11). The substantive effect is to allow copyright owners to charge royalties or other fees for commercial rental of their works.

15. TRIPs requires that service marks as well as trade marks be protected (Article 15).

16. Commercial data submitted for regulatory approval of pharmaceutical or agricultural chemical products shall be protected against unfair commercial use (Article 39).

The two significant WIPO treaties relating to IPR are the WIPO Copyright Treaty (WCT) and the WIPO Performances and Phonograms Treaty (WPPT). The WIPO Copyright Treaty was implemented in US law by the Digital Millennium Copyright Act (DMCA). In March 2000, the European Council approved the treaty on behalf of the European Community. While Gabon's accession in December 2001 provided the necessary 30 countries for the two treaties to enter into force as of 10 February 2006, only 58 countries had ratified the WCT treaty and 57 countries the WPPT treaty.[6]

The treaties clearly articulate the principle that copyright law applies on the Internet as in the off-line world. One stipulation of the treaty is that authors, performers, producers, etc. are able to specify how and when they would like to distribute their music. This exclusive 'making available' right covers many different types of dissemination of music, from listen-only services to those that allow the download of permanent copies. It provides the basis for record companies or licensees to develop different forms of business models, examples of which are currently reflected in ventures such as Music Net (involving BMG, EMI and Warner), Press Play (involving Sony Music and Universal), iTunes (Apple) and a number of ventures by independent record companies.

The WIPO treaties also protect the technologies that enable new uses of copyrighted material. The treaties recognize that copyright holders need to use technical measures, such as encryption, passwords, and scrambling, in order to manage the delivery of their works to consumers, as well as to protect them from piracy and unauthorized copying. Examples of technical measures include the use of copy control technologies and the use of rights management information to identify content and channel payments digitally to the appropriate copyright holders. The treaties also require governments to protect such measures from hacking and circumvention effectively, which should include outlawing the manufacture and distribution of a range of circumvention devices.[7]

Along with the WCT and WPPT treaties, WIPO also helped make great strides towards the development of a global patent system and harmonization of patent law in September 2001. Their efforts included lobbying countries to ratify the Patent Law Treaty (PLT), which harmonized procedures for patent applications; developing measures to reform the Patent Cooperation Treaty (PCT) of 1970; and beginning negotiations on a Substantive Patent Law Treaty (SPLT).[8] This 'Patent Agenda' was designed to address the failure of the patent system to adequately respond to the international nature of business activities, the high costs of obtaining patents, the workload crisis in patent offices, and time-consuming patent office procedures.[9]

Ironically, just one month later, in October 2001, the Canadian government decided to break drug manufacturer Bayer AG's patent on Cipro over concerns of a 'matter of availability' in the case of an anthrax outbreak. One week later, the US government contracted with Bayer AG for 100 million Cipro tablets for $0.95 each, far less than the $1.77 the US government had reportedly been paying prior to the Canadian decision to break the Bayer patent.[10]

The Doha Declaration on the TRIPs Agreement and Public Health, adopted in November 2001, was one of the most important international developments in the area of IPR in WTO since the adoption of the Agreement in 1994. The Doha Declaration was important to developing countries in particular, as the public health consequences have been far reaching. The Declaration has indicated that in cases of conflict between IPR and public health, the former should not be an obstacle to the realization of the latter. This was primarily political in nature, and the economic trade-off between greater patent protection (namely pharmaceuticals) and social welfare was the focus of debate. In affirming that the TRIPs Agreement 'can and should be interpreted and implemented in a manner supportive of WTO Members' right to protect public health and, in particular, to promote access to medicines for all',[11] paragraph 4 provides guidance to panels and the Appellate Body for the interpretation of the Agreement's provisions in cases involving public health issues.[12] This space for interpretation reduces the effect of bilateral pressures, and the risk of potential disputes linked to the TRIPs Agreement and the implementation of national health policies. In addition, least developed countries are not required by the treaty to enforce patent rights on pharmaceuticals until 1 January 2016, and had until 1 January 2006 to apply the basic TRIPs Agreement's provisions. This decision allows developing countries to take necessary steps towards improving health conditions in their respective territories without jeopardizing their economic development.[13]

Over the decade, some European countries have been raising the topic of geographical indications and their scope in international forums. Geographical indications are placenames used to identify the origin and quality, reputation or other characteristics of products. Under the TRIPs Agreement, protection is defined in two articles: Articles 22 and 23. Article 22 covers all products, which defines a standard level of protection. This says geographical indications must be protected in order to avoid misleading the public and to prevent unfair competition. Article 23 provides a higher or enhanced level of protection for geographical indications for wines and spirits. During the Doha round of trade negotiations, the two main concerns over geographical indications were a multilateral register for wines and spirits, and extending the higher (Article 23) level of protection beyond wines and spirits.[14] Disagreement on expansion of Article 23, however, became a thorny issue for many countries, and geographical indications talks have been linked with agricultural negotiations, which makes it even more difficult to find a compromise. Negotiations with respect to a multilateral system of notification and registration of geographical indications came to a halt in July 2006 with the indefinite suspension of the Doha WTO round.[15]

Traditional Knowledge (TK) has become increasingly important in IPR protection as well, although there are no set international standards as yet specifically protecting it. TK is defined through WIPO as any tradition-based literary, artistic or scientific work, such as performances, inventions, scientific discoveries, designs, etc.[16] The TRIPs Agreement does not specifically deal with TK in the formal sense; instead, it grants monopoly rights by way of patents to inventions, whether products or processes, in all fields of technology, only provided that they are new, involve an inventive step, and are capable of industrial application. Because of this and from a lack of other agreements, TK has been forced to go through the 'normal' means of IPR protection as discussed above, such as low-cost patents, trademarks, copyrights and geographical indications. WIPO has presented a set of criteria, however, that could be an important first step towards recognition of TK in the IPR world. It involves splitting TK into two separate categories, the first covering biodiversity and medicine, such as traditional agriculture or medical techniques, and the second covering the arts, such as music, designs and expressions.

Since the late 1990s, preferential trade areas (PTAs)—typically referred to by government bureaucrats as 'free trade areas' (FTAs)—have proliferated around the globe. While PTAs within Asia contain no or very few references to IPRs, the United States has made the inclusion of IPRs a centrepiece of its FTA agreements. The US–Morocco FTA contains the 'gold standard' package of IPR provisions that strengthens IPRs and their enforcement beyond the levels specified in the TRIPs Agreement. The package includes extensions of copyright terms; required membership in the WCT and WPPT treaties; broad provisions mandating national treatment with few exceptions; patent terms extensions for pharmaceutical products delayed by the regulatory process from being marketed; banning the export of generic pharmaceuticals to countries experiencing public health crises; mandating the use of licensed software by government agencies; banning compulsory licensing for retransmission of television signals; mandating use of the retail product price (rather than the price of a pirated copy) in calculations of damages for copyright infringement; allowing customs and criminal authorities to pursue violations without a complaint by the rights holder; and mandating copyright damages to be sufficiently high to deter potential violators. Most of these provisions are included in the US FTAs negotiated since 2000 with Bahrain, Jordan, Morocco, Singapore, Chile, and the countries in the Central America–Dominican Republic FTA (El Salvador, Nicaragua, Costa Rica, Guatemala and Honduras). It is noteworthy that national treatment requires these countries to extend the higher IPR protection granted to the United States to all other countries.

The IPR provisions in the US FTAs are, in some respects, not particularly important, as they affect only a small part of US and APEC trade. They do, however, signal the price that potential APEC partners in an FTA with the United States, e.g. Thailand, Indonesia and Malaysia, would have to pay to finalize an FTA agreement. While some of the provisions—banning compulsory licenses for the rebroadcast of television signals—are likely to be efficient, others—banning exports of generics to countries experiencing public health crises—are more problematic and seem to be in conflict with the Doha Declaration on the TRIPs Agreement and the Public Health (discussed above).

DOES PATENT HARMONIZATION INCREASE GLOBAL WELFARE?

The economics literature is divided concerning the welfare implications of minimum IPR standards and IPR harmonization.[17] Evenson and Westphal (1995) and Taylor (1994) concluded that a well functioning IPR law is a critical component of the institutional package required for economic development. Helpman (1993) used a dynamic two-country (North–South) model to show that stronger IPRs can reduce welfare in the South and reduce global R&D.[18] Grossman and Lai (2004) developed a two-country (North–South) model that yields results similar to those generated by the 1995 TRIPs Agreement. This model is examined in more detail below.

Grossman and Lai's theoretical results

Several authors (McCalman 2002; Grossman and Lai 2004) have investigated the choice of IPR standards by developing and developed countries in the absence of global cooperation on IPR but in the presence of global information, capital, and product flows. Grossman and Lai (2004: 1635–36) observed that '[i]t is not obvious how a government ought to set its IPR policy if some of the benefits of its national innovation accrue to foreigners, if its constituents benefit from innovations that are encouraged and take place beyond its borders, and if domestic and foreign firms differ in their ability to innovate'. They considered a world economy with two countries (North–South) that differ with respect to market size and ability to innovate. Each country has two sectors, one producing a homogeneous good and a second producing a continuum of differentiated products. Designs for the differentiated products emerge from R&D conducted by individual firms; the designs can be imitated by other firms if the designs are not patent-protected. The optimal patent system is derived for each of the two countries for three cases: (1) each country is an autarchy; (2) the two countries trade and independently determine their patent systems; and (3) the two countries trade and agree to use the globally efficient patent system.

In the first case (autarchy), Grossman and Lai (2004: 1637–41) found results broadly similar to those of Nordhaus (1969): optimal patent protection increases as the useful life of the product increases and as the productivity of R&D expenditures increases; and falls as consumer discount rates increase. Market size has indeterminate effects on the strength of patent protection. In their base case, in which R&D is produced using a Cobb–Douglass production function, optimal patent protection is positively related to market size.

In the second case (trade in differentiated goods, national treatment, and no parallel imports), the North adopts stronger patent protection than the South due to its higher human capital endowment and the higher productivity of labour in the North than the South; patent protection is, however, lower in both the North and the South than in the closed economy case.[19]

In the third case (globally efficient patent protection which, by definition, maximizes the sum of North and South welfare), Grossman and Lai (2004: 1647–50) showed that the welfare of the North increases as Southern patent protection increases, while the welfare of the South increases as Northern patent protection weakens. They showed that there is a range of joint patent policies that maximize world welfare but which have vastly different effects on the welfare of each country. Many (but not all) of the welfare-maximizing patent combinations require that the North pay a lump-sum to the South if Southern welfare is to be higher than in the second case discussed above.

Finally, efficient patent harmonization (identical patent policies which maximize the sum of North and South welfare) produces an increase in patent protection in both countries as well as a gain in welfare in the North. The South requires a lump-sum payment from the North to offset the negative effects on Southern welfare generated by the increased flow of royalty payments to the North (Grossman and Lai 2004: 1649–50).

The 1994 WTO Agreement: Trading IPRs for textile markets?

Grossman and Lai's theoretical results concerning the implications of IPR harmonization and strengthening parallels the conventional wisdom on the political economy of the TRIPs Agreement: TRIPs imposed losses on developing countries due to the premature strengthening of their IPRs but those countries were more than compensated for their losses by the provisions in the WTO Agreement providing for the dismantling of the Multi-Fiber Arrangement (MFA) beginning in 2005 (Harrison, Tarr and Rutherford 1997). Table 9.2 provides data on net licensing and royalty payments to selected developed and developing countries. After the implementation of the TRIPs agreement in 1995, the payments data indicate that net payments by developing countries in APEC increased, while the developed countries realized increases in net receipts. Could the dismantling of the MFA provide the lump-sum compensation necessary for developing countries to gain from the TRIPs Agreement?

Prior to the Uruguay Round, textile and clothing trade was governed by the MFA outside of normal GATT rules and standards. Agreed upon as an exception to the GATT of 1974, the MFA established a system of bilateral negotiations that established quotas on imports to four economies (United States, European Economic Community, Canada and Norway) of textiles and apparel made from cotton, wool and synthetic fibre. Quotas were, however, not allocated on the basis of cost efficiency but rather in

Table 9.2 Estimates of net royalty and licence transfers in selected EU and APEC countries (in US$ millions)

Country	1992	1995	2000	2003
United States	15,680	23,370	26,760	28,180
France	–490	–470	270	1,500
Germany	–2,430	–2,790	–2,760	–980
United Kingdom	610	880	1,510	2,520
Canada	NA	–1,511	–1,510	–2,265
Japan	–4,140	–3,410	–780	1,270
China	NA	NA	–1,281	–3,548
Thailand	–271	–629	–701	–1,261
Singapore	NA	–1,645	–3,525	–3,137
Malaysia	NA	NA	–528	–762
Australia	–685.4	–713	–660	–874
Mexico	–387	–370	–364	–524
Chile	–39	–48	–288	–221

Source: IMF Balance of Payments (2004).

response to political pressure and to suppress import surges. Thus the MFA was a significant and longstanding departure from GATT principles of non-discrimination.

Over the past 40 years of the quota system, textiles and apparel were increasingly produced with labour-intensive technologies in developing countries, yet significant production continued in capital-intensive developed countries. Thus the MFA became the quintessential example of how developing countries were not adequately represented by the GATT. The Uruguay Round negotiations included proposals from India, Indonesia, Bangladesh, and the International Textiles and Clothing Bureau, all calling for an end to the MFA. Thus, a major accomplishment of the 1994 Uruguay Round for developing countries was the elimination of the MFA and the phasing out of all textile and clothing quotas by 1 January 2005.

In the interim, the MFA was replaced by the Agreement on Textiles and Clothing (ATC) in which developed countries have agreed to phase out textile and clothing quotas according to the following schedule:

* 16 per cent of products imported in 1990 integrated on 1 January 1995
* 17 per cent of products imported in 1990 integrated on 1 January 1998
* 18 per cent of products imported in 1990 integrated on 1 January 2002
* 49 per cent of products imported in 1990 integrated on 31 December 2004

The WTO's Textile Monitoring Body (TMB) found that textile and apparel importers had lagged behind on their obligations, with the amount of restrained trade left to be integrated by the EU and the US by 31 December 2004 at 80 and 68 per cent respectively. The ATC also provided a special safeguard mechanism that triggers when an overall increase in covered product imports is found to be causing serious damage to the home country's textile or apparel industry.[20]

Neither the WTO negotiators, who ostensibly added the MFA phase-out and the TRIPs phase-in to the 1994 WTO deal to complete the negotiations, nor the economists who subsequently analysed the deal (e.g., Harrison, Tarr and Rutherford 1997), nor the representatives from developing countries with MFA quotas gave much thought as to how the MFA phase-out would affect the developing countries. The simple analysis—that quotas restrain a country's trade—was applied to rationalize the argument that individual developing countries would gain from the removal of quotas. Unfortunately, the economists analysing this issue all failed to address three important factors: (1) the sustained productivity improvements and higher growth in India's economy generated after its landmark 1991 reforms; (2) China's admission to the WTO and its strong economic growth over the 1995–2005 period; and (3) the assignment of textile-apparel quotas to developing countries who were not the least-cost producers in 1974 and are still not the least-cost producers in 2005.

The 1 January 2005 termination of textile-clothing quotas has already generated very uneven effects across developing countries. Over a two- to three-year period, low-cost developing countries are expected to increase production dramatically, while high-cost developing countries, which were previously protected by quota rights, will face closure of a large proportion of their textile and apparel manufacturing plants. A report issued by the US International Trade Commission (2004) concluded that there will be increased sourcing of textiles and apparel from East and South Asia and less sourcing from ASEAN countries, the Andean countries, Sub-Saharan African countries, some Caribbean countries and Mexico.[21]

Moving the geographical locus of textile-apparel production from high-cost to low-cost manufacturers will clearly improve world efficiency by reducing production costs, decreasing prices, and increasing the volume of clothing purchases world-wide. As output is increasingly determined by comparative advantage and less by quota allocations, income will also be redistributed throughout the developing world. Thus, the elimination of the MFA becomes a dubious means by which to compensate developing economies for the large anticipated losses due to higher streams of net royalty payments under the TRIPs agreement. It is estimated that a handful of developing countries—China, India, and Pakistan—will gain handsomely from the MFA phase-out; a few others—perhaps Vietnam, perhaps Indonesia—will retain some textile-clothing export business; and the vast majority of developing countries will see almost all clothing-textile exports totally disappear over the next decade. The stark reality is that the MFA phase-out is likely to deliver large losses to 35 developing countries with MFA quotas in 1995 and gains to just three developing countries— albeit with over 40 per cent of the world's population.[22] Coupled with TRIPs, the MFA phase-out represents a large transfer of wealth from 35 developing countries to three developing countries and to the developed countries.[23] In sum, Pareto optimality fails, big time.

Finally, and most importantly, should the WTO be in the business of forcing developing countries to adopt welfare-reducing IPR institutions in exchange for the welfare-increasing dismantling of non-tariff trade barriers in textiles? In short, probably not, unless it can be shown that the distortions will last for just a short period of time.

Empirical effects of IPRs on trade, investment and technology transfer

Inherent in the inclusion of intellectual property (IP) protection under the scope of the World Trade Organization is the notion that the protection of patents, trademarks, and copyrights is somehow 'trade-related'. Exports embody technology and serve as a means of transferring knowledge to foreign markets. Treatment of knowledge in recipient countries thus intuitively should be linked to trade flows. Protection of intellectual property is also clearly a factor in a firm's decision to transfer technology more directly to those markets through establishments of foreign subsidiaries, franchises, or license arrangements. The second-best nature of IP protection renders quite indeterminate the drawing of theoretical conclusions on just how international flows might be impacted by harmonization of standards.

Very simply, intellectual property protection grants market power to the owner of the invention or creation. The stronger the protection and the enforcement of the property right, the larger the firm's monopoly power. Thus firms may decide to restrict sales in markets where IPRs are strongly protected to extract monopoly rents—a market power effect. That is, the market structure may be less competitive in markets in which foreign imitators are not present, and this might dampen exports as the firm seeks higher cost mark-ups. At the same time, the firm will incur a lower cost of protecting IP in markets with strong protection—an efficiency effect that would expand sales in countries that strengthen IP protection. Thus, a classical ambiguity exists between the level of IP protection in foreign markets and the propensity of knowledge-intensive firms to sell to those markets.

The relationships become more complex when alternative modes of delivery are considered. A firm may serve a foreign market at arm's length with exports, by a local subsidiary with foreign direct investment, or by franchising or licensing relationships with a local partner. Each decision is influenced by the nature of the industry, the mechanisms for the transfer of technology, the IP regime in place, and the methods by which imitation might be conducted. A weak IP regime increases the probability of imitation which dissuades foreign investors. However, stronger IP protection tends to shift the mode of entry from direct investment through multinational enterprises towards licensing. Thus the impacts of strengthened IP protection on exports, foreign investment and licenses are interrelated and complex.

IPR regimes have strengthened dramatically since 1990. The Park–Ginarte Index of patent rights (with zero being the lowest and five the highest) registered just 2.06 in 1960. Developed countries registered 2.5 and developing countries 1.5 in 1960. Despite large increases in world income between 1960 and 1990, the Park–Ginarte Index increased only to 2.46 in 1990. The increase to 3.07 in 2000 reflects a variety of factors, including bilateral pressure from the United States and the European Union, TRIPs, and rising incomes. The gap between developing and developed countries barely changed, with less than 5 per cent of the gap closed over the index's 40-year coverage.

Fortunately, a series of empirical studies has emerged in recent years to clarify the relationships involved. A pioneering effort by Maskus and Konan (1994) found that strong IP protection tends to increase bilateral imports and foreign investment over values predicted for countries by gravity equations. Maskus and Penubarti (1995) refined the analysis by using the Helpman-Krugman monopolistic competition model of trade to predict trade flows in the presence of IP protection and other instrumental variables. They provided strong evidence that stronger IP protection has a positive impact on bilateral manufacturing imports. The impact of IP protection was found to be greater the larger the country's market.

Lee and Mansfield (1996) used US firm survey data to show that the strength of a country's IP protection is positively correlated with the aggregate volume of US foreign direct investment (FDI) inflows to that country. Using a gravity equation approach, Smith (2001) considered how IP protection influences a wider range of modes to supply foreign markets. She found that stronger IP protection within a country increased the propensity of US firms to export to that market. Additionally, with strong foreign IP protection, US firms are relatively more likely to use foreign affiliates and license arrangements rather than export sales. Thus, overall international linkages are strengthened with IP protection, with local distribution being favoured over exports. Yang and Maskus (2001) also found that licensing is more likely to take place when IP protection is stronger.[24]

A survey of US manufacturing firms by Mansfield (1994) and Lee and Mansfield (1996) provided evidence that the importance of IPRs differs across sectors, even those that might be identified as 'technology intensive'. Respondents were far less concerned about IP protection on investment decisions regarding sales and distribution outlets. IP protection was viewed as far more important for investments in manufacturing and production, most especially when technology transfers were involved.

Using an original firm-level survey as well as country-characteristic data for transition economies, Javorcik (2004) considered empirically how IP protection has an impact on the volume as well as the distribution of FDI. She found that strong IP protection is positively correlated with inward foreign investment in sectors that have been identified as 'technology-intensive'. Additionally, the stronger the IP protection, the more likely are high-technology firms to undertake foreign investments in manufacturing plants and distribution sales rather than just in distribution sales.

Will developing countries lose by adopting stronger IPRs? Using a sample of countries with GDPs below the median GDP and an index of average patent protection between 1960 and 1990, Ginarte and Park (1997) found that stronger patent rights had no effect on growth. Maskus (2000) argued that stronger IPRs tend to stimulate economic growth in developing countries that are open to trade and foreign investment. Yet the link between growth and trade has recently been hotly debated. Some economists argue that the chain of causation is from growth to trade; others argue that export-oriented economies promote growth; and a third group notes that both trade and growth are endogenous outcomes of more fundamental economic and institutional factors (Frankel and Romer 1999).

We also note that the causal chain leading from stronger IPRs to more foreign investment and then to stronger (transitory or permanent) GDP growth is tenuous. Even if the empirical literature connecting IPRs and foreign direct investment is well founded, other literature finds only tenuous connections between FDI and growth despite extensive theoretical results pointing to a possible connection (Carcovic and Levine 2005). A series of studies (Moran, Graham, and Blomström 2005; Lipsey and Sjöholm 2005; Blomström and Sjöholm 1999; Long 2005; and Kokko 1994) helps to resolve this dilemma. Lipsey and Sjöholm (2005: 5) found that differences in countries' abilities to benefit from FDI are due to 'varying levels of indigenous human resources, to disparate degrees of private sector sophistication, to differing levels of competition, and to contrasting host country policies toward trade and investment'. Empirical studies by Long (2005) on FDI in China, and by Moss, Ramachandran and Shah (2005) on FDI in East Africa show that 'FDI in which local affiliates operate within a relatively open trade and investment policy framework greatly benefits the host country. FDI in which local affiliates produce for the domestic market behind trade barriers, with joint venture and local content requirements, has a much less positive impact and often subtracts from host-country welfare'. In other words, the effectiveness of stronger IPRs in stimulating growth depends on the capability of the domestic economy to implement the IPRs and to absorb foreign direct investment and foreign technologies efficiently. This leads us to the tentative conclusion that stronger IPRs are more likely to stimulate growth in middle-income developing countries than in low-income developing countries.

GLOBAL COPYRIGHT: FINALLY, IN CRISIS?

Robert Merges (2000) has observed wryly that copyright law is constantly in crisis. The advent of the photocopier in the 1960s and the VCR in the early 1980s brought forth loud protests from copyright industries and from the academy that the 'sky is falling' and that publishing and movie industries would soon fail to be profitable. On the contrary, fair use copying has become the norm, and VCR and DVD players have spawned a huge after-market for films in VCR and DVD formats in both developed and developing economies.

Today's claims concerning a global crisis in copyright law are more ominous: the combination of digitization of creative works and the spread of broadband Internet networks capable of distributing them has dramatically reduced the costs to consumers and intermediaries of copying and distributing copyrighted materials. This combination has dramatically increased rates of consumer piracy in all countries, but particularly in Eastern Europe and the Asia-Pacific region. Table 9.3 provides estimates of piracy rates in APEC countries and finds that they are economically significant in virtually all APEC countries.[25]

Perhaps Merges will again be proven correct. European manufacturers of computers, MP3 players, DVD players, and the like are lobbying the European Commission to repeal copyright levies on the sale of such equipment, which are redistributed to musical and video artists owning copyrights. Their claim is that new digital controls on consumer copying are beginning to alleviate the problem. Musicians are opposed to the repeal.

Consider, however, the possibility that Merges is wrong and a real crisis in copyright exists. Has the crisis been identified and is a multilateral policy response in place or being developed? On the one hand, the speed with which a group of countries moved to ameliorate this problem is amazing and virtually unprecedented. The World Copyright Treaty (WCT) was signed by over 40 countries in December 1996, just two–three years after widespread use of the World Wide Web began, and the United States and the European Union have significantly upgraded their IP laws to implement the treaties. On the other hand, Table 9.4 shows that only a few countries in Asia have signed the WCT or the WIPO Performances and Phonograms Treaty (WPPT).

The US Digital Millennium Copyright Act (DMCA) was passed to clarify the nature of copyright in digital works and to provide support for technological blocks on access to and copying of digital works. It was signed into law on 28 October 1998 as part of US implementation of the WCT and WPPT. The DMCA implemented these recommendations and added more of its own, thereby providing copyright owners with even broader protection than provided in the two WIPO treaties.[26]

The DMCA contains four main provisions:

1. a prohibition on circumventing access controls [1201(a)]
2. an access control circumvention device ban [1201 (a)]

Table 9.3   Estimates of losses from piracy in selected Asia-Pacific countries (2003)

Country	Motion pictures		Records & music		Business software applications		Entertainment software		Books
	Loss US$m	Piracy level %	Loss US$m	Piracy level %	Loss US$m	Piracy level %	Loss US$m	Piracy level %	Loss US$m
India	77	60	6	40	187	73	113.3	84	36.5
Indonesia	29	92	44.5	87	94	88	NA	NA	30
Malaysia	38	50	40	45	77	63	NA	NA	9
Pakistan	12	95	70	100	9	83	NA	NA	44
People's Republic of China	178	95	286	90	1787	92	568.2	96	40
Philippines	33	89	22.2	40	33	72	NA	95	45
South Korea	40	20	3.5	20	275	48	248.4	36	38
Taiwan	42	44	58	42	83	43	261.8	42	20
Thailand	28	60	26.8	41	84	80	NA	82	28
Vietnam	7	100	NA	NA	24	92	NA	NA	12

Source: International Intellectual Property Association.

Table 9.4   WCT and WPPT contracting parties in Asia

World Copyright Treaty		World Performances and Phonograms Treaty	
Contracting party	*Entry into force*	*Contracting party*	*Entry into force*
Indonesia	6-Mar-02	Indonesia	15-Feb-05
Japan	6-Mar-02	Japan	9-Oct-02
Mongolia	25-Oct-02	Mongolia	25-Oct-02
Philippines	4-Oct-02	Philippines	4-Oct-02
South Korea	24-Jun-04		

Source: World Intellectual Property Rights Organization.

3. a copyright protection circumvention device ban [1201(b)]
4. a prohibition on the removal of copyright management information (CMI) [1202(b)].[27]

The first provision prohibits defeating the access control measure that protects or limits access to digital information. Defeating the access control measure, or 'circumventing a technological measure', means to descramble a scrambled work, to decrypt an encrypted work, or otherwise to avoid, bypass, remove, deactivate or impair a technological measure without the authority of the copyright owner. The second provision bans trafficking in devices that circumvent access controls. The Norwegian teenager who found the hole in the DVD encryption code and posted a computer program (DeCSS) allowing DVD decryption would have been in violation of this provision.[28] The third provision bans trafficking in technology that circumvents technological measures that limit the ability to reproduce a copyrighted work. An example of this kind of technological protection is an encoding technique that prevents a music CD from being played on a computer and therefore prevents its songs from being copied to the computer's hard disk. The fourth provision bans the alteration of copyright management information or the provision of false copyright management information. Copyright management information is information conveyed in connection with a copyrighted work for the purposes of identifying its origin: such information could include the title, author, name of the copyright owner, terms and conditions for use of the work, and identifying numbers or symbols referring to the above information.[29] The European Union has passed parallel but slightly different legislation.[30]

On the other hand, despite the speed with which some countries have moved to ratify the WCT and to pass enabling legislation, most countries have not become a party to the WCT, have not passed similar legislation, or have not enforced these laws—and therein lies the root of the problem. These countries can become centres of piracy for individuals in other countries wishing to download copyrighted works. Off-shore sites in international waters with computers linked to the web present additional problems. The problem of piracy has become compounded by the combination of broadband transmission with digitization. A 'window of opportunity' of just an hour could now result in all issues of a leading journal or an entire series of reference works, e.g. North Holland's *Handbook of Economics* series, being downloaded and widely redistributed. With the stock of copyrighted works so exposed, the choices for policymakers are stark.

The first choice is that policymakers could increase copyright terms to provide more protection. Such extensions have been recently granted in the United States and Europe. Cheng (2004) has closely examined the US Sonny Bono Copyright Term Extension Act (CTEA) passed in 1998 which extends copyright terms from life of the author plus 50 years to life of the author plus 75 years. Cheng (2004), Cheng and La Croix (2006), Landes and Posner (2003) and Breyer (2003) all concluded that the effect of a copyright term extension on incentives to produce and market creative works is trivial and that the main reason for the extension appears to be to extend the copyright term of valuable copyrights that would otherwise expire. We can find no efficiency rationales for this type of extension and conclude that retroactivity provisions drove the enactment of the law.

The second choice is that governments could increase penalties for violations of copyright laws and provide additional resources for their enforcement. In countries that are net importers of intellectual property, these will be unpopular measures that could be difficult for the government to sustain, particularly given the decentralized nature of the copyright piracy in most developed and developing countries.

The third choice is that governments could work together to establish new forms of intellectual property for some forms of property that meet consumer needs appropriately, while providing reduced incentives for piracy. Software is one type of work for which copyright protection is obviously too long, and the availability of patent protection for some software may provide protection that is too broad (La Croix 1992). While opening the door to more specialized categories of IPRs may be opening a Pandora's box, the ubiquity and value of software in the workplace and the home calls for more differentiated protection to remedy the ongoing dissipation of rents in the innovation and distribution processes for these products.

CONCLUSION

The 'property rights' approach to economics rightly encourages the establishment of property rights in valuable goods, as well-defined property rights typically maximize the value of the good.[31] This perspective must, however, be modified for goods that are public goods, as one person's use does not deprive another from using the good, as it does with private goods. We conclude that it is important to establish intellectual property rights in intellectual innovations while at the same time limiting those rights to allow widespread access to the new works. Establishing property rights in new products and new intellectual innovations embodied in new products and processes is necessary to establish sufficient incentives for individuals and corporations to undertake R&D. The scope, depth, and enforcement of IPRs is, however, likely to differ across countries according to their economic and political institutions, their per capita income, and their capability to engage in and disseminate the fruits of R&D.

NOTES

The authors thank Matthew Pennaz for excellent research assistance; participants in seminars at the University of Hawaii, the European Institute of Japanese Studies, Stockholm School of Economics, and the 2005 Pacific Asia Free Trade and Development Conference for their thoughtful comments; and Walter Park for supplying us with data. We are responsible for all errors of commission and omission.

1   Article 1, Section 8, US Constitution.
2   The Patent Law of 1836 introduced the modern system of patent examination which provided for examination of patent applications by skilled examiners. Issues previously resolved by expensive and lengthy civil litigation were, after the 1836 legislation, resolved by examiners in the US Patent Office.
3   This helps to explain how Albert Einstein found the time to develop the theory of special relativity and to earn a doctorate while working at the Swiss Patent Office from 1902 to 1909.
4   Books with foreign copyright holders had either to be printed in the United States or to have their printing plates manufactured in the United States. This requirement remained substantially unchanged until the United States joined the Berne Convention in 1988.
5   Major changes included increasing patent terms from 17 to 20 years of protection, mandating patent protection to pharmaceutical products, and establishing a system of IPR protection for plants.
6   Texts of both treaties can be found at <http://www.wipo.int/treaties/en/>; accessed 15 May 2006.
7   <http://www.ifpi.org/site-content/press/20011206.html>; accessed 15 May 2006.
8   <http://www.iprsonline.org/unctadictsd/bellagio/docs/Correa_Bellagio2.pdf>; accessed 15 May 2006.
9   See Memorandum of the Director General, Agenda for Development of the International Patent System, August 2001, WIPO A/36/14, Geneva, para. 17–28.
10   <http://www.fool.com/news/2001/bayzf011025.htm>; accessed 15 May 2006.
11   <http://www.worldtradelaw.net/doha/tripshealth.pdf>; accessed 15 May 2006.
12   <http://www.iprsonline.org/unctadictsd/bellagio/docs/Correa_Bellagio2.pdf>; accessed 15 May 2006.
13   <http://www.ciel.org/Publications/Doha_IP.pdf>; accessed 15 May 2006.
14   <http://www.wto.org/english/tratop_e/trips_e/gi_background_e.htm>; accessed 15 May 2006.
15   Doha Work Programme, Preparations of the Sixth Session of the Ministerial Conference, Draft Ministerial Text, World Trade Organization, 26 November 2005.
16   Intellectual Property Needs and Expectations of Traditional Knowledge Holders—WIPO Report on Fact-Finding Missions on Intellectual Property and Traditional Knowledge, WIPO, April 2001, p. 25.
17   For two empirical studies of the effects of establishing pharmaceutical product patents, see Kawaura and La Croix (1995) and La Croix and Kawaura (1996).
18   See also Chin and Grossman (1990), Rapp and Rozek (1990), Deardorff (1992), Konan, La Croix, Roumasset, and Heinrich (1995) and Scotchmer (2004).
19   Adding more countries into the model reduces optimal patent protection for a small country to zero (Grossman and Lai 2004: 1650–1).
20   Anti-dumping measures and more restrictive rules of origin are being used to replace the quotas in the United States. Developing countries expected to lose productive capacity in this area are asking the US Congress to enact preferential tariff rates to allow them to retain some export business.
21   The large number of developing countries losing from the elimination of the MFA–ATC quotas may help to explain why the quota phase-outs were delayed until 2005: to provide

the losing developing countries with an additional ten years of benefits prior to the phase-out.

22 Thirty-three countries with MFA producer quotas were expected to lose from the MFA phase-out: Bangladesh, Brazil, Colombia, Costa Rica, Czech Republic, Dominican Republic, Egypt, El Salvador, Fiji, Guatemala, Honduras, Hong Kong, Hungary, Indonesia, Jamaica, Kenya, South Korea, Macao, Malaysia, Mexico, Oman, Panama, Peru, the Philippines, Poland, Romania, Singapore, Slovakia, Slovenia, Sri Lanka, Thailand, Turkey and Uruguay. Two MFA countries with MFA producer quotas—India and Pakistan—were expected to gain from the phase-out. China, a country without an MFA producer quota in 1995, was expected to reap a majority of the gains from MFA phase-out.

23 Under MFA, the quota rents were assigned to the developing country. After 1 January 2005, the developing countries that remain in textile-apparel production lose the quota rents but receive producer surplus on their increased production. If the loss in rents is greater than the producer surplus, then *all* developing countries incur losses after the MFA phase-out.

24 See also McCalman (2004a, 2004b).

25 While the United States is not listed in the table, it has economically significant piracy rates in music, consumer software and business software. In a survey of software piracy in 2005, the Business Software Alliance found a US piracy rate of 21 per cent, with losses amounting to US$6.9 billion. See <http://www.bsa.org/globalstudy>; accessed 29 June 2006.

26 <http://www.chillingeffects.org/anticircumvention/faq.cgi#QID123>; accessed 15 May 2006.

27 <http://thomas.loc.gov/cgi-bin/cpquery/0?&&db_id=cp105&&r_n=hr796.105 &&sel=DOC&>; accessed 15 May 2006.

28 For a summary of the US court cases involving the posting of DeCSS on the internet, see <http://www.linksandlaw.com/linkingcases-linkstoillegalmaterial2.htm>; accessed 29 June 2006.

29 <http://depts.washington.edu/uwcopy/Copyright_Law/DMCA/Provisions.php>; accessed 15 May 2006. The first three provisions are distinguishable from the fourth, in that the first two provisions focus on technological protection systems that provide access control to the copyright owner, while the third provision prohibits circumvention of technological protections against unauthorized duplication and other potentially copyright infringing activities. Another DMCA provision is designed to protect Internet service providers (ISPs), allowing them to escape liability for the actions of their users as long as they did not know or have reason to know that their users were violating a copyright holder's rights. The DMCA allows for both civil remedies and criminal penalties for violations under the anti-circumvention provisions. The civil and criminal penalties in the DMCA are well defined, in comparison to the WIPO treaties, with their relatively lax and subjective penalty clauses. In the United States, if the violations of the DMCA are determined to be wilful and for commercial purposes or private financial gain, the court can order significant fines as well as jail time. Civil cases are brought in the federal district court where the court has broad authority to grant injunctive and monetary relief. Injunctions can be granted forbidding the distribution of the tools or products involved in the violation. The court may also order the destruction of the tools or products involved in the violation. The court can also award actual damages, profits gained through infringement, and attorney's fees. If an individual held in violation of the DMCA commits another such violation within the three-year period following the judgement, the court may increase the damages up to triple the amount that would otherwise be awarded. In circumstances involving innocent violators, it is up to the courts to decide whether to reduce damages. However, in the case of non-profit library, archives or educational institutions, the court must remit damages if it finds that the institution did not know of the violation. If the circumvention violations are determined to be wilful and for commercial or private financial gain, first time offenders may be fined up to US$500,000, imprisoned for five years, or both. For

repeat offenders, the maximum penalty increases to a fine of US$1,000,000, imprisonment for up to ten years, or both. Criminal penalties are not applicable to non-profit libraries, archives and educational institutions.

30 Much like the Digital Millennium Copyright Act (DMCA) passed by the United States, the European Community also has their version, called the EU Copyright Directive (EUCD). Differing copyright regimes among European countries were seen as major obstacles to efficient trade, and the EC set about drafting a directive on the subject between 1997 and 2000, which sought to create a level playing field for the enforcement of intellectual property rights in different EU countries, by bringing enforcement measures into line across the EU, especially in those countries where the enforcement of intellectual property rights is currently weakest. The directive covers infringements of all intellectual property rights (both copyright and industrial property, such as trademarks or designs), and concentrates on infringements carried out for commercial purposes or which cause significant harm to rights-holders. The EUCD does *not* cover music downloading or file-sharing (it leaves this up to individual countries to enforce their own laws), but is instead concentrated on provisions of encoding and protections found in the two WIPO treaties and the DMCA. Also, similarly to the DMCA, the EUCD paves the way for injunctions to halt the sale of counterfeit or pirated goods, provisional measures such as precautionary seizures of suspected offenders' bank accounts, evidence-gathering powers for judicial authorities and powers to force offenders to pay damages to rights-holders to compensate for lost income.

31 The establishment of property rights is, however, also costly, and the transaction costs of establishing these rights may limit their scope and delineation.

REFERENCES

Breyer, S. (2003) 'Dissenting Opinion', Eldred *et al.* v. Ashcroft 537 US 186.

Blomström, M. and F. Sjöholm (1999) 'Technology Transfer and Spillovers: Does Local Participation with Multinationals Matter?', *European Economic Review*, 43: 915–23.

Carcovic, M. and R. Levine (2005) 'Does Foreign Direct Investment Accelerate Economic Growth?', in Moran, T.H., E.M. Graham and M. Blomström (eds), *Does Foreign Direct Investment Promote Development?*, Washington, DC: Institute for International Economics and Center for Global Development.

Cheng, X. (2004) 'Intellectual Property Rights, Innovation in Developing Countries, and Copyright Term Extension', unpublished dissertation, University of Hawaii-Manoa.

Cheng, X. and S. La Croix (2006) 'To Infinity and Beyond! Are Ever Lengthening Copyright Terms Efficient?', unpublished manuscript, Department of Economics, University of Hawaii.

Chin, J. and G.M. Grossman (1990) 'Intellectual Property Rights and North–South Trade', in R.W. Jones and A.O. Krueger (eds), *The Political Economy of International Trade*, Cambridge MA: Basil Blackwell Publishers.

Deardorff, A.V. (1992) 'Welfare Effects of Global Patent Protection', *Economica*, 59: 35–51.

Evenson, R.E. and L.E. Westphal (1995) 'Technological Change and Technology Strategy', in J. Behrman and T.N. Srinivasan (eds), *Handbook of Development Economics*, vol. 3A, New York: North Holland Press.

Frankel, J.A. and D. Romer (1999) 'Does Trade Cause Growth?', *American Economic Review*, 89(3): 379–99.

Ginarte, J.C. and W.G. Park (1997) 'Determinants of Patent Rights: A Cross-national Study', *Research Policy*, 26: 283–301.

Griliches, Z. (1994) 'Productivity, R&D, and the Data Constraint', *American Economic Review*, 84(1): 1–23.

Grossman, G.M. and E.L-C. Lai (2004) 'International Protection of Intellectual Property', *American Economic Review*, 94(5): 1635–53.

Harrison, G., D. Tarr and T.F. Rutherford (1997) 'Quantifying the Uruguay Round', *Economic Journal*, 107: 1405–30.

Helpman, E. (1993) 'Innovation, Imitation, and Intellectual Property Rights', *Econometrica*, 61(6): 1247–80.

Javorcik, B.S. (2004) 'The Composition of Foreign Direct Investment and Protection for Intellectual Property Rights: Evidence from Transition Economies', *European Economic Review*, 48: 39–62.

Kawaura, A. and S.J. La Croix (1995) 'Japan's Shift from Process to Product Patents in the Pharmaceutical Industry: a Stock Market Event Analysis', *Economic Inquiry*, 33(1): 88–103.

Khan, B.Z. and K.L. Sokoloff (1998) 'Two Paths to Industrial Development and Technological Change', in M. Berg and K. Bruland (eds), *Technological Revolutions in Europe, 1760–1860*, Cheltenham: Edward Elgar.

—— (2001) 'The Early Development of Intellectual Property Institutions in the United States', *Journal of Economic Perspectives*, 15(3): 233–46.

Kokko, A. (1994) 'Technology, Market Characteristics, and Spillovers', *Journal of Development Economics*, 43(2): 279–93.

Konan, D.E., S.J. La Croix, J. Roumasset and J. Heinrich (1995) 'Intellectual Property Rights in the Asia-Pacific Region: Problems, Patterns, and Policy', *Asian-Pacific Economic Literature*, 9(2): 13–35.

La Croix, S.J. (1992) 'Property Rights in Computer Software: some Comments on the Evolving International Framework', in K. Abe and W. Gunther (eds), *Economic, Industrial and Managerial Coordination Between Japan and the USA: A Comparative Analysis*, New York: Macmillan Press.

La Croix, S.J. and A. Kawaura (1996) 'Korea's Shift from Process to Product Patents in the Pharmaceutical Industry: an Event Study of the Impact of American Pressure on Korean Firms', *International Economic Journal*, 10(1): 109–24.

La Croix, S.J. and D.E. Konan (2002) 'Intellectual Property Rights in China: American Pressure and Chinese Resistance', *The World Economy*, 25(6): 759–88.

Lamoreaux, N.R. and K.L. Sokoloff (1996) 'Long-term Change in the Organization of Inventive Activity', *Proceedings of the National Academy of Sciences*, 93 (November): 12686–92.

—— (1999) 'Inventors, Firms, and the Market for New Technology in the Late Nineteenth and Early Twentieth Centuries', in N.R. Lamoreaux, D.M.G. Raff and P. Temin (eds), *Learning by Doing in Markets, Firms, and Countries*, Chicago: University of Chicago Press, 19–57.

—— (2003) 'Intermediaries in the US Market for Technology, 1870–1920', in S.L. Engerman, P.T. Hoffman, J-L. Rosenthal and K.L. Sokoloff (eds), *Finance, Intermediaries, and Economic Development*, New York: Cambridge University Press, 209–46.

Landes, W.M. and R.A. Posner (2003) 'Indefinitely Renewable Copyright', *University of Chicago Law Review*, 70: 471–518.

Lee, J.Y. and E. Mansfield (1996) 'Intellectual Property Protection and US Foreign Direct Investment', *Review of Economics and Statistics*, 78: 181–6.

Lipsey, R. and F. Sjöholm (2005) 'The Impact of Inward FDI on Host Countries: Why the Different Answers?', in T.H. Moran, E.M. Graham and M. Blomström (eds), *Does Foreign Direct Investment Promote Development?*, Washington, DC: Institute for International Economics and Center for Global Development.

Long, G. (2005) 'China's Policies on FDI: Review and Evaluation', in T.H. Moran, E.M. Graham and M. Blomström (eds), *Does Foreign Direct Investment Promote Development?*, Washington, DC: Institute for International Economics and Center for Global Development.

Mansfield, E. (1994) 'Intellectual Property Protection, Foreign Direct Investment, and Technology Transfer', *International Finance Corporation Discussion Paper* 27, Washington DC: The World Bank.

Maskus, K.E. (2000) *Intellectual Property Rights in the Global Economy*, Washington, DC: The Institute for International Economics.

Maskus, K.E. and D.E. Konan (1994) 'Trade-related Intellectual Property Rights: Issues and Exploratory Results', in R.M. Stern and A.V. Deardorff (eds), *Analytical and Negotiating Issues in the Global Trading System*, Ann Arbor: University of Michigan Press, 401–46.

Maskus, K.E. and M. Penubarti (1995) 'How Trade Related are Intellectual Property Rights?', *Journal of International Economics*, 39: 227–48.

McCalman, P. (2002) 'National Patents, Innovation and International Agreements', *Journal of International Trade and Economic Development*, 11(1): 1–14.

—— (2004a) 'Foreign Direct Investment and Intellectual Property Rights: Evidence from Hollywood's Global Distribution of Movies and Videos', *Journal of International Economics*, 62(1): 107–23.

—— (2004b) 'Protection for Sale and Trade Liberalization: an Empirical Investigation', *Review of International Economics*, 12(1): 81–94.

Merges, R.P. (2000) 'One Hundred Years of Solitude: Intellectual Property Law, 1900–2000', *California Law Review*, 88: 2189–40.

Moran, T.H., E.M. Graham and M. Blomström (2005) 'Introduction and Overview', in Moran, T.H., E.M. Graham and M. Blomström (eds), *Does Foreign Direct Investment Promote Development?*, Washington, DC: Institute for International Economics and Center for Global Development.

Moss, T.J., V. Ramachandran and M.K. Shah (2005) 'Is Africa's Skepticism of Foreign Capital Justified? Evidence from East African Firm Survey Data', in T.H. Moran, E.M. Graham and M. Blomström (eds), *Does Foreign Direct Investment Promote Development?*, Washington, DC: Institute for International Economics and Center for Global Development.

Mowery, D.C. (1983) 'The Relationship Between Intra-firm and Contractual Forms of Industrial Research in American Manufacturing, 1900–1940', *Explorations in Economic History*, 20: 351–74.

—— (1995) 'The Boundaries of the US Firm in R&D', in N.R. Lamoreaux and D.M.G. Raff (eds), *Coordination and Information: Historical Perspectives on the Organization of Enterprise*, Chicago: University of Chicago Press.

Nordhaus, W.D. (1969) *Invention, Growth and Welfare: a Theoretical Treatment of Technological Change*, Cambridge MA: MIT Press.

Rapp, R.T. and R.P. Rozek (1990) 'Benefits and Costs of Intellectual Property Protection in Developing Countries', *Journal of World Trade*, 24: 75–102.

Schiff, E. (1971) *Industrialization without Patents: The Netherlands, 1869–1912, Switzerland, 1850–1907*, Princeton: Princeton University Press.

Scotchmer, S. (2004) 'The Political Economy of Intellectual Property Treaties', *Journal of Law, Economics, and Organization*, 20(2): 415–37.

Siwek, S.E. (2004) *Copyright Industries in the United States.* Available at <http://www.iipa.com/pdf/2004_SIWEK_FULL.pdf>; accessed 29 June 2006.

Smith, P.J. (2001) 'How do Foreign Patent Rights Affect US Exports, Affiliate Sales, and Licenses?', *Journal of International Economics*, 55: 411–39.

Srinivasan, T.N. (2000) 'The TRIPs Agreement: A Comment Inspired by Frederick Abbott's Presentation', Yale University, November, mimeo.

Taylor, M.S. (1994) 'TRIPs, Trade, and Growth', *International Economic Review*, 35(2): 361–81.

US International Trade Commission (2004) *Textiles and Apparel: Assessment of the Competitiveness of Certain Foreign Suppliers to the US Market*, Washington, DC, January.

Yang G. and K.E. Maskus (2001) 'Intellectual Property Rights and Licensing: an Econometric Investigation', *Weltwirtschaftliches Archiv*, 137(1): 58–79.

Zhutshi, B.K. (1998) 'Bringing TRIPs into the Multilateral Trading System', in J. Bhagwati and M. Hirsch (eds), *The Uruguay Round and Beyond: Essays in Honor of Arthur Dunkel*, Ann Arbor: University of Michigan Press.

10 Economic interdependence and security in the Asia Pacific

Rong-I Wu, Chyuan-Jenq Shiau and Chi-Chen Chiang

INTRODUCTION

Historically, economic factors have been applied to explain many security issues, such as the outbreaks of World Wars I and II, Japan's military expansions in the 1930s and 1940s, and US interventions in the post-war third-world countries. The way in which economic interdependence has affected security has been viewed from different theoretical perspectives. In particular, with the end of the Cold War and the development of economic liberalization, regionalization and globalization, many scholars, analysts, and policy makers believe that the increase of economic interdependence would not only raise productivity, efficiency and economic welfare, but also enhance or improve national and international security. But is this really happening in the post-Cold War era?

In the case of the Asia-Pacific region, as economic liberalization and globalization advance, the extent of economic interdependence in the region today is almost unprecedented. Nonetheless, many traditional security issues in the region, including the China–Taiwan rivalry, North–South Korean conflict, South China Sea dispute, Chinese military build-up, and the arms race problem, remain uncertain. More importantly, the increase of economic interdependence seems to extend the impacts of such new security threats as international terrorism, infectious diseases and weapons of mass destruction (WMD), and thus even makes national and international security increasingly sensitive and vulnerable in the Asia Pacific. In this context, whether the increase of economic interdependence really enhances or improves overall security in the Asia Pacific becomes a very compelling question we must explore and understand.

The primary objective of this paper is to examine the relationship between security and economic interdependence in the Asia Pacific after the Cold War. It first reviews the major theoretical perspectives, then examines the development of economic interdependence, and explores power relations and security issues. Because the world is changing, the paper also tries to identify major new security threats challenging the relationship between economic interdependence and security in the region. Based on the findings, the paper concludes with some prospects.

ECONOMIC INTERDEPENDENCE AND SECURITY: DIFFERENT THEORETICAL VIEWS

Has the increase of economic interdependence really changed overall security in the Asia Pacific? The puzzle apparently has to do with the relationship between economic interdependence and security. According to Irwin (1996), the claim of trade influencing political relations has existed for almost two thousand years. Past studies have viewed this relationship in different ways, which are described below.

Positive or optimistic views

In essence, positive or optimistic views argue that the increase of international economic interdependence would reduce the probability of international conflicts, which would thus contribute to security preservation and improvement. Such arguments have mainly come from liberal thinkers or have been influenced by liberal ideas.[1] Nineteenth-century Manchester school liberals, among others, publicly and systematically claimed that 'in the world of shared economic growth and prosperity, war has become increasingly obsolete' (Moon 1998; Mueller 1989).[2] Since then there have been several major claims in this positive or optimistic camp regarding the relationship between economic interdependence and security.

The first claim is that increasing contact between countries via trade contributes to the development of mutual respect and harmonious relations, and fosters a sense of international community (Viner 1985). Increasing levels of international trade thus create more potential for positive interactions between countries, which not only serves as a catalyst for international cooperation, but also a deterrent to future conflicts (Hirschman 1977; Pavehouse 2004). Second, from the perspective of economic opportunity cost, many arguments stress that since trade generates economic benefits for both parties, the anticipation that war will disrupt trade and lead to a trade loss helps to deter countries from easily waging conflicts against trading partners (Oneal and Russett 1999; Polachek 1980; Barbieri and Schneider 1999). They also consider that the mechanism of economic opportunity cost could increase the pressure from domestic interest groups, motivated by gains from trade, to force governments to maintain peaceful trading environments (Rogowski 1989). In other words, the more economically interdependent countries become, the more they will have an interest in maintaining peaceful political relations in order to sustain economic interactions and avoid economic loss (Mochizuki 1998). Another key claim in this camp argues that economic interdependence facilitates and promotes international norms of cooperation, which over time can be for peace by transforming countries' attitudes, preferences, and interests so that international cooperation and accommodation become more likely in the security area (Mochizuki 1998; Ikenberry 1996; Nye 1988).

In short, perspectives in this camp (mostly based on liberal ideas) tend to see the security implications of economic interdependence in positive or optimistic terms. They place emphasis primarily on how transnational economic interactions (especially trade) can mutually benefit and constrain states. At the same time, they hold that increasing economic interdependence not only builds confidence and harmony, but also provides opportunities and norms for international cooperation. Therefore, positive or optimistic views regard international economic competition or interdependence as a positive-sum game, instead of a zero-sum one.

Sceptical or pessimistic views

Positive or optimistic views based on liberalism, however, are not without challenges in elaborating the relationship between economic interdependence and security. For instance, realist[3] and Marxist[4] perspectives are sceptical of the above-mentioned positive views. They even hold pessimistic or negative views on the relationship between economic interdependence and security.

Realist perspectives challenge positive views mainly by emphasizing the anarchic nature of world politics and countries' tendency to maximize national power, reduce dependence on other states, and lessen vulnerabilities. Some realists even argue that countries' increasing dependence and vulnerability caused by rising economic interdependence might 'aggravate' interstate relations and ultimately lead to military hostilities (Mochizuki 1998: 6). After all, for realism, 'power distribution' in the international system is the key to peace or war: economic interdependence may benefit all states in terms of absolute economic gains, but the increase of relative gains is the ultimate assurance for national security (Pavehouse 2004: 249).

More specifically, realists tend to believe that the disparity in relative gains from economic interdependence would finally change the interstate military balance and power configuration, which in turn might give rise to security instability (or security dilemma) and antagonism. This is because, for realists, military power is fungible and economic capability is by and large a subset of military power (Moon 1998). States in the anarchic world will convert industrial and technological resources into military might so as to strengthen their security (Mochizuki 1998: 6). Arms races are accordingly hard to avoid and the probability for conflicts may increase. Moreover, some realists maintain that economic interdependence can directly exacerbate relations among states. Because the world is anarchical, economic interdependence instead makes states more anxious about the costs of depending on other states, and more sensitive and vulnerable to other states' unilateral actions (Waltz 1979: 106). States may thus seek to expand the economic gains from interdependence at the expense of others by adopting such strategies as raising political pressure, conducting military measure, or applying malevolent mercantilism (Gilpin 1987: 404–5). Yet such strategies will hardly promote international cooperation and security.

For realist arguments, transnational economic interactions may not be a deterrent to conflict, but rather a source of tension or instability: the increase of economic interdependence promoting security and peace may be just a liberal myth (Waltz 1970: 205).

Compared with realist views, Marxist views on the relationship between economic interdependence and security are even more pessimistic. For Marxists, as Moon (1998: 9) argues, 'economic interdependence is nothing but a disguised and deceptive expression of the capitalist international or regional division of labour. The expression of the capitalist division of labour undermines security and peace in two different ways. One is the inevitability of hegemonic wars among imperial or neo-imperial powers in search for their market niches, and the other is the deepening of class conflicts and their eventual externalization, both of which threaten national, regional, and international security'.

Even the 'dependency theory' and 'world system theory', two major variants of Marxist tradition after World War II, hold pessimistic views on the relationship between economic interdependence and security. Such thinkers in Marxist tradition as Fernado Cardoso, Samir Amin and Immanuel Wallerstein basically assume an asymmetric economic interdependence between developed (the core) and developing (the periphery) countries. The asymmetric economic interdependence over time would produce dominance and dependency in both national and international economies, which in turn could trigger efforts to break the dependent ties (Pease 2003: 76). Under the circumstances, two types of conflict—internal conflict within the periphery and conflict between the core and the periphery—could endanger national and international security by sharpening domestic and external tensions.

In light of these sceptical or pessimistic views, capitalist market forces will not automatically guarantee peace and security. The relationship between economic interdependence and security is not as positive as liberals imagine. The increase of economic interdependence may even raise the probability of conflict, threaten security and add uncertainty.

Theoretical deficiencies

The numerous studies regarding the tie between economic interdependence and security have resulted in different claims and conclusions, but careful examination shows their theoretical and logical inadequacies. Traditional views or theories usually assume a unilinear or monocausal relationship between economic interdependence and security, and thus—knowingly or unknowingly—neglect other key factors such as domestic variables, decision-making processes, diplomatic alignments, third-party considerations or hegemonic influence. Traditional studies also focus primarily on such traditional security issues as wars, geopolitics and military confrontations. However, the impact of economic interdependence has extended to cover non-traditional security problems such as international economic crises, terrorism, illegal immigration, infectious diseases and natural disasters. Also, past studies, particularly empirical ones, usually examine the tie between economic interdependence and security in 'dyadic' or 'bilateral' settings, and ignore the networking impact of multilateral or regional interdependence on security. More importantly, as the world is changing, the content of economic interdependence has gone beyond mere trade to include investment, finance, flows of people, transportation and communication, and so on. As such, traditional studies regarding trade as the main element of economic interdependence cannot see the whole picture.

Indeed, the relationship between economic interdependence and security should be dynamic, rather than static and unilinear. In particular, with the changing environment of political economy, the content of economic interdependence and the concept of security are changing. Taking this into consideration would thus improve our understanding of the relationship between the two.

INCREASING ECONOMIC INTERDEPENDENCE IN THE ASIA PACIFIC

The world economy has been experiencing the growing mobility of goods, services, capital, technology, information and even labour since the end of the Cold War. This in turn has made the world economy more interdependent by changing the way of trade, the direction of investments, flows of capital, international divisions of labour, modes of production and the format of economic integration. The Asia Pacific economy is no exception and has become more interdependent both externally and internally in the areas discussed below.

Trade

With respect to trade, under the circumstances of liberalization and globalization, the Asia Pacific is more open to, and dependent on, trade than before: the pattern of trade in the Asia Pacific has been shifting with the following characteristics since the end of the Cold War. Trade–GDP ratios have been increasing for most Asia-Pacific economies since the late 1980s (see Table 10.1). Particularly for most developing economies in the region, trade has become very significant to their GDP, the average trade–GDP ratio increasing from less than 50 per cent before 1990 to 82 per cent in 2003. According to APEC, the sole and primary institution for economic cooperation in the Asia Pacific, today the 21 economies of APEC account for approximately 56 per cent of world GDP and 48 per cent of world trade (APEC n.d.). The consequence of the increasingly interdependent trading networks is not just about a greater percentage of GDP, but rather about the increasing and deepening links between national and international economies as well as between high- and low-income countries within or outside the Asia Pacific.

More importantly, as a region, the importance of intra-regional trade for the Asia Pacific has also increased remarkably in the post-Cold War era. For instance, as Table 10.2 illustrates, the number of merchandise exports within APEC has doubled from US$901 billion in 1990 to more than US$2,000 billion in 2001, an increase that is even higher and faster than that of the EU. Its percentage of total APEC exports has increased to more than 70 per cent as well (see Table 10.2). Table 10.3 confirms the increased importance of intra-regional trade in the Asia Pacific by summarizing the 'trade dependence index'[5] of 14 economies in the region: with few exceptions, each economy's trade dependence with other economies dramatically increased through the 1990s.

Capital flows

Apart from trade, a traditional indicator of measuring economic interdependence, capital flows have not only expanded but also made the Asia Pacific much more interdependent both within and outside the region. According to Nicholson, there are three kinds of capital movements: (1) movements of capital across state boundaries for 'real investment' such as foreign direct investment (FDI); (2) exports of capital goods where the commodities used to make further commodities are exported; and (3) speculative moves of capital (1999: 30). The FDI flows in Asia and the Pacific have increased considerably since the late 1980s (see Table 10.4), and the ratio of

Table 10.1   Trade development in selected Asia-Pacific countries (% of GDP)

	1985	1986	1987	1988	1989	1990	1991	1992	1993	1994	1995	1996	1997	1998	1999	2000	2001	2002	2003
Australia	34.72	34.28	34.07	33.44	33.68	33.48	34.27	36.59	37.67	39.31	39.81	39.40	41.38	40.29	42.37	45.74	42.96	41.76	..
Cambodia	..	..	..	12.63	18.76	18.93	25.48	34.32	49.21	65.61	79.94	70.66	80.94	77.36	89.17	113.86	118.88	126.59	..
Canada	54.68	55.22	52.94	53.23	51.83	52.01	51.35	55.17	61.12	67.61	72.28	73.61	77.96	81.89	83.63	86.78	82.46	..	..
China	24.10	26.54	27.32	27.18	26.24	31.85	35.52	37.46	35.67	48.77	45.68	39.90	41.38	39.21	41.49	49.06	48.54	54.77	65.00
Ecuador	51.74	48.37	57.66	59.35	65.01	64.98	67.43	67.21	51.78	50.99	53.99	50.48	51.35	49.85	56.48	68.06	58.13	55.42	52.46
Hong Kong, China	206.69	212.15	232.24	253.71	251.58	255.88	265.12	273.99	267.02	270.14	294.65	278.24	261.42	250.57	254.55	287.41	278.00	293.31	330.60
Indonesia	42.65	39.97	46.33	44.87	45.69	49.06	49.90	52.85	50.52	51.88	53.96	52.26	55.99	96.19	62.94	76.39	77.11	65.09	56.94
Japan	24.88	18.38	17.33	17.42	19.08	19.81	18.26	17.45	15.92	15.99	16.74	18.87	20.34	19.49	18.54	20.10	20.09	21.00	..
Korea, Rep.	62.90	65.83	69.32	65.76	59.94	57.40	55.82	54.93	53.22	54.92	58.75	59.20	65.39	79.46	71.44	78.49	73.31	69.12	73.81
Macao, China	184.94	189.27	185.69	180.58	176.60	164.24	157.01	136.93	126.36	122.83	119.88	119.47	120.75	123.25	133.37	152.68	159.25	161.75	..
Malaysia	103.17	104.95	111.92	122.62	136.69	146.96	159.31	150.61	157.94	179.91	192.11	181.77	185.67	209.49	217.57	229.28	214.48	210.68	204.78
Mexico	25.75	30.77	32.88	38.47	38.06	38.31	35.64	35.51	34.42	38.48	58.07	62.10	60.64	63.49	63.11	63.94	57.26	55.46	58.53
New Zealand	62.63	53.78	50.93	49.30	52.99	53.78	55.87	60.53	58.64	59.87	57.77	56.08	56.29	59.40	63.45	70.80	68.20	64.82	..
Papua New Guinea	94.55	94.93	92.84	95.17	93.40	89.57	94.42	93.55	89.59	94.30	105.62	95.55	92.42	96.52	90.03	..	..	..	..
Peru	39.42	29.27	23.69	41.45	24.64	29.60	26.69	27.99	28.78	28.92	30.70	31.20	32.74	31.99	32.05	34.14	33.63	33.77	34.99
Philippines	45.85	48.68	52.90	55.27	58.78	60.80	62.18	63.16	71.17	73.96	80.54	89.81	108.25	110.93	102.78	108.90	100.30	98.38	99.01
Singapore	277.53	267.32	298.12	328.33	313.24	307.58	289.57	272.04	272.89	282.53	289.25	277.97	269.85	258.36	277.40	297.74	280.13	277.82	..
Taiwan*	..	..	..	..	80.00	76.00	78.00	72.00	72.00	73.00	81.00	78.00	82.00	81.00	81.00	94.00	82.00	86.00	95.00
Thailand	49.16	49.17	57.23	67.41	72.41	75.78	78.47	77.95	80.16	82.59	90.43	84.78	94.60	101.87	104.02	124.91	125.40	122.16	122.35
United States	17.25	17.51	18.59	19.76	20.20	20.62	20.64	20.80	20.93	21.99	23.46	23.71	24.50	23.87	24.19	26.31	24.13	23.63	..
Vietnam	..	23.22	20.80	18.95	57.90	81.32	66.95	73.58	66.21	77.47	74.72	92.71	94.34	97.00	102.79	112.53	111.56	115.01	..
East Asia & Pacific	36.62	37.68	40.70	42.42	44.23	49.46	52.69	53.74	53.52	63.27	63.92	59.70	63.63	70.97	68.37	78.67	77.13	78.17	82.03

Note: .. = Data not available or not applicable. * Data compiled and calculated from the statistics of the Ministry of Finance, Taiwan.

Source: Compiled from World Bank, *World Development Indicators* database.

Table 10.2 Merchandise exports within regional trade blocs

Year	1970	1980	1990	1995	1996	1997	1998	1999	2000	2001
Regions					US$ million					
APEC	58,633	357,097	901,560	1,688,707	1,755,116	1,869,192	1,734,386	1,896,217	2,262,159	2,075,735
ASEAN	1,456	13,350	28,648	81,911	86,925	88,773	72,352	80,418	101,848	91,675
European Union	76,451	456,857	981,260	1,259,699	1,273,430	1,162,419	1,226,988	1,404,833	1,418,149	1,406,859
MERCOSUR	451	3,424	4,127	14,199	17,075	20,772	20,352	15,313	17,910	15,295
NAFTA	22,078	102,218	226,273	394,472	437,804	496,423	521,649	581,162	676,440	639,138
Regions					% of total bloc exports					
APEC	57.8	57.9	68.3	71.8	71.9	71.6	69.7	71.8	73.1	72.6
ASEAN	22.9	18.7	19.8	25.4	25.4	24.9	21.9	22.4	23.9	23.3
European Union	59.5	60.8	65.9	62.4	61.4	55.5	57.0	63.3	62.1	61.3
MERCOSUR	9.4	11.6	8.9	20.3	22.6	24.8	25.0	20.6	20.9	17.3
NAFTA	36.0	33.6	41.4	46.2	47.6	49.1	51.7	54.6	55.7	55.5

Notes: Regional bloc memberships are as follows: *Asia Pacific Economic Cooperation (APEC)*: Australia, Brunei Darussalam, Canada, Chile, China, Hong Kong (China), Indonesia, Japan, the Republic of Korea, Malaysia, Mexico, New Zealand, Papua New Guinea, Peru, the Philippines, the Russian Federation, Singapore, Taiwan, Thailand, the United States, Vietnam; *Association of South-East Asian Nations (ASEAN)*: Brunei, Cambodia, Indonesia, the Lao People's Democratic Republic, Malaysia, Myanmar, the Philippines, Singapore, Thailand, Vietnam; *European Union (EU)*: Austria, Belgium, Denmark, Finland, France, Germany, Greece, Ireland, Italy, Luxembourg, the Netherlands, Portugal, Spain, Sweden, United Kingdom; *Southern Cone Common Market (MERCOSUR)*: Argentina, Brazil, Paraguay, Uruguay; *North American Free Trade Agreement (NAFTA)*: Canada, Mexico, United States.

Source: World Bank, *World Development Indicators 2003*.

Table 10.3   Trade dependence index of 14 economies

	1980	1985	1990	1995	1996	1997	1998	1999
Brunei	17.03	27.20	33.63	59.88	62.05	62.41	33.93	36.47
Myanmar	4.43	2.19	2.20	2.24	1.76	1.40	0.89	0.84
Cambodia	..	..	5.47	53.53	48.67	38.96	41.91	52.67
Indonesia	7.64	5.96	9.91	11.41	12.02	13.70	27.12	23.41
Lao PDR	..	1.89	18.28	31.26	34.82	24.42	43.31	45.13
Malaysia	26.78	30.36	49.72	62.36	61.05	62.42	70.21	78.53
Philippines	6.92	8.55	11.03	16.73	15.93	22.59	29.11	29.99
Singapore	140.24	107.65	112.06	130.61	125.91	124.86	112.95	122.74
Thailand	11.62	11.31	15.76	21.80	20.36	24.01	26.06	29.71
Vietnam		0.98	23.03	37.98	45.79	43.46	38.00	38.76
Taiwan	12.81	10.77	14.71	24.14	23.50	24.96	23.75	25.55
Hong Kong	47.40	71.24	106.56	138.20	130.86	123.69	117.09	121.72
Korea	6.11	7.23	6.84	12.66	13.57	15.77	18.80	17.63
China	3.36	5.23	14.73	14.26	12.36	13.33	11.73	12.06
(average of the above)	25.85	22.35	30.28	44.08	43.47	42.57	42.49	45.37

Note: The table assumes 14 economies as a group to calculate the index.
   .. = Data not available or not applicable.

Source: IMF, Direction of Trade Statistics; World Bank database.

gross FDI to GDP for East Asia and the Pacific has shifted from 0.74 per cent in 1986 to 4.06 per cent in 2002 (Table 10.5). The FDI inflows into Asia and the Pacific reached their highest point of more than US$146 billion in 2000 (see Table 10.4), and China has continued to be the number one FDI recipient in the region in recent years (UN 2004: 49–50). Other private capital flows have been growing rapidly too. As a whole, the ratio of gross private capital flows to GDP for East Asia and the Pacific has increased from 3.87 per cent in 1989 to more than 10 per cent in the 1990s (see Table 10.5). As the capital mobility increases, however, capital flows have at the same time exposed Asia-Pacific countries to external disturbances and destabilizing effects such as massive flows of short-term capital (hot money) and speculative activities, which in turn has brought to the region such financial crises as the 1994 Mexico peso crisis and the 1997 Asian financial crisis, and deepened the region's economic interdependence internally and externally.

People's flows

With the innovations of travelling and transportation technology, the movement of human beings becomes another key aspect of observing economic interdependence. Increasing people's flows, including tourists and migrations of labourers, not only

Table 10.4   FDI flows in Asia and the Pacific (US$ million)

	FDI inflows	FDI outflows
1985	5,468.8	2,860.8
1987	13,431.8	5,650.1
1989	17,328.0	14,133.8
1991	24,348.3	8,013.5
1993	58,954.6	31,173.3
1995	80,280.8	42,250.2
1997	110,349.9	52,770.3
1998	102,449.3	31,591.1
1999	112,884.3	41.,644.8
2000	146,194.8	83,872.4
2001	111,966.1	50,425.1
2003	107,277.6	23,636.9

Source: The United Nations, *World Investment Report 2004* (Geneva: United Nations, 2004).

indicates but also deepens economic interdependence. While the degree of people's flows in the Asia Pacific is not as large as that in Europe or North America, it has been rapidly increasing throughout the 1990s. Advanced countries in the region, including Australia, Canada, Japan, New Zealand, and the United States, had more inflows of foreign workers after 1990 (see Table 10.6). Also, East Asian newly industrialized economies (NIEs) such as South Korea, Taiwan, Singapore and Hong Kong have become major host economies for foreign labourers who are mostly from Southeast Asian countries. For example, foreign labour force of total labour force in South Korea has increased from 0.10 per cent in 1994 to 0.60 per cent in 2001 (World Bank 2004). As well, as Table 10.7 indicates, the number of foreign workers in Taiwan has increased sharply to more than 300,000 in the past decade. On the other hand, more and more overseas workers from Southeast Asian countries have been deployed in the Asia-Pacific area since the 1990s. Overseas workers of the Philippines have not only increased, but also gradually shifted their destinations from the Middle East to the Asia Pacific in the 1990s (see Table 10.8).

Furthermore, the expansion of people's flows in the Asia Pacific can be examined through the growth of international tourism and passengers of air transport. In particular, for most Asia-Pacific developing countries indicated in Table 10.5, both average expenditures of international tourism and passengers of air transport have continued to grow since 1990. All these changes of people's flows have in turn further increased the interdependence of the Asia Pacific both within and outside the region.

Table 10.5 Development indicators of East Asian and Pacific developing countries, 1986–2003

Indicators\Year	1986	1987	1988	1989	1990	1991	1992	1993	1994	1995	1996	1997	1998	1999	2000	2001	2002	2003
Gross private capital flows (% of GDP)	3.61	3.18	3.87	3.87	4.96	5.06	7.50	11.43	11.41	7.85	8.24	11.19	12.86	14.64	13.87	11.32	10.20	..
Gross foreign direct investment (% of GDP)	0.74	1.05	1.43	1.53	1.74	1.96	3.16	5.12	4.64	4.24	4.33	4.57	5.20	4.55	4.21	4.50	4.06	..
International tourism, expenditures (% of total imports)	..	..	..	..	2.35	2.33	3.32	3.24	3.22	3.24	3.42	4.23	4.65	4.68	4.31	4.67	4.40	..
Air transport, passengers carried (million)	34.70	40.00	47.80	44.10	52.20	57.90	69.10	77.20	88.80	104.30	110.90	107.70	106.40	105.50	117.50	129.10	144.10	
GDP growth (annual %)	6.65	8.82	9.98	6.53	5.95	8.15	10.50	10.53	10.37	9.48	8.56	6.43	0.70	5.67	7.10	5.56	6.72	7.73

Note: *East Asia and Pacific region refers to 24 developing countries:* American Samoa, Malaysia, Philippines, Cambodia, Marshall Islands, Samoa, China, Micronesia, Fed. Sts, Solomon Islands, Fiji, Mongolia, Thailand, Indonesia, Myanmar, Timor-Leste, Kiribati, Northern Mariana Islands, Tonga, Korea, Dem. Rep., Palau, Vanuatu, Lao PDR, Papua New Guinea, Vietnam.

.. = Data not available or not applicable.

Source: Compiled from World Bank, *World Development Indicators* database.

Table 10.6   Inflows of foreign workers of selected countries (thousands)

	1991	1993	1995	1997	1999	2001
Australia	..	37.03	34.51	51.93	64.96	81.37
Canada	77.70	65.45	69.69	75.39	85.41	93.08
Japan	113.60	97.10	81.51	93.90	108.04	141.95
New Zealand	..	..	..	30.22	39.17	68.38
United States	229.20	329.29	306.00	90.61	582.52	867.68

Note: .. = Data not available or not applicable.

Source: Compiled from World Bank, *World Development Indicators* database.

Table 10.7   Registered foreign workers in Taiwan, by origin

Year	1996		1997		1998		1999		2000		2001		2002	
Origin	No. (000)	Share (%)	No. (000)	Share (%)	No. (000)	Share (%)	No. (000)	Share (%)	No. (000)	Share (%)	No. (000)	Share (%)	No. (000)	Share (%)
Indonesia	10.2	4.3	14.6	5.9	22.1	8.2	41.2	13.9	77.8	23.8	91.1	29.9	93.2	30.1
Malaysia	1.5	0.7	0.7	0.3	0.9	0.3	0.2	0.1	0.1	0.1	0.1	0.1	0.1	0.6
Philippine	83.6	35.3	100.3	40.4	114.2	42.2	113.9	38.6	98.2	30.0	72.8	23.9	69.4	22.9
Thailand	141.2	59.7	132.7	53.4	133.4	49.3	139.5	47.3	142.7	43.7	127.7	41.9	111.5	36.7
Vietnam	0.0	0.0	0.0	0.0	0.0	0.0	0.1	0.1	7.7	2.4	12.9	4.2	29.5	9.7
Total	236.5	100.0	248.3	100.0	270.6	100.0	294.9	100.0	326.5	100.0	304.6	100.0	303.7	100.0

Source: Council of Labour Affairs, Executive Yuan, Taiwan <http://dbs1.cla.gov.tw/stat/index/ 4602. pdf>; accessed 16 May 2006.

RTAs/FTAs

Unilateral liberalization, multilateral liberalization and regional (or preferential) liberalization are basically three routes to trade liberalization. Despite the establishment of the World Trade Organization (WTO) in 1995, regional trade agreements (RTAs) continue to mushroom across the globe. In the period 1948–94, the General Agreement on Tariffs and Trade (GATT) received 124 notifications of RTAs; however, since the creation of the WTO, there have been over 130 additional arrangements notified covering trade in goods or services. By the end of 2005, if RTAs reportedly planned or already under negotiation are concluded, the total number of RTAs in force might well approach 300.

The rise of free trade agreements (FTAs) in particular is taking alongside the forward movement of multilateral trade negotiations and has become a prominent feature in the WTO era. Against the backdrop of increasing economic interdependence, since

Table 10.8   Overseas workers from the Philippines, by destination

	1990		1996		1997		1998	
	Number (000)	*Share (%)*	*Number (000)*	*Share (%)*	*Number (000)*	*Share (%)*	*Number (000)*	*Share (%)*
Asia Pacific	90.8	27.1	174.4	36.0	235.1	42.3	221.3	39.7
Hong Kong	34.4	10.3	43.9	9.1	..	..	..	..
Japan	41.6	12.4	20.2	4.2	..	..	..	..
Malaysia	4.4	1.3	12.3	2.5	..	..	..	..
Singapore	4.7	1.4	15.1	3.1	..	..	..	..
Taiwan	0.1	0.0	65.5	13.5	..	..	..	..
Other Asia	5.6	1.7	17.4	3.6	..	..	..	..
Americas	9.6	2.9	8.4	1.7	7.1	1.3	8.2	1.5
Europe	6.9	2.0	11.4	2.4	12.6	2.3	15.7	2.8
Middle East	218.1	65.1	221.2	45.6	221.0	39.8	226.8	40.7
Other	9.6	2.9	69.3	14.3	79.9	14.3	84.9	15.3
Total	335.0	100.0	484.7	100.0	555.7	100.0	556.9	100.0

Note: .. = Data not available or not applicable.

Source: Adapted from Goto (2002: 33).

the late 1990s the FTA fashion has also turned the Asia-Pacific region from an empty box in the regional map of FTAs to a region with more than 30 signed FTAs and emerging FTA proposals (see Table 10.9).

The increase of economic interdependence might not be the only or most important factor contributing to the recent proliferation of FTAs in the Asia Pacific. However, since FTAs may contribute to trade creation or diversion, increasing investment flows, future market access, binding and reciprocal commitments, and faster negotiation and liberalization, the economy of the Asia Pacific will likely become further integrated and interdependent as FTAs continue to evolve in the region.

All in all, for the Asia Pacific, international economic interdependence has been on the increase, no matter in terms of trade, capital flows, or people's flows. The increasing economic interdependence has also reinforced cross-border exchanges as well as pushed for such international cooperation as RTAs/FTAs in the region. The question now is whether the increase of economic interdependence has made the Asia Pacific more secure or more stable.

UNSTABLE POWER RELATIONS AND REMAINING SECURITY TROUBLES

During the Cold War, international security and world order were by and large determined or affected by the US–Soviet confrontation, and so was the basis of security and international relations in the Asia Pacific. Yet the break-up of the Soviet Union in

Table 10.9   The proliferation of FTAs in the Asia Pacific

	Within the Asia Pacific	*With non-Asia Pacific partners*
Signed	ASEAN FTA, NAFTA, Australia– New Zealand CER, Japan–Singapore EPA, Japan–Mexico EPA, China– Hong Kong CEPA, China–Macao CEPA, Singapore–Australia FTA, Singapore–New Zealand FTA, Singapore–US FTA, Chile–US FTA, Chile–Canada FTA, Chile–Mexico FTA, Chile–Korea FTA, Australia– US FTA, ASEAN–China FTA, China–Thailand Bangkok Agreement	US–Israel FTA, US–Jordan FTA, US– Bahrain FTA, US– Morocco FTA, Canada–Costa Rica FTA, Canada–Israel FTA, Chile–Costa Rica FTA, Mexico– Israel FTA, Mexico–Nicaragua FTA, Mexico–Bolivia FTA, Mexico–Panama FTA, Mexico–EU FTA, Mexico–EFTA FTA, Mexico–Singapore–Liechtenstein FTA, Singapore–Switzerland FTA, Singapore–Norway FTA, Taiwan– Panama FTA
Under negotiation or study	ASEAN+3 FTA, ASEAN–Japan FTA, ASEAN–Korea FTA, Japan– China–Korea FTA, Japan–Korea FTA, China–Australia FTA, China–Chile FTA, China–Peru FTA, China–New Zealand FTA, China–Singapore FTA, Singapore–Chile FTA, Singapore–Canada FTA, Singapore– Mexico FTA, Singapore–Korea FTA, Singapore–Thailand FTA, Thailand– US FTA, Thailand–Australia FTA, Thailand–New Zealand FTA, Thailand–Chile FTA, Thailand–Mexico FTA, Philippine–Taiwan FTA, Philippine–US FTA, Korea–Mexico FTA, Korea–US FTA, Korea– Australia FTA, Korea–New Zealand FTA, Japan–Philippine FTA, Japan– Malaysia FTA, Japan–Thailand FTA, Japan–Brunei FTA, Japan–Indonesia EPA, Japan–Taiwan FTA, Japan– Chile FTA	ASEAN–EU FTA, ASEAN–India, China–India FTA, Singapore–EU, Singapore–India FTA, Singapore– Jordan FTA, Singapore–Sri Lanka FTA, US–Egypt FTA, Thailand–Peru FTA, Thailand–India FTA, Thailand– Bahrain FTA, Mexico–India FTA, FTAA, Taiwan–Nicaragua FTA, US–North Africa FTA, US–Central America FTA, US–SACU FTA

Source: Various sources.

1991 not only ended the Cold War, but also changed the world order and power configuration overnight. This in turn shook the basis of Asia-Pacific security and immediately created such uncertainties as whether the United States would remain a hegemony in the region and whether a regional power would emerge. This section thus explores whether the basis of Asia-Pacific security is improving in the context of growing economic interdependence by examining the post-Cold War power relations, particularly among the US, China and Japan, as well as reviewing the traditional security troubles in the region.

Unstable power relations

When the Cold War had just ended, the withdrawal of the Soviet Union and the uncertainty of the US commitment to military presence in the Asia Pacific brought a 'power vacuum' that other regional powers, notably China and Japan, might fill. As the most populous nation in the world, China has been widely regarded as the most likely country to fill the power vacuum with its fast-growing economic strength and its military potential after the end of the Cold War. Since its economic reform and open-up policy began in 1978, China has maintained a very high economic growth rate. Based on World Bank's statistics, China's average GDP growth rate in the past decade is about 8.9 per cent, which is the highest in the world. Also, as China continues to open and integrate with the world economy, trade has become increasingly significant to its economy. After the Cold War, China's trade–GDP ratio more than doubled to 65 per cent in 2003. More important is that today Japan and the United States have become China's number one and number two trading partners respectively.[6] The market shares of China's export goods in Japan and the Unites States have climbed to 20 per cent and 13 per cent respectively.[7] Except for Hong Kong, both the United States and Japan are currently the largest FDI providers for China.[8] Under the circumstances of rapid economic growth, China's military expenditure climbed steadily in the 1990s and reached US$32.8 billion in 2003, based on the estimation by the Stockholm International Peace Research Institute (SIPRI) (see Table 10.10). In the face of the rise of China, Asia-Pacific states, especially the United States and Japan, have started to react in various ways, which in turn has affected the security structure of the region.

As the only post-Cold War superpower in the world, the United States has not changed its strategic primacy in the region, although it initially did reduce its military presence in the Asia Pacific. The US even advocated an Asia-Pacific security structure, with the US as the sole leader followed by its bilateral alliances (Wu 2000: 480; Lasater 1996: 14–16). Given this and China's fast-rising power, a US–China struggle for dominance appears to be inevitable. Despite China's constant claim for peaceful coexistence and multilateral security cooperation, the United States has been wary of China's every movement. In particular, China's nuclear tests in May and July 1995 and its series of military exercises and missile tests over the Taiwan Strait in 1995 and 1996 stimulated the United States to send two carrier battle-groups into the area to monitor the situation. Then a strong message was sent not only to China, but also to the rest of the Asia Pacific that the US would not back down on its security commitment to the region and it is in the interest of the US to keep the region's stability and status quo (Mak 1998: 103).

Table 10.10 Military expenditure, selected countries, 1989–2003

	1989	1990	1991	1992	1993	1994	1995	1996	1997	1998	1999	2000	2001	2002	2003
Australia	5,911	5,940	6,042	6,218	6,454	6,526	6,321	6,244	6,354	6,666	6,993	6,973	7249	7624	7821
Chile	[1,786]	[1,835]	[1,891]	[1,958]	[2,006]	[2,029]	[2,078]	[2,156]	2,347	2,502	2,650	2,805	2912	3105	2975
China	[11,300]	[12,100]	[12,700]	[15,300]	[14,200]	[13,500]	[13,900]	[15,300]	[15,500]	[17,800]	[20,000]	[22,000]	[25900]	[30300]	[32800]
Indonesia	[1,436]	[1,587]	[1,615]	[1,739]	[1,670]	[1,845]	[1,942]	[2,110]	1,963	1,545	1,273	1,656	1740	1835	..
Japan	40,140	41,311	42,259	43,278	43,753	43,958	44,398	45,293	45,510	45,394	45,479	45,793	46259	46773	46895
N. Korea	(1,867)	(1,983)	(2,053)	(2,107)	(2,157)	(2,215)	..	..	..	(1,343)	(1,343)	(1,379)	(1439)	(1517)	(1793)
S. Korea	9,475	9,624	9,928	10,506	10,988	11,310	11,897	12,539	12,842	12,398	12,061	12,801	13079	13533	13925
Malaysia	1,057	1,135	1,545	1,535	1,631	1,768	1,879	1,807	1,698	1,248	1,689	1,533	1908	2169	2312
Mexico	[1,722]	[1,788]	[1,972]	[2,183]	[2,386]	[2,978]	2,630	2,763	2,865	2,828	2,991	2,997	3113	2957	2873
New Zealand	(774)	(727)	(691)	647	631	635	647	651	638	639	648	650	636	613	606
Philippines	759	747	684	691	747	797	877	907	808	794	778	819	767	868	[881]
Russia	[93,600]	[79,200]	..	[18,500]	[16,400]	[15,800]	[10,000]	[9,100]	[9,700]	[7,100]	[8,300]	[9,700]	[11000]	[11400]	[13000]
Singapore	1,958	2,248	2,325	2,472	2,550	2,636	3,157	3,459	3,882	4,396	4,478	4,331	4434	4679	4733
Taiwan	8,572	9,047	9,298	9,398	10,664	10,535	9,525	9,606	9,973	9,723	8,377	7,770	7927	7281	7272
Thailand	1,851	1,947	2,148	2,293	2,538	2,540	2,709	2,784	2,736	2,417	2,109	1,843	1773	1847	[1827]
USA	422,133	403,701	354,284	374,386	354,778	334,539	315,107	298,058	296,530	289,658	290,480	301,697	304130	341489	417363
Vietnam	1,018	988	694	437	343	468	..	..	..	..	..	..	..	..	..

Note: Figures are in US$ million, at constant 2000 prices and exchange rates and are for calendar year. ( )=Uncertain figure, [ ]=SIPRI estimate, ..=Data not available or not applicable.

Source: Stockholm International Peace Research Institute (SIPRI).

To further strengthen American dominance over the region, just one month after the Taiwan Strait crisis, the US and Japan signed the US–Japan Joint Declaration on Security—Alliance for the 21st Century. In 1998, to counter both North Korea's nuclear threat and China's missile capabilities, the US joined with Japan to research theatre missile defence (TMD). All of these actions not only deepened China's suspicion of US motives, but also increased China's concerns about Japan (Yang 2003: 307). This is because, in China's perception, the end of the Cold War would likely bring about the rise of China and Japan relative to Russia, and the multipolarization of regional affairs with the growing influence of China, Japan, and ASEAN; however, from Beijing's perspective, the redefinition of the US–Japan alliance is to hamper the multipolarization process, build some sort of 'Washington–Tokyo condominium on regional affairs', and marginalize China (Wu 2000: 487).

The dispute over the Taiwan issue between the US and China was not resolved with the end of the Cold War. Although Washington's 'one China' policy since the late 1970s did serve China's interests and contribute to cross-Strait stability, the US has enhanced political ties with Taiwan, continued to provide military assistance to Taiwan's defence, and strategically viewed Taiwan as a quasi-ally in the region since the end of the Cold War. In the face of expanding political and military relations between Washington and Taipei, Beijing has found it intolerable and has constantly stated that the Taiwan issue is the major obstacle in improving the Sino–US relationship. In other words, as long as the US prefers the status quo to be maintained—the de facto independence of Taiwan—the Sino–US relationship would always find a sticking point.

Certainly, based on recent cooperation and coordination in countering terrorism and dealing with the issue of North Korea via the Six-Party Talks, the Sino–US relationship has been improved significantly since the 9/11 incident. Even so, in the long run, the US still has to face the rise of China and its challenges to American hegemony and dominance in the Asia Pacific in various dimensions. Short-term and ad hoc interest compromise seems unable to ensure long-term stability of the Sino–US relationship. Therefore, as Mak (1998: 88) remarks, 'while the Cold War was an era of USA–Soviet confrontation, the post-Cold War period is likely to be marked by USA–China tensions'. Yet the statement might oversimplify the post-Cold War power relations in the Asia Pacific. As a major power in Asia, Japan has also been forced to react to the rise of China and changing Sino–US relations. In fact, Japan was the first of the Western allies to resume loans for China after the Tiananmen massacre. With the increasing mutual economic interactions, in recent years Japan has emerged as China's greatest trading partner, and China as second biggest to Japan. Coinciding with this has been a corresponding growth in Japanese FDI towards China (total agreed investment from Japan of over US$60 billion by 2004). More than that, until the 1990s China was the main beneficiary of the Japanese Official Development Assistance (ODA). By 2000 Japan had provided free aid of more than 1.1 trillion yen (Yahuda 2004).

Despite this, the growing economic exchange has not led to the emergence of constituencies that have been publicly supporting or improving closer ties between China and Japan. In a recent opinion poll in China, only 5.9 per cent of Chinese said that Japan was 'very friendly' or 'friendly' while 43.3 per cent believed the opposite. In

Japan, there are fewer and fewer people who think that China is friendly, from 75.4 per cent in 1985 to 47.5 per cent in 2001; in contrast, the number of those who think China unfriendly extended to 48.1 per cent in 2001 (Yang 2003: 306). In short, Japan has been worried about the 'China threat', whereas China has increased concerns about the expansion of Japan's military role and political influence. Nevertheless, the contradicting development has much to do with historical problems and uneasiness in new divergences between China and Japan.

For a long time, the treatment of the historical legacy of Japanese invasion of China, including the Japanese textbook controversy and official visit to the Yasukuni Shrine, the Diaoyu (Senkaku) Islands dispute, and the Taiwan issue, have been primary historical problems in Sino–Japanese relations. Unfortunately, none has approached solution in the post-Cold War era and some are even intensifying (Yahuda 2004). Even though these long-term problems are currently under control and not contributing to military conflicts, new divergences, particularly associated with each party's strategic concerns, between Japan and China have continuously emerged since the end of the Cold War. Thus far they have in general included Japanese worries about further Chinese nuclear tests and military activities in the Taiwan Strait and South China Sea; Chinese concerns about the reinvigoration of the US–Japan Security Threat and the expansion of the US–Japan TMD programmes; Japan's identification of China as a potential source of external threat in its Defence White Papers; Japan's fear of China's military modernization and enhancement; and China's warning of Japanese inclination toward militarism (Roy 2004; Yahuda 2004).

Moreover, in order to cope with the soaring demand for natural resources, lately China–Japan disagreement on demarcation of the East China Sea has intensified. Japan favours drawing a line falling at an equal distance from each country's shoreline, whereas China asserts the continental shelf is the demarcation line (Wolfe 2004). The dispute flared further when Japan detected a Chinese submarine in its waters between the southern island of Okinawa and Taiwan in November 2004. At the same time, Japan announced that it would reduce and eventually end ODA to China in the near future. China reacted by saying 'the Chinese people need only rely on their own strength, wisdom, determination and confidence to build their own country' (Wolfe 2004). These latest divergences and disputes add further sticking points and uncertainties to Sino–Japanese relations.

Overall, as Yang (2003: 306) points out, 'China's post-Cold War relations with Japan have been largely stable. Yet this stability can hardly disguise the uneasiness in that relationship'. Lacking mutual trust, closer economic ties between China and Japan seem to have no corresponding spill-over into political, social, and security aspects of bilateral relations. In this context, the Sino–Japanese relations are hardly predictable and stable, but increasingly uncertain and unstable. In other words, together with the sticking Sino–US relations, the situation of big-power relations in the Asia Pacific is more unstable and complex than what some expect in the post-Cold War era.

Remaining security troubles

Apart from power relations, whether or not the security in the Asia Pacific would evolve in a cooperative or conflictual direction also depends on the development of traditional security troubles within the region. Against the backdrop of increasing economic interdependence, what happened to such major security problems as cross-Strait rivalry, the Korean issue, and the disputes of the South China Sea after the Cold War?

Regarding cross-Strait rivalry, the People's Republic of China (China) and Taiwan began to confront each other militarily and politically after World War II. Since then both sides of the Taiwan Strait had had little contact until the late 1980s. Especially after Taipei made the dramatic move of allowing its citizens to visit their relatives in China in 1987, cross-Strait exchanges in economy, culture, education, and so on, increased remarkably in the 1990s. Among others, the development of a bilateral economic relationship is the most momentous, active, and obvious one. China soon became Taiwan's alternative export market as well as its largest investment place, even though Taiwan promoted a 'Southward' policy.[9] Under the circumstances, trade, investment, and people's flows across the Strait have skyrocketed, as Table 10.11 shows.

Two-way trade increased sharply from less than US$3 billion in 1988 to more than US$46 billion in 2003. Today China has replaced the United States as Taiwan's largest export market and received nearly 24 per cent of Taiwan's total exports in 2003 (MAC 2004). In addition to trade, up to 2003 China received at least 47 per cent of Taiwan's approved outward investment (total = US$72.99 billion) and became the number one recipient of Taiwan's foreign investment (MAC 2004). In terms of contract-investing capital, Taiwanese business people have cumulatively poured nearly US$70 billion into China (MAC 2004). In 2002, the number of trips made by Taiwanese people to

Table 10.11   Cross-Strait exchanges, 1988–2003

Year	Two-way trade (US$ million)	Share of Taiwan total foreign trade (%)[a]	Export share of Taiwan's exports (%)[b]	Taiwan investment towards China (realized amount, US$ million)	Taiwanese visits to China (000)
1988	2,720.90	2.47	3.70		4.38
1991	8,619.40	6.20	9.84	844.00*	946.60
1994	17,881.20	10.02	17.22	3,391.00	1,390.20
1997	26,370.60	11.15	18.39	3,289.00	2,117.60
2000	31,233.10	10.84	16.87	2,296.28	3,108.70
2002	37,412.50	15.39	22.56	3,970.64	3,660.60
2003	46,319.70	17.07	24.52	3,377.24	2,731.90

Notes
a   Taiwan's trade volume to China divided by Taiwan's trade volume to the world;
b   Taiwan's exports to China divided by Taiwan's total exports to the world.
*   including data before 1991.

Source: Mainland Affairs Council, *Cross-Strait Economic Statistics Monthly* (Taipei), no. 144, August 2004. Available from <http://www.chinabiz.org.tw/chang/L1-5.asp>; accessed 16 May 2006.

China reached a historical high: 3,660,570. Cumulatively, more than 30 million such trips have been made across the Strait without direct flight (MAC 2004). The two sides of the Strait have never before experienced such a high degree of economic interdependence between them.

Yet disappointingly (especially for liberals and functionalists), increasing economic interdependence has not been sufficient to overcome divergent political and security interests across the Strait. Politically, Beijing still stands tough on its claim of political sovereignty over Taiwan, and continues to squeeze Taiwan's room in the international community by breaking Taiwan's formal relationships with other countries and boycotting Taiwan's entries into international organizations. Beijing has not ruled out the use of military force against Taiwan. More importantly, after the 1995–96 Taiwan Strait crisis, China has positioned numerous (more than 700) truck-mounted short-range ballistic missiles targeting Taiwan along its southeast coast. As the nation becomes richer, China has also been engaged in a rapid military build-up by expanding defence spending and acquiring a huge array of weapons, including SU-27 and SU-30 jet fighters, Kilo-class submarines and advanced destroyers (Miles 2005: 6).

Despite China's political pressure and military intimidation, economic interactions across the Strait have continued to grow. Nonetheless, with Taiwan's smooth and fast democratization, people in Taiwan have been in a process of redefining their identity. Today the majority of people in Taiwan think they are Taiwanese, instead of Chinese.[10] This identity redefinition has not only contributed to Taiwan's nationalism, but also incurred China's worry about the island's formal independence. As a result, Beijing recently has been issuing warning that a *de jure* independence of Taiwan (including a change of name) would mean war. Beijing is even preparing a new anti-secession law to indirectly constrain Taiwan's choices for the future and legitimize its use of forces against Taiwan.

In other words, the rivalry across the Strait has not been eased substantially with the increase of economic interdependence. Rather, tension between China and Taiwan could escalate, even to a point of military conflict that might drag in the US and Japan. In that case, 'the whole region could be plunged into turmoil', as Miles (2005: 3–4) concludes. Even in strictly economic terms, the asymmetry of economic interdependence across the Strait has also made Taiwan's economy overdependent on and vulnerable to China's economy. This has not only brought such threats as industrial hollowing-out and hyper-competition to Taiwan's economy, but has also challenged its economic security. So, has economic interdependence made the Taiwan Strait much more secure? The answer is there.

Besides the Cross-Strait issue, security troubles in the Korean peninsula and the South China Sea have remained unsolved since the end of the Cold War. Despite the increase of economic interdependence in the Asia Pacific, North Korea remains by far the most economically isolated country in the region. During the Cold War, Pyongyang played off Moscow and Beijing to obtain economic benefits from both. After the collapse of the Soviet Union, North Korea began to use its nuclear card to initiate talks with the US to gain access to energy and economic aid (Mochizuki 1998). To avoid another Korean war or a violent collapse of North Korea, such countries as the United States, Japan, China and South Korea have been trying to use economic incentives to steer North Korea towards internal reform, external moderation and dialogues with neighbouring states (Mochizuki 1998). However, from previous four-party talks (the two Koreas, the US and China) to current six-party talks (four parties plus Japan and Russia), North Korea is still reluctant to give up its weapons of mass destruction (WMD) programme, given the offer of energy aid and security guarantee. Consequently, it is hard to see North Korea introducing comprehensive economic reform and fostering normal relations with the US, Japan and South Korea in the near future.

Instead, a crisis may be rekindled if the US escalates economic pressure and pushes international inspections of North Korean ships and cargo movements (Morrison and Baker 2004: 6). Furthermore, as Camroux and Okfen (2004: 169) argue, 'over time, economic problems in North Korea will be aggravated due to the constantly high military expenditures of the government, and so the possibility of collapse in North Korea cannot be ruled out'. If that is the case, the worst consequence could be as catastrophic as a nuclear war.

Another historical security trouble is the South China Sea disputes, which essentially involve two main archipelagos: the Paracels and the Spratly: 'whereas China and Taiwan claim all the archipelagos in the South China Sea, the Vietnamese claim the Paracels and the entire Spratlys. Malaysia, the Philippines and Brunei lay claim to various parts of the Spratly Islands' (Mak 1998: 110). Thus far, there have been various motivations behind these competing claims, such as traditional sovereignty, colonial heritage, coastal jurisdiction, strategic considerations, resources, and economics. Thus a failure to resolve the South China Sea dispute peacefully would have broad regional consequences (Cossa and Khanna 1997: 226).

In order to carry out its 'good-neighbour policy', establish a China–ASEAN free trade area, and increase its political influence in the region, China signed the Declaration on the Conduct of Parties in the South China Sea with ASEAN countries in 2002. The signatories basically declared 'to resolve their territorial and jurisdictional disputes by peaceful means, without resorting to the threat or use of force, through friendly consultations and negotiations by sovereign states directly concerned, in accordance with universally recognized principles of international law, including the 1982 UN Convention on the Law of the Sea' (ASEAN 2002). To further improve its relations with ASEAN, in 2003 China also gained accession to the Treaty of Amity and Cooperation in Southeast Asia. With these, the South China Sea territorial disputes seem to have become less troublesome; however, they are still pending and without effective solutions.

In the long run, to solve the disputes the region must still face some embedded challenges that may alter the consequences significantly. First, the Declaration on the Conduct of Parties in the South China Sea does not apply to Taiwan, a key disputant in the disputes. Without including all parties concerned, the disputes will not be solved. Second, the South China Sea could be rich in oil, gas, fish and mineral resources. As economic growth and interdependence push demands for energy and resources, disputants may eventually collide in competing for resources. Finally, in strategic terms, the South China Sea is not only territorial waters for disputants, but also a gateway to other regions for Japan and the two Koreas. In other words, any decision regarding the disputes would have impacts on non-disputants. For these reasons, the disputes may last longer than expected.

In sum, the end of the Cold War did shake the basis of Asia-Pacific security. Yet the increase of economic interdependence seems unable to do much about the increasingly complicated and uncertain Sino–US, Sino–Japanese, and Sino–US–Japanese relations. Also, even though the current extent of economic interdependence in the region is unprecedented, traditional security troubles in the Taiwan Strait, Korean peninsula and South China Sea still remain unsolved. Economic interdependence, in some cases and to some extent, has further intensified power relations and deteriorated historical security problems.

NEW SECURITY THREATS

Traditionally, security concerns are often bound by military affairs, power relations, political ideologies and rival foreign policies. However, with the demise of the Cold War, the increase of economic interdependence, and the spread of globalization, today we worry about the uncertainty and volatility of the global economy, global terrorism and organized crimes, deadly contagious diseases, ecological disasters, and such chaos as ethnic, religious or cultural conflicts. In other words, as the world becomes interdependent and globalized, the scope of security concerns is more wide and diverse. This is hardly exceptional to the Asia Pacific wherein such new security threats posed by economic volatility, terrorism and infectious diseases have become increasingly salient.

In the Asia Pacific, the Asian financial crisis that erupted in 1997 could be the most vivid case demonstrating the risks and security concerns posed by economic volatility. The crisis began with the tumbling of the Thai baht in July 1997. By the end of July 1997, however, the Philippine peso, the Malaysian ringgit and the Indonesian rupiah all came under attack from international speculators and thus plummeted (Wu 2004: 2). The financial turmoil soon spilled over to Northeast Asia, including Korea, Hong Kong, Taiwan, Japan, and China. South Korea's economy in particular was in serious trouble so that the Korean government finally asked the IMF for bailout in November 1997.[11] As the currency turmoil had become contagious, the New York Stock Exchange and European markets were substantially affected as well. At the end of 1997, 'almost all East Asia had experienced unprecedented significant currency depreciation in a short period of time, coupled with heavy falls in share prices' (Wu 2004: 7).

Thus far there have been several explanations for the Asian financial crisis: huge short-term capital flows, persistent deficits on the current accounts, limited information and transparency, weak surveillance and insufficient regulation, and economic globalization (Wu 2004; Mochizuki 1998). However, as Dr Wu points out, 'the salient feature of this financial crisis is its "contagion effect" due to the integration among the economies and the cross-border movement of capital. No country can escape the impact of the financial fluctuation once the economy is open to international markets' (2004: 7). In other words, as Horst Kohler, managing director of the IMF, argues, 'openness and economic interdependence exacerbate the spill-overs of economic shocks across countries, and amplify domestic economic problems' (Santiago 2004: 34). Therefore, with trade, capital flows, and people's flows becoming interdependent and integrated in the Asia Pacific, economic volatility has become an important origin for security concerns and challenges in the region.

More than that, with the increase of economic openness and interdependence, non-economic factors such as terrorist activities and rapidly infectious diseases are also affecting the security of the Asia Pacific. For instance, despite the terrorist attack of 11 September, 2001 in the United States (the 9/11 incident), with economic interdependence, its impact has been both regional and global. According to the World Bank (2002: 5), the direct cost of the 9/11 incident to the US is about US$25–35 billion (0.38 per cent of GDP). Yet, the 9/11 incident and war on terrorism had brought about worldwide damage to tourism, investment confidence, financial markets and transportation. Based on the World Bank's estimation, the 9/11 incident even caused greater impact on the economic growth of developing countries than on that of the US. The World Bank predicted that the 9/11 incident would reduce American economic growth rate by 0.1–1.0 per cent, but cut 1.3 per cent for developing countries (World Bank 2001: 176, World Bank 2002: 3).

More importantly, with the rising importance of international trade and investment to Asia-Pacific economic growth and prosperity, uncertainty surrounding terrorism has not only increased anxiety about security at the personal level, but has also raised the risks and costs for doing business in the region. Governments are thus forced to impose counter-terrorism policies and measures on economic activities and transactions, because any terrorist attack on American ports is estimated to result in a US$58 billion cost for the American economy, and reduce 1.1 per cent of GDP for such economies as Singapore, Hong Kong and Malaysia (Australian Department of Foreign Affairs and Trade, 2003). However, counter-terrorism measures have generated extra costs for economic transactions, such as higher insurance fees, costly transportation and complex customs reporting. According to American estimation, counter-terrorism measures implemented after 9/11 would increase the cost of trading products by 1–3 per cent (Huisken 2003: 33).

Economic interdependence thus not necessarily preserves Asia-Pacific security; instead, it spreads security anxiety and increases regional uncertainty. A similar argument can also be illustrated by the outbreak of Severe Acute Respiratory Syndrome (SARS) in 2003. As *Asia Pacific Security Outlook 2004* describes it, 'although fewer than 1,000 people worldwide lost their lives to SARS, far less than to ordinary influenza, the novelty and initial deadliness of SARS, the mysterious manner in which it seemed to spread, and the lack of medicines to treat it created widespread fear sometimes verging on panic' (Morrison and Baker 2004: 2). Accordingly, measuring and understanding the full picture of the impact of SARS cannot just rely upon calculating the number of cancelled trips and the decline in retail trade (Lee and McKibbin 2004: 1). Taking the factor of economic interdependence into account would rather help to capture the overall impact caused by the SARS outbreak, which went beyond the direct damages incurred in the affected areas.

With economic interdependence, and its intensive flows of goods, capital and people, SARS spread quickly across countries through networks associated with global travel, and any economic shock to one country was soon spread to other countries through trade and financial linkages. Erupting in China, SARS had spread to almost 30 countries by July 2003. At the same time, there were at least 8,400 probable SARS cases worldwide; 99 per cent of them in the Asia Pacific (WHO 2003). According to Lee and McKibbin's (2004: 123–4) estimation by the G-Cubed (Asia Pacific) model, a temporary shock (six months) caused by the SARS outbreak would reduce the GDP of Hong Kong by 2.63 per cent, much larger than the corresponding loss of 1.05 per cent for China. Taiwan was the next most seriously affected area, losing 0.49 per cent of GDP in 2003, followed by Singapore with a loss of 0.47 per cent of GDP. Hence, as the Asia-Pacific economy becomes more integrated, the cost and security concerns of a highly contagious disease like SARS are expected to rise. Though SARS did not reappear in 2004, an outbreak of avian flu with some associated human deaths in Southeast Asia quickly incurred the region's anxiety and concerns once again.

Therefore, economic interdependence might traditionally be conceived as conducive to diminishing political or military conflicts, and positive to facilitate international cooperation. As indicated above, nevertheless, economic interdependence indeed could spread, and even create security threats. As a consequence, the concept of security is no longer determined by political, military or strategic affairs. Instead, our conceptual understanding of security has been expanding to cover such new security threats as economic volatility, terrorist activities, highly contagious diseases, cultural conflicts, and so on.

PROSPECTS

The relationship between economic interdependence and security has engendered considerable debate in history. While positive or optimistic views argue that international economic interdependence would reduce conflicts, increase cooperation, and contribute to security preservation and improvement, sceptical or pessimistic views hold that economic interdependence provides no guarantee against conflict and may even increase uncertainty and threaten security. For the post-Cold War political economy, however, both views may be too one-sided and oversimplified. The relationship between economic interdependence and security in fact is much more complicated than what both traditional positive and sceptical views perceive.

As indicated above, the economy of the Asia Pacific in particular has become extraordinarily interdependent both externally and internally in trade, capital flows, and people's flows, which has increased cross-border exchanges as well as improved international cooperation in such areas as FTAs, regional economic integration and economic development. Against this backdrop of increasing economic interdependence, nevertheless, power relations (including the Sino–US, Sino–Japanese and Sino–US–Japanese relations) are increasingly complicated and unstable. Similarly, traditional security troubles in the Taiwan Strait, Korean peninsula and South China Sea have not been altered much by economic interdependence. Rather, economic interdependence has spread or generated such security threats as economic volatility, terrorist activities, highly contagious diseases and cultural conflicts, and at the same time widened the scope of security concerns for the Asia Pacific.

As a result, the relationship between economic interdependence and security should be neither unilinear nor monocausal, but dynamic and networking. In other words, economic interdependence in a sense can increase exchanges and provide chances for cooperation, but should not be accepted as a panacea for contemporary security problems. Unmanaged economic interdependence and untamed market forces can sometimes threaten economic security, undermine communal harmony, damage social well-being, and aggravate international peace and security issues (Moon 1998: 12). Security has been gradually regarded as one sort of public good in the context of increasing economic interdependence. International cooperation and coordination are thus essential to manage/govern the contemporary tie between economic interdependence and security. No single country, no matter how hegemonic, could resolve security problems associated with economic interdependence. As Moon asserts (1998: 12), 'there must be coordinated, collective efforts'. No stakeholders can be excluded for any reason; otherwise the efforts will eventually fail.

In the Asia Pacific, the ASEAN Regional Forum (ARF), established in 1994, is currently the only official venue to discuss security matters. The ARF members thus far have included 10 ASEAN countries and another 14 dialogue partners.[12] Except Taiwan, all stakeholders associated with (potential) conflicts in the region are now members. Although the ARF was established to promote 'preventive diplomacy', build confidence, and manage or peacefully resolve conflicts, it had nothing to say on the 1996 Taiwan Strait crisis, did nothing about North Korea's WMD programme, and had little to do about countering terrorism and other new security threats. The ARF 'has therefore been accused of being unstructured, under-institutionalized, and therefore ineffective' (Mak 1998: 117). Given its current institution, what the ARF can do most is probably to build confidence via the process of socialization that is, however, also its major obstacle to addressing immediately pressing issues or crises. In short, the Asia-Pacific region has been lacking an inclusive, responsive and effective multilateral regime for security cooperation since the end of the Cold War.

In the face of remaining security troubles and potentially serious security threats and uncertainties, and given the weak institution for security cooperation, the Asia-Pacific region is compellingly in need of cooperation mechanisms to address increasingly multi-faceted and pressing security issues responsively and effectively. Some have proposed establishing new regional mechanisms for security cooperation; some have argued to strengthen the current ARF or to extend the existing APEC to address security problems. However, no matter what the region prefers, 'non-exclusiveness' should be the principle and all relevant stakeholders should be taken into consideration, because collective effort is imperative to manage the increasingly dynamic and complex relationship between economic interdependence and security.

Having proper cooperation mechanisms, including all relevant stakeholders might be necessary, but it is still not sufficient to address the security problems associated with economic interdependence. To improve the efficiency and effectiveness of international cooperation and coordination in this regard, capacity-building should not be neglected either. In particular, as the origin of security threats moves from traditional to non-traditional concerns, security threats delivered via economic interdependence could be prevented, contained or reduced if individual states' related capacity is sufficient. This is why APEC, ASEAN or ASEAN+3[13] recently have gone beyond traditional economic cooperation to focus on capacity-building in such areas as financial reforms, accommodation to globalization, social security, countering terrorism, health security, and disaster preparation and responsiveness. In spite of this, such efforts have been by and large fragmented, sporadic and framed around each issue area. The capacity gap among Asia-Pacific countries has also made the region far from creating and sustaining a cooperation mechanism to cope with insecurity related to economic interdependence. Narrowing the capacity gap or capacity building thus becomes desperately needed, but such a transition cannot be undertaken without international cooperation or assistance.

In sum, as economic interdependence increases and security becomes more like public good in the Asia Pacific, international cooperation and coordination are essential to manage the link between economic interdependence and security as well as cope with relevant insecurity. However, to initiate, sustain and reinforce such international cooperation and coordination, the principle of non-exclusiveness and the improvement of capacity-building must be emphasized.

NOTES

1   This is because liberals typically assume that: (1) human beings are 'good' in nature; (2) conflict and war are not inevitable; (3) human beings are likely to make progress, particularly for a better life; (4) the state is not a unitary actor; (5) a free market and absolute gains are admirable (Jackson and Sørensen 1999: 108–10; Viotti and Kauppi 1999: 199–200; Kegley 1995: 4).

2   Manchester school refers to 'the movement in England from 1820 to 1850 which was inspired by the propaganda of the Anti-Corn Law League' (Bannock *et al.* 1992: 268). The school basically 'believed in free trade and political and economic freedom with the minimum of government restraint' (*ibid.*).

3   In contrast to liberal assumptions, most realists basically assume that: (1) people are by nature sinful and wicked; (2) states are the principal actors that consist of an international system characterized by anarchy; (3) international politics are essentially and necessarily conflictual, in which states rely on their own capabilities (mainly political and military) to struggle for power and seek security and survival; (4) states are both unitary and rational actors; (5) relative gains are key to a state's power; (6) politics are more important than economics so that economic activities need to accommodate national (political) objectives (Jackson and Sørensen 1999: 68–9; Dougherty and Pfaltzgraff 1997: 58–9; Viotti and Kauppi 1999: 55–7; Gilpin 1987: 31–4).

4   Most variants of Marxist tradition share the following central propositions: (1) economic determinism at both domestic and international levels, e.g., economic production determines the institutional and ideological structures of society—whoever controls the economic system also controls the political system; (2) all history is a history of class struggle between a ruling group and an opposing group, e.g., the bourgeoisie vs. proletariat; (3) states are not autonomous and instead are driven by ruling-class interests (Dougherty and Pfaltzgraff 1997: 217; Jackson and Sørensen 1999: 185).

5   Trade dependence index is defined as the number of exports and imports of a country with a particular trading partner as a percentage of the country's GDP.
6   This estimation is based on data from *China Foreign Economic Statistical Yearbook* and *China's Customs Statistics*. The data are also available from *Cross-Strait Economic Statistics Monthly*, <http://www.chinabiz.org.tw/chang/L1-5.asp>; accessed 16 May 2006.
7   Japan Customs, Ministry of Finance, Japan; and USA Customs Statistics. The data are also available from *Cross-Strait Economic Statistics Monthly*, <http://www.chinabiz.org.tw/chang/L1-5.asp>; accessed 16 May 2006.
8   This estimation is based on data from *China Statistical Yearbook*, *China Foreign Economic Statistical Yearbook*. The data are also available from *Cross-Strait Economic Statistics Monthly*, <http://www.chinabiz.org.tw/chang/L1-5.asp>; accessed 16 May 2006.
9   The policy is to encourage Taiwanese businesses to expand trade and investment relationships with Southeast Asian nations to avoid overdependence on the Chinese market, which may threaten Taiwan's national security.
10 Based on the surveys conducted by the Election Study Centre of Taiwan's National Chengchi University, in the past 12 years the number of those identifying themselves as Taiwanese has risen from 17 per cent to 41 per cent, whereas those who regard themselves purely as Chinese have dropped from 26 per cent to 6 per cent (Miles 2005: 5).
11 The bailout plan was to settle with US$57 billion, which was also the largest international aid programme in history at that time (Wu 2004: 4).
12 ARF members are: Australia, Brunei Darussalam, Cambodia, Canada, China, European Union, India, Indonesia, Japan, Democratic People's Republic of Korea, Republic of Korea, Laos, Malaysia, Myanmar, Mongolia, New Zealand, Pakistan, Papua New Guinea, Philippines, Russian Federation, Singapore, Thailand, United States, Vietnam.
13 'ASEAN+3' means the cooperation mechanism among the ASEAN, China, Japan and South Korea.

REFERENCES

APEC (n.d.) 'What is Asia-Pacific Economic Cooperation?'. Available from <http://www.apecsec.org.sg/content/apec/about_apec.html>; accessed 2 June 2006.

ASEAN (2002) 'Declaration on the Conduct of Parties in the South China Sea'. Available from <http://www.aseansec.org/13163.htm>; accessed 16 May 2006.

Australian Department of Foreign Affairs and Trade (2003) 'The Costs of Terrorism and the Benefits of Cooperating to Combat Terrorism', Information Report submitted to APEC Senior Officials Meeting I, Chiang Rai, Thailand, 20–21 February. Available from <http://www.dfat.gov.au/publications/costs_terrorism/costs_of_terrorism.pdf>; accessed 2 June 2006.

Bannock, G., R.E. Baxter and E. Davis (1992) *The Penguin Dictionary of Economics*, London: Penguin Books.

Barbieri, K. and G. Schneider (1999) 'Globalization and Peace: Accessing New Directions in the Study of Trade and Conflict', *Journal of Peace Research*, 36(4): 387–404.

Camroux, D. and N. Okfen (2004) 'Introduction: 9/11 and US–Asian Relations: Towards a "New World Order" ', *The Pacific Review* 17(2): 163–77.

Cossa, R.A. and J. Khanna (1997) 'East Asia: Economic Interdependence and Regional Security', *International Affairs*, 73(2): 219–34.

Dougherty, J. and R. Pfaltzgraff (1997) *Contending Theories of International Relations: A Comprehensive Survey*, 4th edn, New York: Longman.

Gilpin, R. (1987) *The Political Economy of International Relations*, Princeton, NJ: Princeton University Press.

Goto, J. (2002) 'Economic Interdependence and Cooperation with Reference to Asia', presented at Capacity Building Workshop: Trade Policy Issues, 25 February–1 March 2002, Singapore.

Hirschman, A.O. (1977) *The Passions and the Interests: Political Arrangements for Capitalism before its Triumph*, Princeton, NJ: Princeton University Press.

Huisken, R. (2003) 'The Threat of Terrorism and Regional Development', in K. Chang (ed.) *Political and Economic Security in Asia Pacific*, Taipei: Foundation on International & Cross-Strait Studies, 25–39.

Ikenberry, J. (1996) 'The Myth of Post-Cold War Chaos', *Foreign Affairs*, 75(3): 79–91.

Irwin, D.A. (1996) *Against the Tide: An Intellectual History of Free Trade*, Princeton, NJ: Princeton University Press.

Jackson, R. and G. Sørensen (1999) *Introduction to International Relations*, New York: Oxford University Press.

Kegley, C.W. Jr. (ed.) (1995) *Controversies in International Relations Theory: Realism and the Neoliberal Challenge*, New York: St. Martin's Press.

Lasater, M.L. (1996) *The New Pacific Community: US Strategic Options in Asia*, Boulder, CO: Westview Press.

Lee, J-W. and W.J. McKibbin (2004) 'Globalization and Disease: the Case of SARS', *Asian Economic Papers*, 3(1): 113–31.

Mainland Affairs Council (MAC) (2004) *Cross-Strait Economic Statistics Monthly* 144 (August). Available from <http://www.chinabiz.org.tw/chang/L1-5.asp>; accessed 16 May 2006.

Mak, J.N. (1998) 'The Asia-Pacific Security Order', in A.G. McGrew and C. Brook (eds), *Asia-Pacific in the New World Order*, New York: Routledge, 88–120.

Miles, J. (2005) 'A Survey of Taiwan', *The Economist*, (15 January): 3–12.

Mochizuki, M.M. (1998) 'Security and Economic Interdependence in Northeast Asia', working paper, Asia/Pacific Research Center, Stanford University.

Moon, C. (1998) 'Market Forces and Security', United Nations University Report. Available from <http://www.unu.edu/unupress/marketforces.html>; accessed 19 April 2006.

Morrison, C.E. and R.W. Baker (2004) *Asia Pacific Security Outlook 2004*, Tokyo: Japan Centre for International Exchange.

Mueller, J. (1989) *Retreat from Doomsday: The Obsolescence of Major War*, New York: Basic Books.

Nicholson, M. (1999) 'How Novel Is Globalization?', in M. Shaw (ed.), *Politics and Globalization: Knowledge, Ethics, and Agency*, New York: Routledge, 23–34.

Nye, J.S. Jr. (1988) 'Neorealism and Neoliberalism', *World Politics*, 40(2): 245–51.

Oneal, J.R. and B. Russett (1999) 'The Kantian Peace: the Pacific Benefits of Democracy, Interdependence, and International Organizations, 1885–1992', *World Politics*, 52(1): 1–37.

Pavehouse, J.C. (2004) 'Interdependence Theory and the Measurement of International Conflict', *The Journal of Politics*, 66(1): 247–66.

Pease, K-K.S. (2003) *International Organizations: Perspectives on Governance in the Twenty-First Century*, 2nd edn, Upper Saddle River, NJ: Prentice Hall.

Polachek, S.W. (1980) 'Conflict and Trade', *Journal of Conflict Resolution*, 24(1): 55–78.

Rogowski, R. (1989) *Commerce and Coalitions: How Trade Affects Domestic Political Alignments*, Princeton: Princeton University Press.

Roy, D. (2004) 'Stirring Samurai, Disapproving Dragon: Japan's Growing Security Activity and Sino–Japan Relations', *Asian Affairs: An American Review*, (June): 86–101.

Santiago, T. (2004) 'Political Risk Could Cost World Economy $1 Trillion', *Electronic Engineering Times*, (9 February): 34.

United Nations (UN) (2004) *World Investment Report 2004: The Shift Towards Services*, New York: the United Nations.

Viner, J. (1985) 'Peace as an Economic Problem', in R. Art and R. Jervis (eds), *International Politics*, 2nd edn, Boston: Little, Brown, 291–302.

Viotti, P. and M. Kauppi (1999) *International Relations Theory: Realism, Pluralism, Globalism, and Beyond*, 3rd edn, Boston, MA: Ally and Bacon.

Waltz, K. (1970) 'The Myth of National Interdependence', in *The International Cooperation*, Charles Kindleberger (ed.), Cambridge: MIT Press, 205–23.

—— (1979) *Theory of International Politics*, New York: Random House.

Wolfe, A. (2004) 'The Potential Deterioration of Sino–Japanese Relations', *The Power and Interest News Report (PINR)* (6 December), available from <http://www.pinr.com/report.php?ac=view_report&report_id=242&language_id=1>; accessed 16 May 2006.

World Bank (2001) *Global Economic Prospects and the Developing Countries 2001*, Washington, DC: World Bank.

—— (2002) *Global Economic Prospects and the Developing Countries 2002: Making Trade Work for the World's Poor*, Washington, DC: World Bank.

—— (2004) *World Development Indicators 2004*, available at <http://www.rrojasdatabank.org/wdi04toc.htm>; accessed 16 May 2006.

World Health Organization (WHO) (2003) 'Cumulative Number of Reported Probable Cases of SARS'. Available from <http://www.who.int/csr/sars/country/2003_07_11/en/>; accessed 16 May 2006.

Wu, R-I. (2004) *Collection of Papers on 1997–98 East Asia, Russia and Latin America Financial Crises*, Occasional Paper Number 1, Taipei: Taiwan Institute of Economic Research.

Wu, X. (2000) 'US Security Policy in Asia: Implications for China–US Relations', *Contemporary Southeast Asia*, 22(3): 479–97.

Yahuda, M. (2004) 'The Limits of Economic Interdependence: Sino–Japanese Relations'. Available from <http://www.isanet.org/archive/yahuda.doc>; accessed 16 May 2006.

Yang, J. (2003) 'Sino–Japanese Relations: Implications for Southeast Asia', *Contemporary Southeast Asia*, 25(2): 306–27.

Policy perspectives

11 Practitioner's perspectives on trade and development

Mari Pangestu

I write this chapter not as an academic, but as a policymaker, to ask how developing countries can manage the process of globalization so that its benefits outweigh its risks.

BENEFITS OF GLOBALIZATION

Research leaves little doubt that increased trade and investment lead to growth and development. We also know that the underlying drivers of globalization—rapid change in technology, communication, and transport and the behaviour of multinational companies—permit greater fragmentation and specialization in production of goods and in the provision of services, and that this opens new opportunities for developing countries.

To benefit from increased integration with the world economy, a country needs to attract investment. However, the issue is no longer about simply liberalizing foreign investment policies. More critical is the provision of soft infrastructure, and efficient services and infrastructure to ensure the competitiveness of industry. It is no longer necessary to have integrated production links between upstream and downstream sectors, nor are economies of scale and volume necessarily sources of competitive advantage. What matters more nowadays is time to delivery, how fast we can adapt to changes in technology and tastes, and how our industries can be part of the so-called value chain of any sector.

Within Indonesia, the debate among policymakers is what kind of industrial and trade policy we should have, given these trends and our commitments under international agreements. Should we establish clusters of upstream and downstream industries—a traditional industrial tree—or facilitate more flexible, dynamic structures of industry, where the goal is no longer graduating slowly up a value-added ladder, but rather finding niches in the value chain? The latter requires the country's industry to be more agile, but it may be better for developing countries and especially their small and medium-sized enterprises. Fragmentation and specialization of production give more opportunity for developing countries to leapfrog certain sectors or subsectors of the development process, and gives more opportunity for SMEs to participate. At the same time we must create jobs for the more than two million new entrants into the labour force every year, as well as the 10 per cent of the labour force that remains unemployed.

RISKS OF GLOBALIZATION

We also face inherent risks from globalization. Research on the risks of globalization, especially since the failed WTO ministerial meeting in Seattle, suggests that trade should not be seen as an end but as a means. Openness is not, on its own, a guarantee of sustained growth or poverty reduction. (To be sure, there is also no evidence that closed economies achieve sustained growth.)

The crucial issue is the process of opening up—how broad based it is and, most importantly for policymakers, what complementary policies and institutions are adopted to make the impact as beneficial and widespread as possible. In many countries, and Indonesia is no exception, the easiest policy to use is trade policy, so that too much burden is put on trade policy as a means of achieving competitiveness and growth. Trade policy on its own is a very blunt instrument, and is a poor policy for achieving growth and equity. It needs to be accompanied by investment and complementary policies in other areas, such as human capital, hard and soft infrastructure and technological capability—in other words, a combination of policies that target both openness and other drivers of growth. At the same time, there must also be explicit policies to address equity as part of the development strategy. These should be separate, targeted policies.

A further point in the debate on trade and poverty is that developing countries are not homogeneous. The conventional wisdom before the Asian crisis of the 1990s was that poor countries that followed market-oriented policies and good governance would automatically experience sustainable growth, provide basic needs, and alleviate poverty. This may have happened to an extent in East Asia, but there were many other developing countries and regions where these linkages did not take place. For instance, much of sub-Saharan Africa faces structural problems that are beyond its control; good governance and good policies were not enough. In contrast to the structural adjustment programmes of the 1980s, or the IMF and World Bank programmes of the 1990s, the alleviation of poverty is not just about good policy and good governance, but must include efforts to deal with the root causes of poverty, such as war, geographical constraints, disease, and excessive reliance on traditional primary products.

POLICIES TO MANAGE RISKS

Several types of policies are needed over and above trade policy to make globalization lead to genuine development. First, we need to invest in human development. Second, we need to help farmers raise their productivity and break out of subsistence farming. Third, we need to target industrial development policies on non-traditional private sector activities, including a range of policies that support SMEs—export-processing zones, tax incentives, R&D and the mobility of unskilled labour. Fourth, we must also address equity, environmental sustainability, and urban management—the broader context of sustainable development.

We are currently having an important debate in Indonesia over industrial development policy. In today's world, the Japan and Korea Inc. models no longer apply, because the policy space for government interventions is very limited. For example, it is no longer possible to use local content rules or export subsidies.

Furthermore, budget constraints mean that even if subsidies were still permitted, they would be a limited instrument. So what can governments do? There are still those who believe that we can select winning sectors, but even if we could, what instruments or incentives could we use to promote them? Given the severe limits on sector-specific government policies, isn't it better to focus on providing the right investment environment, the right infrastructure? Perhaps the most important goal that government can pursue is to make sure that once goods leave the factory, they get to the harbour efficiently. That includes ensuring adequate physical infrastructure, removing bureaucratic bottlenecks, and making customs work efficiently. In the contemporary value chain, speed and reliability of delivery are critical factors.

What then can governments do to ensure that we benefit from globalization while managing the risk? More importantly, how do policymakers sell their case domestically? It is not enough to tell people—as economists sometimes do—that the benefits of liberalization come mostly from a country's own liberalization rather than liberalization by others.

The ideal approach for a country—especially one facing the pressures of globalization at the same time as it engages in regional, bilateral and multilateral negotiations—is to adopt a clear national strategy for sequencing the liberalization process. The strategy must determine what institutions or policies need to be in place before the liberalization process begins, anticipating risks by sector, by groups of stakeholders and by region.

Indonesia is already a very open economy. Tariffs are on average only seven per cent. The foreign investment environment is also very open, including in the sensitive services sector. However, many Indonesians think that we should not open further, and in some sectors, especially agriculture, there remains a great deal of protection or control. As we address the liberalization of these sectors, we must ensure that policies are in place to meet the needs of the people who will not benefit, getting them to engage with the policy by ensuring that they feel comfortable with the compensation offered.

Allow me to provide two specific examples. Indonesia banned the export of raw rattan a few years ago in order to help its furniture makers, in effect to lower the price of their raw material to enable them to compete with Chinese and other lower-cost furniture makers. In fact, furniture makers only use 30 per cent of the raw rattan, so 70 per cent is now supposedly not exported. It is likely, however, that some of this was exported illegally. The fact is that Chinese producers are still making furniture with Indonesian rattan. The question is whether we should remove the export ban on rattan, and if so, how we could do that without adversely affecting furniture makers. The ban and limitations on rattan exports came at the cost of the rattan harvesters, many of whom are in Sulawesi and Kalimantan, while the furniture makers are in West and East Java. The other stakeholders are environmental groups.

What is the 'win-win' policy solution? The solution was a compromise consisting of several elements. First, the quota for rattan exports was increased and broadened (still maintaining the ban on raw rattan exports), based on the estimated need for ensuring domestic supply. Second, furniture makers were provided with support to become more competitive by upgrading their productivity and quality. This included a programme of technical assistance to enhance design capability and promotion efforts, and a general policy to reduce the costs of doing business as part of the broader government reform agenda. Third, investors and furniture makers, including from China, were invited to relocate in Indonesia, where the raw materials are produced.

The second example comes from the services sector. In Indonesia, there is widespread concern that modern hypermarkets, such as Giant and Carrefour, take business away from traditional markets. There is also the issue of fair treatment of domestic suppliers, who are allegedly facing stringent and unfair trading terms. These are issues faced by many countries. Some popular demands include halting the growth of the modern retail sector, asking modern hypermarkets to provide space to the small retail sector and suppliers, or regulating the trading terms of hypermarkets. One must indeed find solutions that allow traditional markets and small shops to grow in tandem with modern retail. Surveys have shown that in developing countries there is still market segmentation, and different types of retailers serve rather different consumer needs. Even if products overlap, consumers continue to shop in both traditional and modern retail markets.

The popular solutions will not solve the competitiveness problem of traditional markets versus hypermarkets. The approach that is being developed involves, first, improving the domestic distribution system so that the supply of goods to domestic retailers is of competitive quality and price. Second, it involves improving and empowering traditional domestic markets so that they are clean, well-ventilated, well-organized and comfortable places to shop. Third it requires improving the management of traditional markets. Fourth, it requires guidelines for zoning the location of modern and large hypermarkets, and for partnerships between them and small and medium-sized enterprises. Finally, it involves addressing fair competition and trading terms through competition policy and monitoring by the Fair Trading Commission.

The policymaker must also deal with the implications of globalization strategies for institutional reform. Related to this is the balance between national autonomy and sovereignty, and the international discipline that flows from multilateral, regional or bilateral commitments. As I already noted, there remains little scope for a country in terms of industrial policy. We are therefore moving away from sectoral to general approaches. Given our democratic context, we are also moving toward greater transparency in decision-making.

Countries that acceded to the WTO recently, such as China and now Cambodia, have used WTO accession as a framework for domestic reform. Countries such as Indonesia, which have already acceded to the WTO, have also used commitments in APEC, the WTO or in ASEAN to shape their domestic reform efforts. Nevertheless, the fact is that there has been a considerable backlash against international institutions since the Asian financial crisis and post-Seattle, and so there is much less sympathy for using international commitments as a framework for policy reform. So the challenge we face as policy makers is public education—keeping the public informed on what we are doing to manage globalization, and how we are making sure that our national interests are addressed in international negotiations as well as in our national policies.

INDONESIAN TRADE POLICY

Let me comment now on the role of Indonesia in regional, bilateral, and multilateral negotiations. In recent months, we have reviewed our policies and Indonesia is now following a cautious, multi-track strategy of bilateral, regional and multilateral negotiations. We think that they can be complementary and WTO-consistent, but how can we make sure that is the case?

Bilaterally, we have entered into negotiations with Japan, and with the US we are still accelerating the TIFA, as the first step of a potential bilateral FTA. If one asks how a developing country should enter bilateral negotiations, the ideal is to 'practise' with smaller partners before entering negotiations with large countries such as Japan. Unfortunately, that luxury is no longer open for countries that are only beginning to consider bilateral negotiations. This is because many of the other ASEAN countries have already entered or completed their bilateral negotiations. Singapore already has a bilateral agreement with Japan, the US, and a number of other countries. Thailand has a bilateral agreement with Australia and is negotiating with the US and Japan; Malaysia has completed its negotiations with Japan and is negotiating with the US, and the Philippines is negotiating a bilateral agreement with Japan. This implies that countries like Indonesia have to adopt a parallel track strategy whereby our negotiations are still anchored within the multilateral WTO framework and the regional agreements with ASEAN as the centre, but also include bilateral negotiations. On the bilateral negotiations, given limited resources and the fact that many of our competing neighbours already have negotiations in place with large trading partners, we need to limit our focus on the priority markets, beginning with Japan.

On the ASEAN front, we are moving rapidly on the ASEAN-plus-one model. To ensure best practice in such ASEAN-plus-one or bilateral agreements, it is important to have consistency among agreements. Rules of origin negotiations are a recent example. ASEAN has liberal rules of origin—40 per cent cumulative content—which we are trying hard to maintain. We were able to achieve that in the ASEAN/China agreement, but India insisted on complex, sectoral rules of origin. We won that battle, conceding only an exclusion list of some sort. But that has led to a debate over how extensive that exclusion list is going to be. We are trying to maintain best practice in regional agreements and, as ASEAN's largest country, we feel the responsibility to take a leadership role.

On the multilateral front, the aim is still to successfully complete the modalities for negotiations, but what needs to happen, if this is to be a real development round, is that progress has to be made on all five areas of developing-country issues. In particular, as coordinator of the G33, I am responsible for special products in the agriculture negotiation. There is great political need to address this issue in developing countries, much as developed countries need some kind of 'sensitive products' list. The challenge is political—each side has to sell its WTO commitments domestically—but the solutions should not be so disruptive of trade as to defeat the purpose of the negotiations.

Another issue for developing countries in the WTO negotiations involves changes in their bound concessions. On paper, many agreements now being negotiated on market access and services involve reducing such bound concessions, but in fact most developing countries, with the exception of those that acceded to the WTO recently, have bound tariffs at high rates. Therefore, reducing bound rates will not involve giving up much in terms of changing actual applied rates.

There is a similar issue in services: our commitments and offers are much more limited than the actual situation allows. While research shows that the gains from opening up result from a country's own liberalization, negotiations do not work this way. And so policy makers have to explain somehow—domestically, politically—that reducing bindings is not tantamount to 'giving away the goods'. That is one of our biggest challenges, because to benefit economically from the negotiation often requires reducing bindings.

CONCLUSIONS

The real difficulty facing those involved in trade policy today is to convince the domestic constituency that opening up, with the right sequence and complementary policies and institutions, can lead to broad-based benefits. How one compensates losers and ensures that the benefits are widely shared becomes a challenge. Furthermore, acceptance of the ideal policy is often out of reach because of considerations for sectoral, group and regional interests. The reality is that we do live in a second-best world. The challenge for the policy maker is to find a politically acceptable second-best policy that involves the least distortion and hopefully also becomes a stepping stone to first-best policy when and if domestic constituencies and institutions are ready. An alternative is to find compensatory mechanisms that allow the first-best policy to be reached.

Another real difficulty for smaller developing countries is negotiating in the complex world of multilateral, regional and bilateral negotiations. We must always keep in sight what will benefit us, and avoid complex regional agreements that lead to higher costs of doing business and administrative complexities that inevitably stretch our limited capacities.

12 US trade strategy and the Asia-Pacific region

Lisa Coen

In recent years, the trade strategy of the United States has been simultaneously global, regional, and bilateral—much like the approach endorsed by Minister Pangestu.

Our discussions at this conference have made it clear that trade is controversial in the Asia-Pacific region, and this is also the case in the United States. Our system in the US requires close partnership with Congress, which delegates key aspects of trade negotiating authority to the President. We also work closely with business and other interest groups. Even in the highly politicized environment that typically surrounds trade efforts, we have accomplished a great deal, and it is worth reviewing some of the results.

POLICIES UNDER PRESIDENT BUSH

Our most important priority has been the Doha Development Agenda, in which we have played a leadership role since it began in 2001. We now have free trade agreements (FTAs) with 14 countries and are working on agreements with an additional 12 countries. In 2001 the US implemented the Jordan FTA and the Vietnam Bilateral Trade Agreement, and the China Permanent Normal Trade Relations agreement (PNTR) went into effect. In 2002, we got a boost when, after a hard-fought battle, Congress approved the Trade Promotion Authority (TPA), a new fast-track authority enabling the President to pursue a broader trade agenda. That year we announced the Enterprise for ASEAN Initiative, which allows us to work with ASEAN countries that are committed to openness and economic reform, and potentially an FTA relationship with the United States. In 2003, Congress approved both the Singapore and Chile FTAs.

In 2004 the TPA really began to pay off. The Australia and Morocco FTAs were approved by Congress. We also concluded the DR–CAFTA and Bahrain negotiations, and hope to have the agreements approved by Congress shortly. The Doha framework was agreed on in July, and we then launched negotiations on the Thailand, Andean and Panama FTAs. At the same time we notified Congress that we would begin negotiations on UAE and Oman FTAs, building on the President's Middle East Free Trade Area initiative (MEFTA). Based on the progress with Morocco and Bahrain, we see a good deal of potential in this approach. We also continued work on the South African Customs Union (SACU) and Free Trade Area of the Americas (FTAA) agreements.

PRIORITIES IN THE ASIA-PACIFIC

In the Asia-Pacific region, in addition to cooperation with our FTA partners, Thailand and Singapore, we are continuing our broad engagement, often via Trade and Investment Framework Agreements (TIFAs), with the Philippines, Malaysia, Indonesia, Brunei, New Zealand, Taiwan, and Korea. We also have a regulatory dialogue underway with Japan, and are working with China through the Joint Commission on Commerce and Trade (JCCT) and on WTO implementation issues. With ASEAN countries, our hope is to step up efforts further, to participate in senior official forums, and to pursue our Enterprise for the Americas Initiative (EAI) goals.

These initiatives are working. For example, in 2004 US exports to Chile, Singapore, and China increased much more rapidly than US exports to the rest of the world. Our exports to Chile grew by 33.5 per cent; to China by 22.4 per cent; and to Singapore by nearly 19 per cent. The cumulative weight of all of our FTAs is also significant. Taken together, the 26 countries with which we have concluded an agreement or with whom we are negotiating comprise the third largest US export market, and our sixth largest trading partner. In the Asia-Pacific region, our goods exports to ASEAN were up six per cent last year and, taken as a group, ASEAN is now our fourth largest export market.

The opening of agricultural markets and the creation of more opportunities for service providers are among our key objectives. The US now runs surpluses in its global agricultural trade as well as its services trade. Our state-of-the-art intellectual property (IP) commitments, with both developed and developing countries, are also critical in addressing business concerns.

While our FTAs are comprehensive, we do not see them as static. For example, with Thailand we have a new group on cooperation involving small and medium-sized enterprises (SMEs), modelled on our trade capacity building efforts with CAFTA. We are also trying to address corruption issues. In other words, we are continuously updating our model, adapting it to circumstances.

GOALS FOR THE FUTURE

Looking ahead, our highest priority remains the successful conclusion of the Doha Round. Ambassador Zoellick had set up small group meetings at Davos in January 2005 with a number of key ministers, including many from the Asia-Pacific region, and recently Acting United States Trade Representative (USTR) Peter Allgeier met again with key leaders in Geneva. They are laying the groundwork for the WTO Ministerial Conference in Hong Kong, with the aim of making progress in all five key areas. With eight APEC economies accounting for nearly half of world trade, the economies of the Pacific Rim have an especially large stake in achieving success at a global level.

At the same time, we will continue to pursue our bilateral and regional agenda, including the EAI, the MEFTA, the FTAA and bilateral FTAs. We have recently discussed the possibility of opening FTA discussion with Korea. We have talked to Malaysia and Brunei under our TIFAs, and hope to do so with Indonesia shortly. By helping to coordinate positions in the Pacific basin, APEC can also play a key role in building a more favourable environment for the expansion of trade in the region.

13 Balancing regional and multilateral commitments: the case of Iceland

Geir H. Haarde

Taking part in an academic forum like this is refreshing although very different from the ministerial meetings I have attended regularly over the past seven years at the IMF, OECD, Nordic Council of Ministers, EFTA and a myriad of other organizations, formal and informal. It seems to me that the proliferation of international gatherings and groupings, large and small, dealing with economic, financial and trade issues is in itself a sign of the growing interdependence and globalization we have witnessed over the past few decades.

ICELAND'S EXPERIENCE IN THE WORLD TRADING SYSTEM

I will make just a few remarks on the situation of my own country, Iceland—distant though it is from the Asia-Pacific region—with respect to trade liberalization, and then offer some comments on regional FTAs as well as the urgency of bringing the ongoing Doha Development Round within the WTO to an early and successful conclusion.

The trend toward freer trade has been an irreversible element in international relations since World War II. While the global framework for this was not formalized in its present form until the mid-1990s in the WTO, the less formal General Agreement on Tariffs and Trade (GATT) as well as regional organizations have been around for much longer. Iceland has been a member of one of those, the European Free Trade Association (EFTA), since 1970. EFTA dates back to the Stockholm convention of 1960, originally with seven members, several of whom later joined what would become the European Union. While today's EFTA is a much smaller organization than at the outset with only Switzerland, Norway, Iceland and Liechtenstein as its members, it is still an organization of some consequence. Its total trade, exports and imports, is greater annually than that of Russia or all of Africa taken together. The EFTA countries, apart from Switzerland, come together with the countries of the EU in the so-called European Economic Area, which essentially incorporates all 28 countries in a single market for goods, services, capital, and labour. As a result of this beneficial arrangement, Iceland has not seen any need to apply for membership of the EU, which would both be costly and result in the transfer of control of our vital fisheries resources to the EU, an unacceptable proposition to most Icelanders.

I have noticed in the debate at this conference a certain lack of enthusiasm, to say the least, for regional free trade agreements. This is understandable, as a global approach is in theory much more desirable. However, the world is not perfect. What may be desirable is not always attainable and hence theory is not always the same as practice. For this reason many countries have sought to seek quicker benefits by seeking to negotiate FTAs with trading partners. This is true for EFTA whose members remain, of course, committed to the success of the more cumbersome and time-consuming multilateral approach while at the same time seeking the advantages FTAs may bring. In December 2004 I had the pleasure of signing, on behalf of EFTA, a new FTA with Tunisia, thereby completing a series of agreements between EFTA and several Mediterranean countries. Earlier, agreements had been made with the countries of Central and Eastern Europe as well as more distant ones such as Mexico, Chile and Singapore. Work is under way on agreements with Canada, South Africa, and South Korea. So EFTA has clearly contributed to Bhagwati's 'spaghetti bowl' of FTAs even if it accounts for only a fraction of the 260 or so FTAs that have been notified to the WTO.

THE IMPORTANCE OF THE DOHA ROUND

Yet clearly the more important task is to move forward on the multilateral front under the auspices of the WTO, as so eloquently outlined by Director General Supachai in his opening remarks at this conference. (I might add in passing that Dr Supachai used to be a student of former World Chess Champion Max Euwe in the Netherlands and is a formidable chess player himself, a skill which is not useless in complicated multilateral trade negotiations!) The success of the current Doha Round of trade liberalization is of tremendous importance for future world prosperity and is to be seen in the context of other commitments set forth by world leaders in the Millennium Development Goals, the Monterrey Consensus and the Johannesburg Declaration.

These documents and action agendas renew the commitments of the world community to economic development and poverty reduction. International trade, every one agrees, is a powerful engine of global growth, which in turn is a *sine qua non* for the alleviation of poverty. The World Bank has in its *Global Economic Prospects 2004* simulated the impact of the Doha Round and concluded that it would reduce the number of people living on less than two dollars a day by some 144 million. The greatest reduction in absolute terms would take place in Sub-Saharan Africa. This is in addition to the impact on richer parts of the world.

How can anyone or any government not be willing to contribute to such an outcome? The national sacrifices required to attain this seem insignificant compared to the global progress to be made in the crucial battle against destitute poverty and human suffering, which surely is one of the most pressing international problems of our day.

The conference theme asks whether trade delivers what it promises. I believe it truly does. What we need to do is to make sure that the conditions for unimpeded delivery are in place worldwide.

14 Globalization and politics

Doug Bereuter

Recently there has been much debate about globalization, not only about its definition, but also about whether it is actually occurring, its significance, and how it shapes our future. Let me begin this paper by defining globalization, based on the work of Steven Flanagan, Ellen Frost and Richard Kugler under the auspices of the US National Defense University, as the process of the widespread growth of international activity.[1] Globalization is creating ever-closer ties, enhancing interdependence and generating greater opportunity and vulnerability for all. Events at the far corners of the earth are now affecting each other. Countries and regions are being drawn closer together. Key trading nations are interacting as never before, and the pace of change is accelerating.

These are important issues for me. My largest single focus in the US Congress has been trade. In fact, much of the leadership on trade liberalization over the last 20 years has come from Midwestern congressmen like me: along with eight other members of the House and the Senate, I am even a veteran of the Seattle WTO meetings of 1999.

Globalization encourages greater economic efficiency and productivity. It makes foreign goods and capital available to us, and reduces consumer prices. It breaks down barriers dividing nations and peoples. However, it also has a downside: it increases competition for jobs from countries with lower wages; it weakens, at least in the short term, labour and environmental standards; it makes global financial markets vulnerable; it makes us more exposed to economic and political turmoil overseas; and it exacerbates trans-national security threats, especially to the stability of rigidly controlled or weak states.

GLOBALIZATION AND SHIFTING POLITICAL POWER

Globalization not only shapes the world economy, it also shapes international politics and security affairs. In the medium term, globalization contributes to several tensions in international politics. Paradoxically, it leads to both fragmentation and integration, to globalization and internalization, and to decentralization and centralization. Globalization not only speeds up the pace at which integration occurs, but also provides an environment conducive to disintegration.

Globalization is therefore creating a new context for the exercise of national power. Regional and international institutions, local governments, and non-state actors—

particularly large trans-national corporations and non-governmental organizations—are using the instruments of globalization to diminish the nation-state's monopoly on power. They are often not conscious of serving as such instruments; it is simply the result of their activities.

As a result of globalization, some power is shifting to the international arena, for example, the fight against organized crime and terrorism. However, some power is also shifting down to local levels, for instance, citizen mobilization through emails and the Internet. New powers are being created as large corporations and NGOs use information tools to shape policy outcomes; the events of Seattle provide an example of this trend.

At the same time, regional economic agreements are becoming much more dominant in Europe, Latin America, and Asia. For example, within Europe, the European Union and the European Commission are playing a larger role relative to national legislators, resulting in a shift toward centralization. Nevertheless, regional free trade agreements that regulate trade and competition create multiple sets of rules, and may siphon off negotiating energy that would otherwise be devoted to global free trade initiatives.

To some extent, therefore, we have a bifurcation of the world order. The world is divided broadly between countries that are integrated into and committed to the norms of a global economy, and countries that are left behind by, or seek to challenge, those global norms. The first group consists of nearly 100 countries, including the members of the OECD. However, broad swathes of the world are still not integrated, and have modest prospects for becoming so—including much of Sub-Saharan Africa, parts of the former Soviet Union and the greater Middle East.

THE ROLE OF THE ASIA FOUNDATION

At The Asia Foundation, we are working to ensure that the countries where we work do integrate successfully into the global economy. Some of our offices are located in developed, prosperous countries and our activities there may need to be rethought. I would like to make those countries our 'Partners in Asian Development', and marshal their resources—human and financial if possible—on behalf of the less developed countries of Asia. In addition to our programmes in South Korea, Japan, Taiwan, and Hong Kong, we hope that we might also have that kind of presence in Singapore, Australia and New Zealand in the near future.

Let me then briefly describe the Foundation, which is currently celebrating its 50th anniversary. Headquartered in San Francisco, we have 450 employees, and 17 offices in Asia. We work on four priorities. The first and largest interest is governance, civil society and rule of law; the second is women's empowerment, our fastest growing area, which includes programmes to counter trafficking of women and children; the third is economic reform and development; and the fourth is international relations. We also run exchange programmes for other foundations in addition to our own programmes.

We are especially proud of our Books for Asia programme, which has placed more than 40 million books in secondary schools, colleges, universities, and national libraries across Asia. Nearly all of these are new books, donated by American publishers. Four years ago, we also formed a subsidiary called Give2Asia. This provides ways for

Americans to take advantage of our federal incentives to make charitable contributions for projects and programmes in Asia, often in the country from which they or their ancestors immigrated.

Although we are not an emergency relief organization, we have also found ourselves involved in the tsunami crisis. With networks in many of the countries affected, we were one of the few nongovernment organizations from the United States with a long-term, on-the-ground presence. For example, working with a moderate Muslim mass action group in Indonesia, we quickly moved some 150 volunteers with emergency relief and medical skills from other parts of Indonesia for disaster relief. We also did work like this in Sri Lanka, Thailand and to some extent in India.

Some further examples of our work include:

- In Mongolia we are building a dialogue on economic policy issues and are working to remove impediments to the growth of small and medium-sized enterprises.
- In the Philippines we focus on promoting engagement with business, involving professional people and associations in policy debate. Many of these are small, demonstration projects that we hope to emulate more widely in Asia.
- In Sri Lanka we promote private development by improving the local business environment and assisting small businesses through the removal of key constraints.
- In Vietnam, we have programmes to counter the trafficking of women across the Cambodian border and elsewhere.

I am glad that the conference examined the phenomenon of globalization. Globalization presents us with many challenges, but it is inevitable and irresistible. What we have to be concerned about is the dislocation that occurs in each country, and the differences or disparities that this creates within and among them. Many countries may be left behind, unless some dramatic changes take place, and that will require considerable assistance to be directed their way.

NOTES

1   Flanagan, S.J., E.L. Frost and R.L. Kugler (2001) 'Challenges of the Global Century: Report of the Project on Globalization and National Security', National Defense University: Institute for National Strategic Studies, available at <http://www.ndu.edu/inss/books/Books_2001/Challenges%20of%20the%20Global%20Century%20June%202001/GloCenCont.html>; accessed 7 September 2006.

Business perspectives

15 New dimensions of globalization

Narongchai Akrasanee

For the past 30 years, my work has involved managing the impact of globalization, particularly in Thailand, but sometimes also in other ASEAN countries. People in those nations tend to react negatively to the idea of globalization. I have come to appreciate that they think of it as a loss of status for their nation-state and for local control. To understand how these concerns arose, we need to study past experience. To understand why these concerns are important now, we need to examine why globalization might involve even more loss of control in the future.

GLOBALIZATION IN RETROSPECT

In the nineteenth century the British asked Thailand to open its markets. Thailand negotiated and finally agreed, signing the Bowring Treaty in 1855. That was the country's first FTA and it changed its production structure. If Thailand had not agreed, it would have become a British colony. By contrast, China refused, so the British moved on Beijing and occupied the country. Thus, this first experience with globalization was intimately tied to colonization.

In the twentieth century, Asian globalization was quite different. It involved the realignment of global power and global political philosophy; it was about the triumph of democracy over autocracy, capitalism over socialism. Against this background the world established a global trade order under GATT, a global financial order under the IMF, and a global development order under the World Bank. These institutions oversaw steady liberalization, now known as the Washington Consensus. While some countries managed to handle liberalization better than others, on the whole the impact has been positive.

In global finance, however, the impact has been mixed. Until 1997 Thailand did not see it as a problem, but at that point the global financial system became unfriendly. We do not blame American banks for this. They offered countries such as Thailand vast amounts of money when it opened its capital markets. At first Thailand said 'no', but they insisted, and Thailand gave in. Then came the collapse. Thailand concluded that global finance, as managed by investment bankers whose only interest was in commissions, worked against Thai interests. Now Thailand has a great deal of work to do to restore financial order.

In development, the results were also generally satisfactory. Overall, one can conclude that Asia came out quite well at the end of the twentieth century.

NEW DIMENSIONS OF GLOBALIZATION

The twenty-first century presents quite another scenario, in which the nation-state is becoming both the corporate state and the cyber state. In this world, globalization is very much driven by business and, increasingly, industrial policies are determined by corporations, not by governments.

Let us examine some of the issues. The most important factors in the corporate state are capital and technology, and if developing countries generally import capital and technology, they will have concerns over these new aspects of the terms of trade, the terms of risk and terms of intellectual property. Intellectual property in particular has become very important, and is something that we do not know how to price or manage.

In the nation-state, we managed at borders i.e. by setting tariff rates or other barriers at the borders where goods move in and out of the country. But in the corporate state, managing must be done behind borders. Competition policy has become a key issue. To give an example, Thailand is negotiating an FTA with the United States, in which the US is asking for the liberalization of the financial sector. People in Thailand believe that such an agreement will destroy Thai banks, leaving American banks as the principal banks in Thailand. The question is how will we then control the monopoly power of these corporations?

In the cyber state, natural barriers for trade and services are disappearing. We are losing control of many markets, whether we explicitly liberalize them or not. An example is the outsourcing of services: an X-ray is taken in Thailand but read in India; a legal agreement in Thailand is drafted in the United States, and so on. Legal services, medical services, and insurance are only some of the things that can be handled via the Internet.

Many corporations do not even produce goods or services now: they outsource production to someone else. Nestle does not produce anything in Thailand: it just manages its brand. Thailand produces the milk products for them, and invests in the fixed assets required for production, because Nestle judges that too risky.

As in international trade, the corporate and cyber state also produces great pressure for simultaneous factor price and product price equalization. The question is whether this produces net welfare gains, and for which party. I am sure that the gains are positive for the service provider, but not so sure whether service users always benefit.

In conclusion, the issue in the twenty-first century is about how we manage globalization in the context of the corporate state and cyber state. Much of what we have discussed at this conference addresses that difficult question.

16 California: a microcosm of Pacific Rim trade issues

Richard M. Rosenberg

This is written from the perspective of a business person living and working in a Pacific Rim country, and specifically in California, a state that represents most of the political, economic, demographic and environmental issues found across the entire spectrum of the Pacific. One in every eight Americans is a Californian, and the state offers a wonderful model for most of the issues that have been addressed in this conference.

CALIFORNIA AND PACIFIC RIM TRADE

If it were a separate nation, California would be the sixth or seventh largest nation in the world as measured by GDP. Of its more than 35 million citizens, less than 50 per cent are Caucasian of non-Hispanic or Latino background, with a very large ethnic representation from Asian and Hispanic populations. In fact, demographers predict that by the year 2010 the largest group of individuals living in California will have an Hispanic background.

California's export and import totals are representative of the imbalance in global trade faced by the entire United States. In 2002, for example, as the economic recovery in the US began to take hold, imports flowing through the ports of San Francisco, San Diego and Los Angeles/Long Beach, which is the second largest port of entry in the US, totalled US$218 billion. However, exports of Californian products passing through those same ports totaled only US$111 billion. Air cargo flowing both ways tended to be more balanced, but the net result was a very substantial trade imbalance between the United States and the nations on the other side of the Pacific.

These data come, of course, as no great surprise to this group. But what I would like to focus on here are the internal political ramifications and the political impact of global trade and its imbalance, as they affect the United States, and California in particular.

POLITICS OF CALIFORNIA'S INTERNATIONAL LINKAGES

Let us first discuss an issue that does not actually show up in the merchandise trade numbers, but has a huge political impact on the lobbying efforts of companies who are affected by trade flows: student visa requirements.

The catalyst for this issue is the homeland security effort in the US. This endeavour, combined with the Patriot Act passed by Congress, has had a negative impact on the number of visas issued to attend Californian universities, as well as the number of H1B visas issued to foreign nationals to work in Californian technology companies.

Since Californian universities such as Caltech, UC Berkeley, UC San Francisco, UC Los Angeles, University of Southern California and Californian technology companies are natural magnets for students and engineers from other Pacific Rim nations, the new visa requirements have a disproportionate effect in this state. The visa issue ranges from a minor annoyance to such a perception of problems that students are inclined to obtain their education in another nation.

Student visa difficulties also have a political impact. The same technology companies, aided by prestigious universities, that are bitter about their inability to import human capital are equally bitter about what they perceive as unfair competition in their export markets. The unfair competition ranges from unique restrictions on Californian exports to non-free market currency manipulations, to outright piracy of intellectual property. Consequently, Congress and the administration are receiving mixed messages from their most important constituencies and financial supporters. A mixed political message in the US is not a good message for global trade.

The signature industry for California, is, of course, semi-conductors. The famous Silicon Valley was the original home of Fairchild and later, Intel. Yesterday, we heard that only 314,000 jobs had been lost to outsourcing in this manufacturing area, or only 11 per cent of all manufacturing jobs in the US. However, there is danger in using aggregate numbers. In some industries, outsourcing or off-shoring has a much greater impact than 11 per cent and it is in those industries where the political impact of free trade has the greatest effect.

Nonetheless, outsourcing is not what killed the semi-conductor industry in the Silicon Valley and left all those empty buildings. You and I know it, but perception is reality and in the world of politics, outsourcing is a wonderful, evil word to use against corporate America and its supporters.

Let us now shift from technology to agriculture, since farmers remain a potent political force in virtually every nation in the world, as we heard yesterday. In California, congressmen and congresswomen represent agricultural districts as diverse as growers of table grapes to wine grapes, to growers of high value vegetables to rice. Clearly, each of these groups has different interests in the success or failure of global trade. For example, table grape growers are being driven from the market because they cannot compete with offshore labour costs of growers from abroad. The end users of wine grapes, wineries, have been equally hit by low cost, foreign competition to the point where many wineries believe their only solution is to actually sell the company to a foreign wine company. Thus, some of the oldest and proudest names in the Napa Valley in California are now subsidiaries of foreign companies. This often does not sit well with local politicians and free trade is blamed as the culprit, regardless of the facts.

Unfortunately, Professor Lin's free trade party does not yet have a chapter in the Napa Valley to provide education and pressure to support free trade.

So far, the high-value vegetable growers have not been affected to any great extent. Consequently, while some of their neighbours are using every bit of political pressure to have their congressional representatives pass agricultural trade protection laws and create barriers to trade, another segment of that same congressman's constituency is applying political pressure and financial muscle to lobby against any potential barriers, which might be retaliated against by creating trade barriers for their own products.

These are but a few on-the-ground examples of the cross currents faced by Pacific Rim nations with their own politicians, but they all come together in the nation-state called California.

GLOBAL TRADE AND 9/11

Global trade is the movement of merchandise from one geographic location to another. The movement of that merchandise into and out of California, as it is in every Pacific nation, is handled overwhelmingly by ships and aircraft.

However, another critical political aspect of global trade that we have heard about only peripherally during this conference is global terrorism. Yet there is nothing that could be more disruptive to global trade than the political structure reacting to an actual act of terror, or a strong perception that an act will occur. We heard yesterday what happened at the Mexican and Canadian borders after 9/11.

Let me set the stage for you in this terror scenario using California, once again, as the example. In the Los Angeles/Long Beach port, on an average day, there are 300,000 containers, either sitting on the dock, being loaded or unloaded from a ship, or on board a ship that is alongside a dock. At the present time, US Coast Guard officers are attempting to do some pre-screening of those containers at some of their ports of origin in Asia, but it is far from an effective process. The X-ray screening technology being used at the Los Angeles/Long Beach port is improving each month, but, with more than a quarter of a million containers a day with which to contend, the odds of *preventing* a terror action emanating from a container is far from assured.

Concurrently, each day thousands of air freight units also pass through the international cargo terminals at the San Francisco and Los Angeles airports.

Given this situation, US senators from California have been conducting a campaign for better security of global trade as it affects California, but with very limited success. Their actions have been resisted by a wide variety of business interests, ranging from port operators to retailers, who all recognize that every action that increases security is going to result in increased costs for the end product, and, therefore, lower profits, unless the total costs can be passed through to the consumer, which is highly unlikely.

Thus far, since 9/11, with no terrorist actions occurring in the sea or air cargo areas, there has been no political backlash to this very limited and inadequate security. But if there is, you can be assured that the voices of the Californian senators will be heard, and Pacific nations counting on increased exports to the single largest importer in the world, California, can expect substantially reduced trade at worst, or more expensive trade at best.

Outsourcing, currency manipulation, weak labour laws: all will fade as political factors relative to the political impact of an action of terror.

I am sorry to end on such a disturbing note. However, I did want to share with you just a handful of the political issues facing global trade in the Pacific that those of us in business in California are concerned about every working day.

17 Globalization at the University of Hawaii

David McClain

Professor Paul Samuelson (2004) cites Alan Greenspan, Jagdish Bhagwati, Greg Mankiw and others as proponents of the view that economics recognizes that some groups can be hurt by free trade, but generally vindicates 'creative destruction' by arguing that the gains of winners are large enough to compensate losers.

Professor Samuelson believes this view to be wrong, in that it is not *necessary* for winnings to exceed losses, as he showed in his Nobel lecture of 1972 and elsewhere (Samuelson 1972). In fact, the reason the United States has benefited so much from trade in the recent past is that it had a wide advantage over other economies at the end of World War II in terms of its productive capacity, educational system, and other assets. Now that many countries have caught up, other outcomes are possible: for example, certain kinds of technical change in China relative to the US could generate net losses in US welfare over reasonably long periods, such as 10, 20 or even 30 years.

The point is, of course, that globalization exerts direct pressures on individuals and institutions, even in large economies such as the United States, and we must all find ways to stay competitive in this context. Let me therefore talk about how we cope with globalization at the University of Hawaii. We are a billion-dollar operation: if we were a company, we would be the fifth largest in Hawaii. We have 80,000 students, of whom 50,000 are earning degrees and another 30,000 take not-for-credit courses. On any day, we serve about one in every 12 adults in the state.

Globalization has already played a large role in our university. We have about 400 visiting scholars each year, many of whom make essential contributions to our scientific leadership in areas such as vulcanology, oceanography, and astronomy. We also have over 100 exchange agreements with universities throughout the region. In my time at the business school in the early 1990s, I oversaw our Japan- and China-focused MBA programmes. More recently, as Dean of the Business School, I helped to start an MBA in Hanoi with the Hanoi School of Business. At least once a month we get an offer from a Chinese university to collaborate on a new MBA. Globalization offers enormous opportunities.

But as a consequence of 9/11, we have also seen a decline in the number of overseas students. Because of a general surge in enrolments in recent years, this decline has so far been reflected mainly in reduced diversity in our classrooms. About one-third of our students are now from out of state. While the split used to be half-half from the US mainland and Asia, it is now two-thirds from the mainland and one-third from Asia.

The movement of scholars has also become more difficult. The federal support we receive for research has doubled over the last five years, to around US$330 million. But the effectiveness of our research enterprise does depend on collaborations that are at risk because of visa problems. Research funding itself has come under pressure, with constraints on federal research budgets. The National Institutes of Health (NIH) budget, which doubled in the past five years, is now barely growing, and the competition for the limited funding available from the National Science Foundation (NSF), National Aeronautics and Space Administration (NASA), and the National Oceanic and Atmospheric Administration (NOAA) is becoming increasingly intense.

Another interesting dimension of globalization is the concern that the US is losing its leadership in higher education. There are now data that show that we are falling behind in some subject areas, and that other countries attract increasing numbers of students who might have studied in the United States. This has given rise to growing demands for accountability in higher education. The measurement of accountability, as put in place at lower levels in the 'No Child Left Behind' initiative, will no doubt extend shortly to the first two years of college, and eventually to the next two. Margaret Spellings, the new Secretary of Education, told the American Council of Education that she believed we were falling behind, and that she would propose greater accountability as a solution.

This raises questions about our public school system. As we talk about upgrading curricula in universities, we need to worry about the competence of the students who are coming to us from lower levels of education. Our data show that the challenge is large: 90 per cent of students entering community colleges need remediation in math, 75 per cent in writing, and 60 per cent in reading.

The University of Hawaii has rethought its strategic plan as a result of globalization. When I arrived in 1991, we saw ourselves as a bridge between East and West. With the advent of globalization of the last 15 years, however, many bridges have been established between East and West. As we revise our strategic plan, we now see our identity defined by the fact that we are an island society, populated initially by the indigenous people of these islands. In that context, our plan has given a larger role to the values—respect and care for our limited resources—that are associated with island societies generally and Hawaii in particular. We think that this view is not only locally responsive, but also globally significant for island Earth—and will give us a special position in competing in a highly globalized environment.

REFERENCES

Samuelson, P.A. (1972) 'International Trade for a Rich Country', lecture before the Swedish–American Chamber of Commerce, New York City, 10 May 1972, reproduced in *The Collected Scientific Papers of Paul A. Samuelson*, Volume 4, Cambridge, MA: MIT Press, Chapter 250.
—— (2004) 'When Ricardo and Mill Rebut and Confirm Arguments of Mainstream Economists Supporting Globalization', *Journal of Economic Perspectives* 18(3) Summer: 135–46.

18 Competition and fairness in the execution of globalization

Arthur L. Goldstein

Much of this conference can be characterized as presenting a 'top down' view of the global trade picture. I would now like to offer a 'bottoms up' point of view, looking at things as they happen on the ground, based on my experience in a 44-year career in international business. I would also like to encourage inviting more business people to future PAFTAD conferences to provide additional dimension and scope to these deliberations and discussions.

Let me begin my remarks with a personal observation regarding a simple but fundamental premise that I believe provides the driving force and rationale for international trade, and that is that modern and emerging countries and their people aspire to a rising standard of living for themselves and their families. It also seems clear that the key to a rising standard of living is economic prosperity and growth. For a country, economic prosperity and growth is directly related to productivity, to what I will call 'the incremental economic value' or the 'value-added benefit' which may be attributable to the products and services of that country as a result of benefits such as lower costs, greater natural resources or a broader technology base.

The real or perceived value-added of the products and services of a given country plays a major role in determining the demand for those products and services in international markets, and therefore provides a major driving force for trade between countries around the globe.

DETERMINANTS OF ECONOMIC SUCCESS

The factors that ultimately determine economic value-added are constantly changing in every country, but I believe there are four attributes or measurements relating to 'capital', broadly defined, which are constants and always come into play. (Note that for this analysis I have excluded 'natural resources', because some countries do not have natural resources.)

The first attribute is the climate for the availability of financial capital. This reflects the overall health of the financial infrastructure, the health of the banking system, the appetite to take financial risk, the availability of private and public equity, the presence of a financial marketplace, and the presence or absence of appropriate controls to protect the investing public from fraud or misuse of funds.

The second attribute is 'intellectual capital'. This measurement includes the output from the educational system, the status within the country of science and technology, the level of investment in research and development, and the system for, and degree of protection of, intellectual property.

The third attribute is the availability of 'labour capital'. The measurement of labour capital reflects the availability and number of skilled and trained workers, and the labour 'culture', which I define as the willingness of labour and management to work together to agree on appropriate levels for wages that reflect the underlying value and demand for the products or service in the marketplace.

The fourth attribute is 'political capital', the degree to which the political system of a country, through its culture, laws, treaties and policies, determines whether financial, intellectual and labour capital are promoted, held back or ignored.

In my judgement, in a given country, the extent to which these four attributes of 'capital' are present, and are in harmony and in sync with each other, determines the attractiveness, or lack thereof, of the goods and services of that country, highlights the advantages or disadvantages of exporting or importing goods or services, and broadly predicts the health of the economy and trade.

However, getting the four capital elements in sync is not easy or automatic for any country. The process is delicate, it takes time, and it can be destabilized very quickly. Destabilization can cause a cascade of devastating repercussions throughout an economy from which it may take years to recover.

Let me illustrate my view of the general process of developing national economic-value-added by examining the four elements of capital and their role in the growth of the US economy over the past 60 years.

The development process began to accelerate in the aftermath of World War II. Spurred on by the impact of wartime production and investment, financial capital became more available in the 1950s and 1960s. Technology was being developed at an increasingly rapid pace in several different fields. New inventions were patented and protected. The political system encouraged the process. The economy began to boom. For a wide array of products and services, the US was initially the inventor, the designer, the manufacturer of the capital equipment, and the source of the labour to produce the product. US-based economic-value-added rose rapidly. US-originated products were desired by other countries. For a time, the economic system was in good balance among the four elements of capital.

This snapshot did not last for very long. As the US economy grew, it became clear that for certain products manufactured in the US, the wages being demanded by workers were too high to produce the most economically competitive products. This situation resulted in the loss of US jobs as US-designed manufacturing equipment was shipped to lower-labour-cost countries. Throughout the 1990s, which was a period of continuing rapid development and growth, such displacement of labour was usually quite temporary and was quickly reversed as the momentum of R&D and investment brought a continuous stream of additional products and services to the market.

EROSION OF US DOMINANCE OF WORLD MARKETS

Over time, the economic 'balance' continued to evolve and change. The value-added equation for the US continued to erode gradually as US-designed manufacturing equipment began to be fabricated outside the US. This was followed shortly thereafter by the design of the equipment being done outside the US. The net result was that over a 30 or more year period, many products previously designed, built and manufactured inside the US were now being designed, built and manufactured outside the US.

Today, a significant and rising percentage of the new products coming to market around the world are invented outside the US. In the past 60 years, the only way for the US economy to not slow down, or to not experience a devastating economic impact from the downsizing of industries such as steel, textiles, semi-conductors, tyres and many others, was to invent, to design, to provide new financial capital and to produce new businesses and products at a pace which could overcome the steadily rising economic-value-added of other countries that was being created overseas by emerging financial capital markets, increasing intellectual capital, lower labour costs and a supportive political climate.

For most of this period, the US was able to outrun the value-added crunch, but in recent years it has become clear that this is no longer the case. The US can not sustain the higher pace now necessary to invent or invest its way out of this problem. As a result, the US has been gradually and steadily losing the battle for manufacturing supremacy. This has manifested itself in a very rapidly rising trade imbalance, exemplified by the billions of dollars of products imported from China, and the billions of dollars of services obtained from India—and all of this is happening while the US dollar continues to weaken.

Many people would say that in the era of global agreements and trade, the changes I just described were understood and inevitable, and that the shifts now underway in the sources of labour, financial capital, and intellectual capital from one nation or region to another is exactly what should be expected. I would mostly agree with this view, particularly to the extent that there is a healthy global economy based on open competition for the highest value-added products and services properly enforced by treaties such as what was intended with NAFTA and the WTO agreements. Under these treaties it was expected that each affected country would prepare itself and its citizens to withstand the challenges of adjustment, at a certain pace, to new economic realities, whether that represents new hardships or new benefits. In entering into global agreements, each nation explicitly accepts the risk of undertaking these challenges.

Unfortunately this has not been the end of the story. It is clear that major problems in adjusting to the new challenges occur when the infrastructure or the political system in a given country allows its companies or its citizens to avoid their obligation to play by the rules. This laxness, plus the absence of appropriate systems and controls to enforce treaties by one nation forces the counter-party to take responsive action and often to over-react in a way that makes the initial problem worse. These real-world actions exacerbate the labour and capital issues in those countries feeling the most pain and prevent them from having the expected ample time for adjustment and recovery.

POLITICAL FAILURES IN INTERNATIONAL TRADE RELATIONS

There are many examples where unwillingness or an inability within the political system of certain countries to follow the rules and the spirit and substance of global or bilateral trade agreements has brought much more pain than was ever bargained for by the parties to the agreement. Let me offer a few.

A major issue is intellectual property. This includes patents, trade-marks, copyrights, know-how, and licenses. A lack of respect for these assets and the absence of enforcement allow certain countries to benefit at virtually no cost from the inventions, capital investment, brand-building, and labour made in other countries. We have seen this in the copying of computer chips, computer designs, machine designs, music and movie DVDs, and many other products. In certain cases, it is nothing short of outright cross-border theft.

A second major issue is the failure to comply with environmental and pollution-control standards stipulated in treaties such as NAFTA and WTO. This puts the complying country at a significant economic disadvantage to the non-complying country, which achieves lower costs primarily by its failure to invest in abatement equipment. As the former Chairman and CEO of a manufacturer of such equipment, I have seen this matter first-hand.

A third important issue involves decisions made in the political arena to avoid or delay free market adjustments to currency valuations. Artificial pegging of one currency to another, particularly when billions of dollars of trade are involved, creates economic distortion and trade deficits that are unsustainable over the long term. This makes the ultimate economic corrections even more painful.

A fourth issue relates to adherence to foreign corrupt practice prohibitions. The fact that some nations do not have, or do not enforce, laws to fight corruption has a major impact on the idea of a 'level playing field' which can overcome all the advantages that a country playing by the rules may have.

I have focused on a businessman's view of the economic model, and how the value-added concept is augmented or impeded, in order to highlight some of the real-world problems of globalization and what can happen when there is unmanaged, uncontrolled so called 'free-trade'. I have focused on the forces at work, not because I am against the goals of free trade and globalization, but because I believe improvements need to be made to the execution process if globalization and FTAs are to achieve their goals within an acceptable level of local dislocation and disruption. At bottom, if managed and controlled well, free trade and globalization represents the proper vehicle for the long-term growth and economic evolution of countries and regions. What we must correct are those situations that cause an unfair loss of jobs, investment capital, and intellectual capital when certain countries do not play by the spirit, rules or legal aspects of trade agreements.

US companies have employees and shareholders who do not do well in accepting such pain. It may very well be that the only way to deal with this unfairness is to slow down certain portions of the globalization process and to apply tariffs, sanctions and penalties unless and until non-compliance is corrected. Only in this way can free trade and globalization proceed and become successful without causing undue and unwanted hardships to those nations which, for many years have been supplying a major portion of the financial, intellectual, productivity and political capital to the rest of the world.

19 International opportunities and national choices

Pang Eng Fong

While international trade does not necessarily make a country richer, there is evidence that countries that isolate themselves from international trade will become poorer. North Korea and Myanmar are good examples. There have been many positive recommendations for globalization, but some countries have decided that adjusting to it is not worth the long-term benefits. In the last couple of months I have visited three very different countries, and would like to describe how their experiences appear in global perspective.

The first was Bhutan, where the king has decided to open up the economy to the world. This is a country of 600,000 people, which does not have a single traffic light and has little idea of environmental management. It aspires to maximize 'gross domestic happiness'. Yet it is beginning to get connected with the world. The Internet has now arrived in Bhutan.

The second was Georgia, which experienced its Rose Revolution a little over a year ago. Its new president has had to build entirely new institutions—he fired some 80 per cent of the police force to fight corruption and ensure security. The president understands the necessity of opening up to the world, but the country is simultaneously grappling with its new identity as a sovereign state in a volatile region. Georgia sits at a strategic crossroad and attracts much political attention—from Russia, its largest neighbour, the United States, which has troops there, as well as Iran and Turkey. It is a poor country, exporting little—mostly food products, wine and spirits to Russia. How will it handle globalization? Many Singaporeans, Malaysians, and Indonesians and others in the PAFTAD region know globalization cannot be wished away. Georgia increasingly understands this imperative. It cannot turn away from the world. But to improve living standards and the challenges of globalization, it must have security and have in place functioning state institutions.

The third was Dubai. Dubai, which is part of the United Arab Emirates, is a booming desert city with cranes everywhere you look. Its huge, gleaming airport is almost totally dependent on imported labour—90 per cent of Dubai's work force is foreign. The country has adapted remarkably well to globalization, despite having no resources. Compared to its neighbour, Abu Dhabi, it does not have much oil, yet it has succeeded in transforming itself, through sheer willpower, into a throbbing hub of the Middle East. If one wants to fly to the Caucasus, Africa, Central Asia and many Indian cities, the best connections are through Dubai. The economic model it appears to have adopted is that of Singapore, which welcomes foreign capital and talent and prospers by constantly reinventing itself to serve the region and the world.

The different responses of the three places suggest that globalization certainly opens opportunities. The benefits, however, are not immediate and there are certainly costs. The path to integration is open, but it will not be taken just because it is there. Each country has to make hard decisions to take it or risk being left behind. The Asia-Pacific region has benefited greatly from globalization, but even here past success does not guarantee that the adjustment process will not become more difficult as competition intensifies for capital, markets, and talent. The challenge for them, as for the three countries I have discussed briefly, is to maintain openness, while minimizing the problems that openness inevitably brings. All over the world, people want a better life for themselves and their children. Their leaders fail them when they shy away from embracing global integration. The challenge for the global community is to help countries evolve conditions where leaders can make the right choices on global integration.

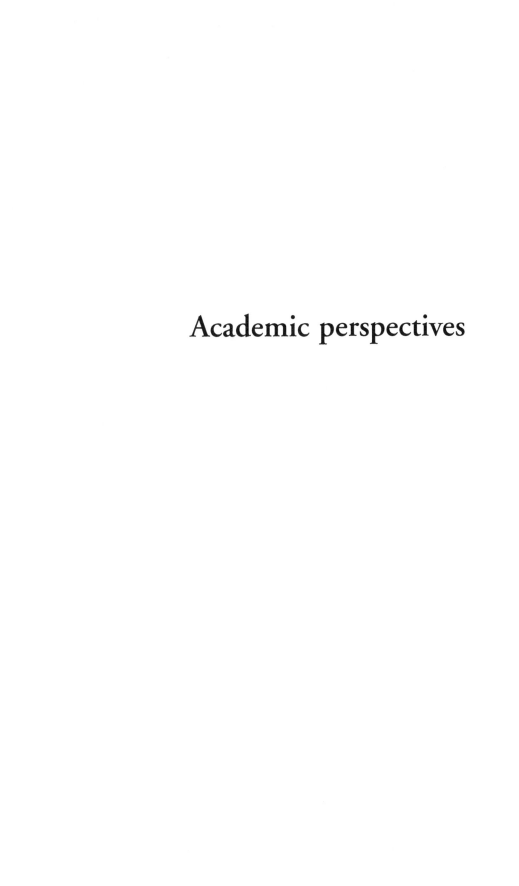

Academic perspectives

20 Adverse trends in trade negotiations

Peter Drysdale

REASONS FOR OPTIMISM?

One point that has been made at this conference is that inexorable forces—related to the technology and the communications revolution of the last half century—now secure the benefits of open trade and investment, and that there is no retreat politically from that process. It was further suggested that we see the current pause in this progress at the multilateral level as merely a slowdown in the expansion of trade and international economic interaction. There is certainly validity in this view. There are many interests and forces in economies throughout the world that work to achieve the benefits from trade and investment liberalization internationally. However, not all the forces at work are congenial to liberalization.

A key policy question in this context is how to manage adjustment and compensate losers. This question is frequently asked in industrial countries, and is particularly important in political democracies. Yet I do not conclude that the use of trade measures, including safeguard measures, is the right way to manage adjustment. As economists, we know that safeguards are a suboptimal way of managing compensation and, in my view, we should advocate superior ways of dealing with the problem. The expansion of contingent protectionism, and especially its impact on the trade access of developing countries, remains a huge problem for the system.

A second point made at the conference is that there is now institutional entrenchment of open trade in the framework of the WTO system, which protects against backsliding through legal processes. That is true, but that system also has many gaps. In the context of RTAs and FTAs, for example, the rules are so weak as to be meaningless. There is no discipline on the structure, speed or manner in which countries enter into these arrangements. Thus there are serious questions still about the strength, resilience and permanence of the institutional entrenchment of a regime that protects and encourages trade.

A third point, a corollary to the second, is that there is now less need for reliance on beneficent hegemonic leadership. In the post-war period, the system that produced the regime in which Japan and the other East Asian economies prospered was managed under the political leadership of the United States. It was aimed at strengthening confidence and engagement in the international economy, regionally and globally.

According to the argument, we are now less reliant on a single power for securing the trade regime. But this is an open question. The concentration of political and security power today is difficult to square with the idea that multi-polar support for trade is sufficient. Much still depends on how the United States decides to play the game.

A final point is that RTAs are an effective substitute for multilateral progress. However correct that may turn to be out in the long run, the transition path is what is important. I will come back to that, particularly in the context of the economics and politics of East Asia.

SYSTEMIC ISSUES

There are several systemic problems with our system of trade negotiations. The first problem is the trend toward bilateralism. The sanguine view is that, by and large, we observe falling trade barriers and protectionism despite, or alongside, the rise of RTAs and bilateral trading arrangements. This is not how it was in the 1930s, when trade barriers and protectionism arose under bilateral and bloc arrangements. But this view may not apply in some important circumstances. In particular, we have had no adequate review of the impact of contingent protectionism on developing countries, which is so important in today's debate. Average tariff levels, quota arrangements and so on— at least those formally under the WTO—are superficially low. But what matters for development is trade access, and that is sensitive to contingent protection.

A second problem is issue selectivity in negotiations. Even in beneficent negotiations, such as the successive rounds of GATT and now the WTO, the agenda tends to be driven by major players—by the political economy of the negotiating process. Issue selectivity really means developed country interest. Not surprisingly, this distortion has led to great dissatisfaction in developing countries. Issue selectivity disadvantages development and biases the way in which the WTO trade regime works.

A third problem is partner selectivity and asymmetric bargaining. By partner selectivity we mean who does deals with whom. In the most frequent cases the powerful do deals with the weak, creating hubs with weak spokes. This is happening not only in Europe and to a lesser degree in North America, but also now in East Asia.

Asymmetric bargaining between the hub and the spokes becomes evident in the structure of the arrangements which, even between such developed partners as the United States and Australia, excludes many barriers important to trade creation. An independent estimate shows that the impact of the US–Australia arrangement is on balance either neutral or trade-diverting. This is so because sugar is excluded from the agreement, and the phasing periods for many agricultural products are over 20 years. Over time this will cause problems to an important political relationship.

Issue and partner selectivity problems affect all bilateral arrangements that are proliferating today. Their impact may endanger the coherence of ASEAN and the region's economic and political future. East Asian growth depends on the growing fragmentation of trade, that is, on increasingly fine specialization among countries such as China, Korea and Japan. If these economies are not coherently connected—and at the moment we would need a political miracle to achieve that—the obstacles to fragmentation will multiply, and could sap the energy of East Asian development.

POLITICAL CONSEQUENCES

There are potentially serious political consequences issuing from these problems. Economic contests between competing hubs get mixed up with political contests. These contests are made worse by the introduction of outside pressures, particularly in the context of conflicts between Japan and China. Yet they are evident even in how Australia relates to the region. For instance, as Australia moves to negotiate an FTA with China, the debate about the arrangement—which is much in Australian interests both politically and economically—has been largely political. Because of this, we can imagine there may be trouble down the track.

It is possible to resolve these issues, but it will require deliberate political effort and considerable energy and initiative. It will require intellectual effort of the kind we have undertaken in other contexts over the years in PAFTAD. But this is not only a job for technocrats; what is urgently needed is political leadership. APEC can play a role in that, as can ASEAN+3.

While Washington has recently viewed these developments as benign, I now detect a shift. This is driven partly by ignorance of the developments in East Asia, but it is also driven by a sense of threat from East Asia. The United States recognizes that East Asia is now replicating arrangements that have long been a part of American policy. The potential for missteps is great; we will have to think about these developments more deeply than we have for many years.

21 Sustaining the multilateral trading system

Hugh Patrick

I want to make five general points.

First, most of us are policy-oriented economists. That means we are paid to worry about what is going wrong or might go wrong in terms of the efficient and effective allocation of resources, not just nationally but regionally, and most importantly globally. We worry particularly about protectionism, trade diversion, discrimination against non-members of any preferential—or to use the Brown and McCulloch term— discriminatory trade agreements. So it is important from time to time to step back and do an overall appraisal of where we are and where we are probably going with respect to global efficiency.

Second, regarding our question 'Does Trade Deliver What It Promises?', the answer in the Asia-Pacific has to be a resounding 'yes': trade has delivered much more than trade theory, static as it was, initially predicted. The Asia Pacific has been and will continue to be the most rapidly growing, economically successful region of the world, and that growth has been built upon a strong export orientation, increasing openness and quite rapid reallocation of resources to accommodate evolving comparative advantage. The success of Asian-Pacific growth has generated new, more dynamic trade theories. What we tend to forget, or take for granted, is that export-oriented growth was possible precisely because of the post-war GATT-based global multilateral system which has provided tremendous, and increasing, market access opportunities to all who were capable of grasping them. The global trade system is not perfect, not a panacea, as we all know, but it is far better than the alternatives. Thank goodness for GATT and now for the WTO. Even if WTO is 'resting'—and I think that is too negative a judgement—it is a strong, healthy multilateral trading system, and will remain so.

Third, as we know, change imposes costs as well as benefits. But non-change— autarchy, isolation from world markets as exemplified by North Korea and Myanmar— causes even greater costs, with virtually no economic benefits. The biggest source of change—of job loss as well as job gain—in the US and elsewhere is technological change, as is well known. Look at the impact of the IT revolution, Automatic Teller Machines replacing tellers, and so forth. However, trade frequently becomes the culprit because we all too easily, if unfairly, blame the bad behaviour of foreigners.

Fourth, relatedly, we have not developed effective policies to ameliorate the costs and enhance the adjustment of those who do lose jobs as a consequence of change, including trade liberalization. It used to be thought that change was gradual enough, and people died early enough, that adjustment through attrition, retirement and intergenerational occupation change was sufficiently effective to cope with the adjustment problem. No more: economies grow and change their structures more rapidly, and technological progress proceeds quickly. The best way to adjust is to grow fast, so that new winner industries bid labour away from loser industries, as happened for example in Taiwan, Hong Kong, Singapore and Korea. Japan's approach was to redirect industrial policy, designed for winner industries, to subsidize and slow the adjustment process of loser industries such as coal and shipping—for too long, in my estimation. We need a combination of adjustment policies in phasing in trade liberalization, as in agriculture over a period, of, say, ten years or so; sunset provisions for all adjustment programmes, including FTAs as Peter Drysdale proposes; and better programmes to retrain older workers—not from steel workers to computer programmers but to, say, commercial truck drivers. The point is that some of the benefits of trade liberalization should be spent, for welfare and income redistribution reasons as well as for political reasons, to help the afflicted workers.

Finally, the development of FTAs, PTAs, discriminatory trade and economic arrangements on a bilateral or regional basis, on net balance, are more likely, I fear, to undermine the benefits of the globalization process than to enhance them—despite Narongchai's clever use in Thailand of such arrangements to circumvent existing high barriers in agricultural trade. The only hope is that these restrictive agreements will be used to bring about effective domestic structural adjustment more rapidly than would occur in the long, drawn-out WTO Doha multilateral negotiating process.

While I am sceptical as to the net benefit of FTAs—I see them as competitive to rather than complementary with the WTO—the reality is that we are now already down the road of creating many more FTAs. Basically I blame the EU and the US for heading us down that meandering path. In the East Asian context, I foresee two possible outcomes. One is that the FTA terms will be so weak that their effect will be inconsequential, as companies properly focus on the global market place. The other is that FTAs will become really consequential, that rules of origin will be special and differential, and that we will be in a serious Bhagwati spaghetti bowl mess. After 10 or 15 years of that, the FTA approach will have to be junked, and WTO-based globalization will once again become the name of the game.

22 Adjustment, compensation and contingent protection

Peter A. Petri

The question of this conference—'Does Trade Deliver What It Promises?'—has been largely answered 'yes', particularly for PAFTAD's region. But an important consequence—and downside—of rapid integration is rapid adjustment. Adjustment problems have cropped up in many papers, and explain many of the tensions we uncovered. For example, adjustment concerns are clearly significant in Japan- and China-bashing. Adjustment is also at work behind the negative reactions to outsourcing, and it may help to explain why the WTO negotiations are proceeding slowly and FTAs play an increasing role.

ACCELERATING ADJUSTMENT SPEED

In assessing adjustment costs, what really matters is not the eventual scale adjustment, but rather its speed. For various reasons, the faster adjustment occurs, the higher its cost. If change occurs quickly, dislocations are larger than if change can be anticipated and implemented slowly. This is why econometric models often portray adjustment cost not as proportional to adjustment, but as an exponential of the rate of adjustment.

Is there something about the global economic environment that has caused adjustment to accelerate? I will argue that there is. This has implications for policy responses and the processes of international policy making. It also has implications for analysis: we need to pay more attention to the factors that determine the speed of adjustment and the policy processes that minimize adjustment costs.

The acceleration of change is a common feature of economic phenomena. There are many reasons for this, but an important underlying factor is the ease of communication about economic events, decisions and policies. It is now commonplace for economic developments in one country to be instantaneously communicated to the whole world, and to trigger potential reactions everywhere. In the World Bank exercise on the 'East Asian Miracle', for example, we noted that the time it took for the world's leading developing economy to double its income has halved every couple of decades. Countries such as China today make that extraordinary breakthrough in a decade or two, as opposed to nearly a century in the case of the United States a few centuries ago. To the extent that speed matters, adjustment costs are thus much greater today than in the past—even over the span of our own experiences as policymakers and students of policy.

GOVERNMENT'S ROLE IN ECONOMIC INTEGRATION

The factors that drive adjustment are also changing. In the post war decades, when the United States and other countries set out to build a global trading system, the task was to remove policy barriers to integration. We did that through the large comprehensive trade rounds of GATT. Today, decentralized economic processes—grassroots business forces—drive integration. It is no secret to business that international trade and investment offer major profit opportunities. While policy no longer needs to lead globalization, it is increasingly called on to respond to its side effects.

Because the natural rate of integration is high, the negative consequences of rapid adjustment—and public pressure for addressing its costs—are widespread. Rather than acting as the accelerator of the globalization process, policy has come to be a brake. This may also explain why countries are reluctant to undertake or to finish global negotiations, and are more willing to adopt regional or bilateral approaches. Smaller agreements with preferred partners allow countries to control what they liberalize and how fast they liberalize it. The net effect is less progress than in the comprehensive, reciprocal rounds that dominated international negotiations in the past. Nevertheless this may be a rational and even efficient way to handle rapid change and high adjustment costs.

OPTIMALITY WITHOUT COMPENSATION

To understand the possible optimality of slow adjustment, consider the issues involved in redistributing the benefits from winners to losers. All of our theorizing on the benefits of international trade is contingent on compensation. One cannot say that a post-trade regime is better than a pre-trade regime, or that a less restricted trade regime is better than a more restricted regime unless there is compensation from the winners to the losers. In any realistic transition there are winners and losers. Thus, in the absence of compensation, nothing can be said about how overall welfare has changed.

Furthermore, there is reason to prefer the status quo to change. This is because greater weight usually needs to be assigned to the larger welfare losses of losers than to the smaller gains of winners. Welfare analysis suggests that large losses have greater utility consequences than small gains distributed widely across many winners. Policy therefore needs to be more concerned with losers than winners, even if net change is positive.

None of this would matter if there were effective compensation. But there usually is not, because it is very difficult to create an efficient compensation system. Once a system for compensation is established, many people will ask for it, even those who are not hurt. In addition, some will change their behaviour (inefficiently) to qualify for compensation. Given these problems, it is often irrational to offer compensation. In other cases, the 'best' compensation scheme will be less than perfect in order to reduce its deadweight costs.

In short, we live in a world without effective compensation, where adjustment is rapid, and adjustment costs are exponentially related to adjustment speed. In this world, slowing the pace of adjustment may be the best that can be done. Slowing change is, of course, second best compared to compensation, but it is not necessarily suboptimal given the constraints that surround policy.

Pushing this argument further, in an imperfect world there is significant payoff to making the 'brake' as efficient (in the overall welfare sense) as possible. This means, for example, making the mechanisms of contingent protection transparent, time-limited, and focused on sectors where there is tangible and significant cost. In other words, if contingent protection is inevitable, then much can be gained from designing a system that approximates optimal compensation, minimizes collateral damage and encourages long-term adjustment.

The WTO is making progress precisely in this direction. It is making contingent protection, including safeguards, anti-dumping subsidies and so on, damage-related, more transparent and subject to time limitations. It would be hard, for example, to imagine today the kind of protection that the steel industry received in developed countries for several decades in the pre-WTO era. Contingent protection subject to the WTO is much more likely to dampen, rather than eliminate, adjustment.

In sum, given wide agreement on the value of trade, an increasingly important role for policy is to seek better distribution of the benefits of trade, and this may require limiting the speed at which adjustment occurs. There is an important role here for analysis—for understanding more fully the limits on compensation, the determinants of adjustment costs, and mechanisms that can slow adjustment without stopping it.

23 First- and second-order adjustments to globalization

Hadi Soesastro

In Chapter 4 in this volume Professor Okamoto classifies countries as globalizers and non-globalizers, and categorizes Indonesia in the non-globalizer group. In my view, Indonesia sees itself as a country trying to participate in the globalization process—after all, globalization is a fact of life we have to take part in—but doing so involves complex adjustments given Indonesia's circumstances.

FIRST- AND SECOND-ORDER ADJUSTMENTS TO GLOBALIZATION

With regard to the management of globalization, a developing country such as Indonesia needs to recognize that there are important groups in the country that are opposed to globalization. The government understands this well, so in order to participate in globalization, it knows that it also has to develop policies to manage opposition to it. In effect, there are two levels of adjustment that it needs to make, which I call 'first-order' and 'second-order' adjustments.

First-order adjustment involves opening up the economy through an effective process of liberalization. Second-order adjustment consists of making the domestic changes that are needed to deal with the impacts of first-order adjustments, that is, to make the necessary changes in the social and political arena that make liberalization politically possible and economically efficient.

Indonesia has been rather successful in making first-order adjustments, as have many other Southeast Asian countries. However, when it comes to making second-order adjustments, the larger a country is, the more difficult it seems to be to make such changes. This may be why we have done less well here. In the absence of compensation mechanisms, we have not found effective ways to respond to groups that oppose globalization.

The same model of first- and second-order adjustments also applies to the broader international setting. Regional and international cooperation have come to be seen in Indonesia and the other ASEAN countries as the way to respond to globalization. When in 1992–93 the ASEAN countries decided to move towards greater integration through the establishment of an ASEAN Free Trade Area, we justified it mainly as a way to respond more effectively to globalization. In fact we stated explicitly at the time that this was how we, as a group, thought that we could participate most effectively in the globalization process.

First-order adjustment involves the region's general integration into the world economy. Second-order adjustment involves finding ways within the region to give ourselves a stronger position in the global context. We see regional integration as a means by which we can achieve a better economic base for global integration. In particular, we envision a strategy involving concentric circles, starting with ASEAN, then APEC, and finally multilateral integration.

SECOND-ORDER ADJUSTMENT IN AFTA

Within AFTA, the contingent protection issue is an important one, because we do not have a compensation scheme in ASEAN. In fact, governments have been very reluctant to talk about introducing into ASEAN transfer mechanisms of the kind that have been developed in the European Union that would benefit the less developed members of the group.

Thus ASEAN from the very beginning adopted an approach that defined areas to be put on a so-called *sensitive list*. Other items would be placed on a temporary *exclusion list*. Everything else would fall into the *inclusion list*: here we could begin to talk immediately about tariff reductions, and also work on non-tariff barriers.

We also agreed from the start to bring down the numbers of items on the exclusion list and agreed on a schedule to achieve this. Later we would do the same for the sensitive list. So items would be moved according to an agreed schedule from the sensitive list to the exclusion list, and then from the exclusion list to the inclusion list. If, at the outset of the process, countries were unable to determine how much they were going to achieve, then they agreed to have a review process by a certain date.

This process of opening up as a group has worked well for ASEAN so far. The same approach has been adopted for the ASEAN–China Free Trade Agreement, and this seems to be making good progress too, because agreement has been reached on when and how much to do—that is, to limit the items in both the exclusion and sensitive lists, and to move items forward from one list to the other.

SECOND-ORDER ADJUSTMENTS WITHIN COUNTRIES

Second-order adjustments within countries have also been envisioned in our regional agreements, but in implementing these we have remained quite backward. In 1998, ASEAN economic ministers decided, despite the financial crisis, to implement AFTA and indeed to bring the dates forward. But they concluded that we also had to do something to manage second-order adjustment issues, and proposed an ASEAN social safety net. Unfortunately, nothing has happened since. It is becoming increasingly clear that the second-order concerns are very important within the region and will need to be implemented in order to make further progress on trade agreements.

In sum, in assessing how countries such as Indonesia have met the challenge of managing globalization, we find that they have done well in first-order adjustments. But we still have a long way to go in making second-order adjustments, and these will be necessary if we are to make further progress in fully participating in global economic integration.

24 Managing adjustments to globalization

Kim Song Tan

The first issue of the *Economist* magazine in 1843 asked what the remedy for increasing trade restrictions was. The question is as relevant today as it was then. Much the same too can be said about the answer: compensation and the facilitation of adjustment remain the very crux of the matter. Like domestic political negotiations, the success of international trade negotiations ultimately hinges on the trade-off between efficiency and equity. Often, greater efficiency can not be achieved without due attention to equity issues.

From a policymaker's perspective, trade negotiations are about coping with domestic adjustments. To understand—and support—policy decisions better, more attention should be devoted to understanding the best practices and mechanisms of adjustment to free trade and globalization. Much of the discussion in the international trade literature focuses on the best practices in improving the efficiency of the trading system. More attention should be devoted to the best practices in managing the equity issues that arise from such adjustment. Indeed, whether the WTO is able to deliver on its promises depends to a large extent on how much leeway it gives member countries in making such compensation and adjustment.

In this regard, one should not view the 'proliferation' of regional free trade agreements (FTAs) too negatively, even if they run contrary to the basic non-discriminatory principle of the WTO. Policymakers are pragmatic, and regional FTAs offer them more control over the negotiation process and hence a more effective alternative than global trade negotiations in managing domestic adjustments arising from trade liberalization. As long as countries adopt an 'open-regionalism' approach and are WTO-consistent in their FTA negotiations, some of the feared 'spaghetti effect' in the long run may be avoided. In fact, it is not clear how severe such spaghetti effects may be, given the lack of empirical evidence on this issue. Meanwhile, the benefits that FTAs have brought about appear to be more visible. It is not clear at all that doing nothing while waiting for a more definite conclusion from the WTO negotiations represents a better outcome for the member countries.

More importantly, it has been shown that it is possible to see FTAs as an intermediate step towards a freer global trading system eventually—as the FTAs are intended to be in the first place. An example is the ASEAN–China Free Trade Agreement negotiations. The template of the agreement is similar to that of the ASEAN Free Trade Agreement.

This reduces the likelihood of spaghetti effects while expanding the coverage of free trade area. Indeed, if successful, the negotiations could even help to strengthen the free trade mechanism within ASEAN. The 'early harvest program' on agricultural products that China agreed to include in the negotiations could significantly free up trade in the agricultural sector—traditionally one of the most heavily protected sectors both within and outside East Asia. The proposed Singapore–New Zealand–Chile three-way FTA, arising from the integration of two separate FTAs (Singapore–New Zealand and Singapore–Chile) provides another example of how regional free trade arrangements can be meaningful building blocks for an eventual global free trade system.

While the WTO might be taking a rest now, as some speakers have noted, it is certainly not dead. Even as it rests, the WTO continues to provide the framework and maintain the 'minimal acceptable' standard on which member countries should conduct their trade. WTO-consistency remains the key word in many regional FTA negotiations. Much more needs to be done to inject dynamism into the WTO negotiation process. But just as the world has learned enough about the operation of monetary policy to avoid a repeat of the 1930s Great Depression, it is inconceivable today that a global calamity could hit the world as a result of mistaken trade policies. The continued existence of the WTO helps ensure that such a calamity will not happen.

Index

Printed in the United States
by Baker & Taylor Publisher Services